THANK YOU FOR
THE DAYS

THANK YOU FOR THE DAYS

A BOY'S OWN ADVENTURES IN RADIO AND BEYOND

MARK RADCLIFFE

SIMON &
SCHUSTER

First published in Great Britain by Simon & Schuster UK Ltd, 2009
A CBS COMPANY

5 7 9 10 8 6 4

Simon & Schuster UK Ltd
1st Floor
222 Gray's Inn Road
London
WC1X 8HB

www.simonsays.co.uk

Simon & Schuster Australia
Sydney

A CIP catalogue for this book is available
from the British Library.

ISBN: 978-1-84737-350-2

Typeset by M Rules
Printed in the UK by CPI Mackays, Chatham ME5 8TD

For Holly, Mia and Rose

'Thank you for the days
Those endless days, those sacred days you gave me
I'm thinking of the days
I won't forget a single day believe me'

Ray Davies – 'Days'

CONTENTS

INTRODUCTION

I don't want you to think of this book as an autobiography because that makes it sound much more full of itself than it is. I've written about lots of stuff that has happened to me here but I make no claims that any of it adds up to anything remotely momentous.

On the other hand, the odd interesting or funny or embarrassing thing has occurred during my first fifty years. I had my car stolen from outside an early U2 gig and was consoled by the kindly and still hair-topped The Edge, I went for a curry with Kraftwerk, I met the original four members of The Kinks and they were still arguing, I made a speech for the BBC at the Houses of Parliament, I lay back and smelled burning as a laser corrected my eyesight. I made some radio programmes too.

Of course, like everybody's life, 99 per cent of mine has been fairly dull and routine, so there was no way I wanted to link these episodes into one continuous narrative. I'm not trying to tell my full life story because a good deal of it isn't that interesting even to me, so there's no reason why anyone else should want to hear about it all.

What you have here are snapshots from different periods of my life which have become lodged in my memory, and which give a pretty rounded picture of who I am, should that be of interest to you at all. So it's a bit like an autobiography, but not quite as grown-up as that. I hope you enjoy it. If you bought it, thanks, and I hope you consider it reasonable value. If you received it as a gift I hope you weren't too disappointed.

Before we begin I want to say some thank-yous if you'll bear with me. You can skip this bit if you like, unless you think you might be in it.

I want to thank my agents Caroline Chignell and Jenny Rhodes at PBJ Management who have never stopped believing in me and have never complained when I have denied them all the percentages of all the things I've turned down.

I'm also grateful to Angela Herlihy for her continued, and some might say misplaced, faith in my abilities as a writer. I am also indebted to Kerri Sharp and Rory Scarfe at Simon & Schuster for knocking this all into shape.

Deepest gratitude must of course go to my family who made me the way I am in the first place, if that's something to celebrate. Thanks then to Mum, Dad, Jaine, Joe and also to Harry, Esther, Doris and George, my grandparents, who I remember with great love and affection.

I also need to thank the friends who've been with me all down the days, in particular my best mate for over thirty years Phil Walmsley; my old university pal Jamie Whitmore; Julian Bellerby, who personifies the early Manchester radio years; and Andy Batten-Foster, who was the like-minded soul I needed when I first went to work for the BBC in London.

I'm also grateful for the camaraderie and counsel of my fellow members of The Family Mahone: Chris Lee, Dave Russell, Paul Cargill, Jock Watson, Russ Mabbutt and not least Don Allen with whom I started the band when we found ourselves leaning on the same bar over a decade ago.

I must also thank everyone I've worked with in my broadcasting life, who are, of course, too numerous to mention.

However, personal thanks are due to my current colleagues Stuart Maconie, Viv Atkinson, Ian Callaghan, Jon 'Memory Stick' Lewis and especially the ever patient and cheerful Lizzie Hoskin.

I should also thank Tony Hawkins, the man who gave me my first job in the media, Johnny Beerling who initially took me into the BBC, and Jenny Abramsky who made it possible for me to stay there.

I'm also deeply indebted to the following people, without whom my radio life would have been very different: Marc Riley, John Leonard, Matthew Bannister, Lesley Douglas and the late Richard Sinton. Cheers also to Gareth Davies for many years of sound and gentlemanly advice.

I haven't written here about my other life as a husband and father because I didn't feel I had anything profound to say on these subjects that you haven't thought or experienced your-self, and, anyway, these are private matters. I want to send love and thanks to Bella and though it seems odd to exclude the most important days before we've even begun, I want to dedicate this book to the three days of my life for which I'm most thankful:

13 March 1988
7 January 1999
11 June 2002

Mark Radcliffe. Cemaes Bay, Anglesey. March 2008.

1. THE DAY I MET THE BAND WHO CHANGED MY LIFE

Dr. Feelgood were a rhythm and blues quartet from Canvey Island in Essex. That might not make them sound like a remarkable proposition, but believe me, they were. Their 1975 debut album *Down by the Jetty* was unlike anything I'd heard before and makes the hairs on the back of my neck stand up to this day.

Obviously I'd already had lots of exposure to all kinds of bands by the time I came across the Feelgoods. When the album came out I was seventeen and had become a voracious consumer of music and regular gig-goer. A lot of these were local events for local people and local bands, several of which I'd been a member of, Berlin Airlift and Billy Moon being two that spring to mind.

Then at Bolton Albert Halls you might get a strictly second-division touring band like Judas Priest or Trapeze or Budgie. They weren't earth-shatteringly brilliant but they seemed like superstars to us as they had record contracts and T-shirts for sale and fat roadies with gaffer tape and pliers hanging off belts slung low under their beer-guts.

There was also B.I.T., Bolton Institute of Technology, where you could see a band every Saturday night. This was predominantly the domain of multitudinous progressive jamming hippie collectives like Hawkwind, Gong or Amon

Düül. I actually retain great affection for the works of Hawkwind, who cast themselves as Tolkien-esque space travellers taking their blissed-out stoner racket to other galaxies. How grateful people in other galaxies would have been for this kind of missionary work is open to hypothetical question, but it had to be better than seeing Captain Kirk turning up and trying to teach the ways of human love to the high priestess, who was, as I understand it from my limited knowledge of *Star Trek*, a kind of space Lady Mayoress wrapped in cooking foil. Their 1971 album titled, naturally, *In Search of Space*, is arguably the definitive album of that genre and certainly presents a vivid snapshot of those dreamy, mystic, hairy, slightly malodorous times.

But my dalliance with this cluster of bands didn't seem destined to last, even at the time. I enjoyed going to watch them while consuming lots of cheap cider, but I didn't feel there was any emotional connection between us. They didn't speak directly to me in any way and said nothing that reflected the life I was leading, the feelings I was feeling. Amon Düül came from a radical political art commune in Munich. I came from a neat semi-detached house on Towncroft Lane. Gong had found their saxophonist Didier Malherbe living in a cave. Berlin Airlift had found our bass player Andy Wright in the sixth-form common room of a respectable sandstone grammar school. We seemed to share little common ground.

Of course there were lots of other kinds of music we could experience from northern soul to glam rock, but for those of us who loved seeing bands live, these presented limited opportunities. Northern soul nights consisted, as far as I could see, of drinking Lucozade and watching someone put records on. I knew nothing of amphetamines and back-flips. And they weren't even dancing with girls half the time. So that was no good.

Glam rock was another alternative but bands like Slade and T. Rex played only the big venues in the big cities, so these events were always going to be few and far between. Of course that made them even more special and going to see David Bowie in 1972 at the Manchester Hard Rock, now a branch of B&Q, remains perhaps the high-water mark of my gig-going life. The downside was that after seeing Ziggy Stardust in all his spangled, supercharged pomp, nothing on the local glam scene could come close. This was perhaps inevitable, as glam is something that only works on a big stage. There are genres of music that seem purpose-built for small, sweaty venues with inadequate toilet facilities. Rhythm and blues is one, heavy metal, with certain provisos, another and clearly punk, which only really works in such surroundings.

Glam rock doesn't because it is as much about presentation as music. This means it has to have impressive batteries of equipment, lots of bright-coloured lights and a cast of heavily made-up, dandified, strutting peacocks in the band itself. It's like pantomime in some ways, as anyone who's ever seen Queen or, if you've been really unlucky, Kiss will testify. You can't reproduce this sort of spectacle in the Dog and Duck. You can't suspend belief if the rhythm guitarist in, say, Moonage Madmen is the bloke who gave your dad's off-side-front Cortina tyre a remould last week wearing his girlfriend's Lurex tank top and some hastily applied eyeliner. It just doesn't work.

Heavy metal may be the brand that most easily straddles both sides of the divide like a denim-clad Colossus of Rhodes, and in fact this much-discussed wonder of the ancient world may well be the origin of the genre. The original statue, constructed between 292 and 280 BC, was over one hundred feet high and was made of iron and bronze. Metals. And heavy. You see where I'm going with this? The subject was the Greek god of the sun Helios, under whose crotch sailors would pass going in or out of Mandraki harbour. So you would look up and see the testicles of this golden, illuminated deity. Compare this with being at the front of the stage staring up at the flaxen-maned Robert Plant caught in the spotlight in his tight jeans. Do you see? Not only that, the Colossus was felled by an earthquake and snapped at the knees, and how many times have you seen a lead guitarist, lost in the emotion of a tortured solo, drop to his knees in exaltation?

Rooted in Greek myth or not though, heavy metal was never really my thing. I think Deep Purple had some truly exhilarating moments on the *In Rock*, *Fireball* and *Machine Head* albums. To not have some place in your heart for a little AC/DC is, frankly, ridiculous. And to fail to appreciate the force of nature that was Black Sabbath, whose *Master of Reality* was the first LP I ever bought, seems downright rude. Tony Iommi had his fingertips replaced with metal ones in pursuit of that sound, following a machine tool accident, so the least you can do is give him the respect he deserves.

But metal, like prog, still felt like your older brother's music somehow. Not that I had one of course, but when I went to a gig everyone seemed older and taller with bigger hair. I was seventeen, getting ready to go away to university the following year, and was desperately searching for the soundtrack that would define these life-changing times in the same way that Bowie had set my early adolescence to music. Once again I needed music that felt like mine. Something that gave voice to the impatient energy I was feeling. And that's where Dr. Feelgood came in.

When I saw them on the telly, it was literally a 'Eureka' moment. One of those instances where you weren't sure exactly what you were waiting for until it came along and everything suddenly slotted into place. Initially it was the look that caught my attention. The drummer and bass player, The Big Figure and John B. Sparks, were dressed in suits that looked like they'd come from the local charity shop, topped off by haircuts that might have been executed by the adjoining charity barber, if such a thing had existed. Centrestage, taut, twitching, wiry and weasel-like, stood the stick-thin, glaring front man, Lee Brilleaux, in an under-sized jacket that may once have been white. He gripped a microphone in one fist, down which he barked the vocals when not wiping the sweat from his face with the back of his hand, and a harmonica in the other, with which he punctu-ated the songs with frenzied bursts of blues harp. The three of them would have presented enough of an arresting spectacle on their own, but to Brilleaux's right stalked the once seen, never forgotten guitarist Wilko Johnson. Dressed in a black suit, with a black pudding-basin haircut, Johnson skittered up and down the stage fixing the audience with a wide-eyed stare, while ripping shards of contorted R & B riffage from a Telecaster with his bare fingers. I watched them in rapt awe. They were unlike anything I'd seen before. They had none of the corny showmanship of the bands I'd been used to, just a sheer, sweating, gritty charisma that pumped out of the TV. They looked like they'd been born to do just this. There didn't seem to be any artifice or concept to it, just four guys playing as if their very lives depended on it.

I began to hear more of them on the radio, and then I bought what I consider to be one of the top ten British albums ever made in *Down by the Jetty*. Its title came from their home of Canvey Island, located off Essex in the Thames Estuary and riddled with petrochemical terminals. It was a landscape that had utterly infused the songs of Wilko Johnson in the same way that Salford had captured the eye of L.S. Lowry. The record was described by Andy Childs, writing in *ZigZag* magazine, as 'loud, dirty, mean, raw, vicious rock and roll'. He was right, but it was more than that. It was also quintessentially English. The band may have been influenced by Howlin' Wolf, but their take on the blues couldn't have been less American. Paul Weller, a huge admirer of Wilko's unique guitar style, paid Johnson the highest compliment when he said he thought of him as the English Chuck Berry at that time. Chuck Berry is, to my mind, the single most important person ever to have existed in rock and roll. He made a white audience consider the possibility of listening to 'black' music, brilliantly captured for the first time what it felt like to be a teenager, and wrote numbers so great and ubiquitous, 'Johnny B. Goode' and 'Roll Over Beethoven' amongst them, that they have almost become folk songs. They are so familiar and perfect that it's easy to think they've been around forever, handed down from generation to generation. But no, Chuck sat down and wrote them all. And Weller is entirely right to put Wilko Johnson in the same league. For a time, back there in the grimy mid-seventies, Wilko captured the essence of small-town English life better than anyone had done since Ray Davies.

Of course, you couldn't look at Wilko's words and say they exactly mirrored my life in Bolton. But they did express that disenfranchised feeling you get as a teenager, where you don't know quite how you're going to fit into the world, but you know you have to leave home and start looking. His songs, and the band's sound, mirrored my own restlessness.

To some extent my life, and not just in the musical sense, falls into BF (Before Feelgood) and AF (I imagine you can work out what that stands for). Things would probably have changed for me when I went away to college anyway, but the sound of Dr. Feelgood is the sound of life changing. And it's not just me that feels that way. The music journalist Charles Shaar Murray talks of the Feelgoods standing at a crossroads in British music, into which a lot of things fed in and a lot of different things led out. You can argue that punk, the biggest seismic change since the beat boom, originates somewhere at that junction. Dr. Feelgood, though outsiders, were operating on the London pub rock circuit from time to time. This scene, though still slightly woolly, hairy and reeking of hippy residue, did start to present a more honest version of rock and roll. Venues were smaller and seedier, bands were less flash and pompous, and the audience were closer to the action and therefore an integral part of the event rather than mute witnesses. Some of the characters who participated in this world and went on to much greater recognition include Elvis Costello, Nick Lowe and Ian Dury.

All of these appeared on what many regard as the doyen of all British independent labels, Stiff Records, and if anything symbolized the DIY ideology that was so important to punk it was Stiff. All right, they didn't have The Sex Pistols or The Clash, though they did have The Damned. But they were the chosen home for artists who wanted to do things their own way. The Pistols, you could argue, were anything but an expression of this new honesty. Yes, they were raw, obnoxious, brimming with attitude and made a string of classic primal pop singles. But elements of their story smack as much of manufacturing as Westlife. Svengali Malcolm McLaren put Johnny Rotten in the frame, and Glen Matlock, the one who took charge of the song writing and played pretty nifty bass, was replaced by Sid Vicious, who was incapable of either of those things, because he fitted the image better. Whether that makes the scam more or less brilliant is open to question, but the band certainly weren't four old schoolmates who'd grown up together and were making all their own decisions. In some ways, McLaren was the Simon Cowell of his day. Both had a vision of how the music business could be manipulated and both exerted freakish control over their artists. Where McLaren wins out of course is that his aim was to impose change, whereas Cowell's master plan is to prevent it. McLaren was a true revolutionary in that he didn't care whether he benefited from the new order, he just wanted to clear the space so that things could grow. It was a kind of benevolent nihilism. In my opinion, Cowell wants us to buy the processed schlock he peddles to make himself ever richer. His legacy will be the methods he employed to create transient pop stars, not the records. It's a sound business proposition, but let's not make the mistake of thinking it has anything to do with music. His records will never be regarded as classics and cherished down the years, and will never provide a snapshot of their times like 'Anarchy in the UK'. It's often said that the music business is a jungle. Well, up to a point, but it's not the greatest of analogies. Untamed things thrive in a jungle. Cowell and his ilk want to tarmac over the jungle so things can only grow where they decide to allow it. McLaren wanted to tear down the jungle and leave a barren wasteland so fresh things could grow unfettered. The real desire to make honest music, unencumbered by people telling you not to break the rules, is what punk was all about, and what Stiff Records encapsulated perfectly. And how did Stiff come into being? With a loan of £400 from Lee Brilleaux, that's how.

I saw Dr. Feelgood in concert many times and they never failed to thrill me. These four strangely unremarkable and yet remarkably strange geezers, crackling with nervous energy and exuding a vague sense of menace, paved the way for punk and were the first band that I felt belonged to me in some way. Yes, I'd thrilled to The Beatles and The Stones and The Kinks and T. Rex and Led Zeppelin, but they never felt like they were exclusively mine like the Feelgoods did. I was a massive Bowie fan, but you could never feel close to a star as big as that. The Feelgoods were so close you could practically touch them. Not that you particularly wanted to, but that was another ground rule of punk. The artists had to be accessible to the fans, not remote tin gods in their luxury hotel suites.

That classic line-up of the band recorded three more albums, *Malpractice, Sneakin' Suspicion* and the number-one live set *Stupidity*, before Wilko left in late 1976. Rather gloriously they had imploded just as the punk revolution got under way. Numerous fine guitar players filled out the Feelgood ranks over the subsequent years, but it was never the same. Gradually they became a blues band like dozens of others. They were never less than a good live act, and as long as Lee was up front, there would be reminders of the glory days. But, inevitably, the spark had gone. Perhaps it was better that Johnson had departed as that left their early body of work perfectly preserved.

In 1994 Lee Brilleaux, one of the greatest front men this country has ever produced, succumbed to lymphoma and died aged forty-one.

For years I'd had the idea of going on a road trip to Canvey Island, to see first-hand where this unique sound had developed. It was a notion that predated having anything to do with radio, but was something I'd never got around to doing. So when I was asked by Radio 2 if there was anything I really wanted to do, it came back to me in a flash.

My companions on the trip would be my long-time producer and confidant 'Juke Box' John Leonard, and my best mate for over thirty years Phil 'Wammo' Walmsley.

Phil and I had met in September 1976 in a hall of residence at Manchester University. That's us in the photo at the start of this chapter. We had clicked immediately through a shared sense of humour, half each, and a mutual love of noisy guitar bands and best bitter. We lived in opposite rooms in Lindsay House at Woolton Hall, and started to go pretty much everywhere together. Well, except during the day when he went off to his endless building technology lectures and I hung about thumbing through *Washington Square* on the off chance I had a tutorial that week.

We started to play music together straight away. He was a guitarist of no little ability, and I was a drummer who'd had to leave his kit in Bolton, as I'd come to live in a single room. You weren't allowed drums in college rooms because of the obvious volume issues. This was fair enough, although I doubt I'd have been as loud as my next-door neighbour Rick DeNezza, an American who appeared to have wired his hi-fi through Jefferson Airplane's PA system.

So, drumless, I had to become the singer in our two-man band, which was just as well as Phil's voice sounds something like a young pig undergoing castration. We were both big fans of The Stones, so we could have aspired to being Keith and Mick, although drinking the amount of beer we did and staying that thin would prove to be problematic. We also loved The Who, so could have harboured aspirations of being the new Daltrey and Townshend, though you wouldn't have seen me dead in one of those tasselled leather jackets, and Phil's nose wasn't big enough anyway. We both watched *Opportunity Knocks* so could have dreamed of becoming the new Millican and Nesbitt, though neither of us were coal-mining crooners from the Northeast with poor taste in knitwear. In reality we had only one overriding thought. I was always going to be Lee to his Wilko. We thought that image-wise we were halfway there as the requisite ingredients were things we were already in possession of: dodgy barnets and even dodgier suits. But Brilleaux and Johnson were the best front pairing we knew, and those were the heights we aspired to.

Going back to our old rooms in the hall of residence to record the opening of the programme felt odd. We hadn't set foot in there since 1978, and yet walking back into the grounds it was as if we'd been strolling those pathways only yesterday. I have no idea how these things work but it seems to me that if a place is associated with the best, or I suppose worst, times of your life, then it must make a stronger impression somewhere in the brain. On that corridor I spent a year as happy and eventful as I've experienced in my entire life.

Phil and I sat in his former room with a copy of *Down by the Jetty* playing on a Dansette record player, exactly as we'd done three decades earlier. Some aspects of the surroundings had altered a bit over the years, but there was a limited amount of change you could inflict on a single study/ bedroom. Not that it had fulfilled its study designation during Phil's tenure, the only things having been closely studied in there that academic year being the chords for Dr. Feelgood songs, the bra clasp barring access to Christina Hetherington's chest and the whereabouts of the lost underpants that were filling the room with a foul odour.

Some of the fixtures were exactly the same though. The old sinks were still there, and so were the bookcases on which we'd stacked our coursework, coffee cups, beer bottles and records. I took a moment to stride across the hall and stand in the room that had been my home in that former life. We'd arranged to start the programme in Phil's quarters because that was where we tended to plot our escapades. Initially this was because Phil had his Dansette, whereas I only had a cassette player. Eventually I did get a stereo system, but we still gravitated towards Phil's place which, given the smell, seems an odd decision now. It was just habit I suppose. The pungent aroma comforting somehow.

Standing in my old bedroom, as alone as I'd been when my mum dropped me off there in September 1976, was a bittersweet experience. Running my fingers along the cracked veneer of the dusty bookshelf or the worn stainless steel of the taps, it was just so strange to think that the last time my hand had touched those things it had been on the end of the

arm of an eighteen-year-old with his whole adult life in front
of him. I've never felt my age more keenly than I did at that
moment. My spell at uni was such an exciting and absorbing
time, and one I feel a real sense of privilege at having experienced. There was no one telling you what to do or what
times you had to come in or go out. The freedom came
without much responsibility though, which made it all the
more delicious. You had no bills to pay or job to worry
about, and everybody wanted to be your friend. Even some
girls. It was heaven from the very first day, and standing there
as a middle-aged man I was forcibly struck by the realization
that I would never be as free as that ever again, or as intoxi-
cated by the limitlessness of possibility. Then again, if
someone had taken the pimply undergraduate aside and laid
out what would happen in the following thirty years, well, I'd
have happily settled for that.

And so, from Woolton Hall in the South Manchester
suburb of Fallowfield, we began our journey to Canvey
Island, a place which had attained almost mythical status in
our own minds. The programme included interviews with
Nick Lowe and Charles Shaar Murray, as well as Bob Geldof
and Paul Weller, all of whom shared our regard for this precious little band. That made us even more confident that
we'd been right all along. We never really doubted it of
course. We knew that Dr. Feelgood were one of the greatest
beat groups of all time, but to know they'd inspired others
was the icing on the cake.

Driving on to the island, and it is an island, felt slightly
anticlimactic. I suppose we were expecting it to be a place of
romantically dishevelled art-deco hotels and rusting fairground attractions. It had, after all, been a popular resort for
Victorian Londoners eager to escape the foul, stodgy air of
the fetid capital. At first glance it had little you could call
romantic. In fact the grim Canvey scene of 1953, when the

North Sea breached the defences and caused widespread flooding, seemed a closer point of reference. You couldn't help but notice how flat it was, with the oldest houses seemingly dating from the 1950s, and small, tired parades of shops and takeaways interspersed with the occasional amusement arcade. Over towards the charcoal smudge of the Thames flickered the flames of the oil-cracker chimneys, blinking into the drizzly gloam. Look, I'm not trying to paint a grimmer picture than is absolutely necessary. I'm sure it's a wonderful place to live with great community spirit and all that, but it wasn't pretty. I'm a real fan of the British seaside, with a particular penchant for stepping out across storm-tossed promenades and esplanades that have seen better days, but even I was struggling to be seduced by Canvey Island that grey afternoon. And yet, you could see how it could inspire the renegade rock-and-roll spirit. It was a very unusual and distinctive place, and one which would form the backdrop for Wilko's immortal tales of little lives and love affairs in a bleak industrial landscape down by the oil terminals at the water's edge.

We were staying at the Oysterfleet Hotel, run by the band's long-time manager Chris Fenwick, who had arranged for the three surviving members of the original quartet to come and talk to us. I can hardly express what a big deal this was to Phil and I. You're probably thinking that I'm getting a bit carried away here, it not being the remaining Beatles or anything, but I'm deadly serious. We all have people who've influenced or touched our lives in some way. Some of them might be world-renowned musicians, sportsmen, artists, writers, architects or inventors. Others might be individuals who aren't famous at all but who've still had a profound effect on our lives: teachers, parents, siblings, friends, lovers, cosmetic surgeons, that kind of thing. The Feelgoods fell between those two camps. They weren't the most famous people in the world. They may not even be the most famous people from Canvey Island, as one-time England football caretaker-manager Peter Taylor hails from there, but they'd shaped the musical lives of Phil and I more than just about anybody else.

First to arrive was The Big Figure. His real name is John Martin, but everybody referred to him by the shortened version of his stage name 'Fig'. He looked quite a lot different. The bear of a man with opaque shades and untamable mop of unruly curls had been replaced by a slimmer, silver-haired gentleman in a smart black shirt and dapper loafers. He was unrecognizable from the album sleeve. Polite and dry, he was living in France and seemed the most contented of the three. He liked a pint.

Next to bowl up was bassist John B. Sparks, probably the unsung hero whose distinctive rhythmic playing gave the band its engine. He was a small man, which having seen them live many times we already knew, and was greyer of hair and thicker of girth, like the rest of us. He was bluff and affable and still lived, as a single parent, on Canvey. I thought there was a slight sadness about him, but I could have been wrong. Perhaps going over the old times was as strange for him as standing in that hall of residence room had been for me. Bittersweet, as I say. He liked a pint, or two, too.

We sat and talked with the sturdy men of the rhythm section for a while and waited for Wilko. Unbeknownst to us, he had had some last-minute doubts about taking part in the programme and there was some talk of him not turning up. The long-suffering and dedicated Chris Fenwick had shielded us from this however, and so we just passed perhaps twenty minutes in easy conversation with Sparko and Fig.

And then he arrived. Quite how he managed it I don't know, and it's possible that I only imagined it as I was so excited to meet him, but he seemed to enter the room with a bit of a flourish. He moved quickly and with a jerky motion that suggested there'd been nothing contrived about his on-stage movements. He was tall, thin, still bug-eyed and still wearing a black suit, shirt and Chelsea boots. He was completely bald, but otherwise looked more or less exactly the same, resembling an overworked undertaker or some character patrolling shadowy, distant cloisters in Gormenghast. He shook our hands and was voluble and friendly, though agitated. And not just with us. He greeted his old band mates in similar fashion. He was obviously pleased to see them, and they him, but there was the unmistakable sense that amongst the memories of the good times that were flooding back were some darker moments. One could imagine, in the nicest possible way, that he might not be the easiest of people to share a Transit van with for weeks on end.

Before we started to record the interview Wilko ordered a large brandy and proclaimed himself starving. A large ham salad baguette was duly produced, heavy with coleslaw and mayonnaise, which he seized upon with the relish of a man who hadn't eaten in a while. Dollops of condiment plopped onto his dark materials creating splatters Jackson Pollock would have been proud of, to the consternation of everyone but the band. Sparko and Fig had evidently seen it all before. Wilko appeared not to have noticed, and scoffed the lot in what seemed like seconds.

We talked for about forty-five minutes after that. They recalled their childhood days on Canvey with stories of little boats and home-made rafts weaving and bobbing along the many channels. It sounded a bit like *Swallows and Amazons*, and strangely idyllic. Fig, as a kid, had actually been rescued from the flood waters. They talked of their schooldays, and Wilko's difficulties in getting to the grammar school on the mainland when the fog closed around the island. In contrast to the others (and who knows if this threw up another barrier between them), Johnson had pursued his education with some zeal. He'd not only been to grammar school, but also went to university in Newcastle. Obviously a man of some culture, his monologues were peppered with surprising references. When I asked him how he developed that peculiar way of getting round the stage that had been christened 'skittering', he mused on the origins of that word and surmised it had first appeared in William Langland's *Piers Plowman*. You began to see that his deceptively perfectly simple songs came from a deep mind. How many blues guitarists can you think of with a working knowledge of the Middle English allegorical narrative tradition?

We heard of their early musical adventures in jug bands and skiffle groups, and Wilko's recollection of his first meeting with the younger Lee whom he remembered as inquisitive, 'weaselly' and 'having something about him'. Indeed.

They reminisced about the endless nights, weeks and years on the road where Sparko, to Lee's eternal irritation, would find it easy to curl up, dormouse-like, and sleep peacefully for hours, even over the throb and grind of the noisiest diesel engine.

We asked about the gestation of the album we loved so much and were enthralled to learn that it wasn't mixed quaintly in mono, as it said on the sleeve, but in fact in stereo with, as Wilko said, 'everything in the middle'. Brilliant. That made it even better somehow. It meant that the cherished record, though based in strong musical traditions, had been made under wilfully perverse circumstances. It had pulled off that great trick of being simultaneously retro and absolutely of the moment.

After the interview finished we had one more task to undertake. All those years ago we'd looked at the grainy black-and-white photograph on the front cover of *Down by the Jetty* and wondered who these strange guys in this strange place making this earth-shattering music were. It was as un-showbiz a picture as has ever adorned an album sleeve. Arranged in an artless line with windblown hair and nonde-script suits and ties, they appear to be huddling together for warmth as a stiff squall lashed the estuary waters, pipelines and refilling tanker moored over their shoulders. Their lack of pretension and disregard for pop posing seemed so refresh-ing at the time. Lee looks positively seasick, and we learned that the photo had been taken early one morning after a heavy night's gigging and boozing followed by the long drive back over the causeway. The inspiration for the shot comes from Wilko's words to the song 'All Through the City':

'Stand and watch the towers burning at the break of day,
Steady, slowing down, been on my feet since yesterday.'

And so they had. Perfect.

That photo had become so mythologized by Phil and I that we asked if it would be possible for them to take us to where it had been snapped. Despite the inclement weather, they agreed. It took about fifteen minutes to get there, a journey I undertook in the back of John B. Spark's well-worn Jaguar, with Wilko in the front passenger seat pointing out their childhood haunts. The formative years of the Feelgoods came back to life against that backdrop with a running commentary from the animated guitarist, by now unstoppable in his anecdotage, delivered in a laconic, estuary drawl, not a million miles from Mick Jagger.

Eventually we arrived at the car park of a coastal boozer called the Lobster Smack. The oldest building on the island, it had had a licence since the time of Elizabeth I. It is widely accepted that Dickens stayed there while writing *Great Expectations*, and looking out across those will-o'-the-wisp infested mud flats, it was not hard to see where the inspiration for the opening scenes of that book might have come from.

We ascended a concrete staircase to the sea wall and took the full brunt of the gale. Fig, though never less than genial, looked like he might have preferred to be back in France, and it was hard to blame him. Sparko, amiably resigned, bore it stoically. Wilko though was a man possessed. He hopped about making sure everything was in as close to exactly the same place as it had been on the original photograph. There was no oil tanker in dock, and the sea wall had been built up, but other than that, Johnson made fastidiously sure that everything was as it had been on the cover. Yet, of course, it could never be. Lee Brilleaux would never be able to re-create that photo again and that must have been difficult for them. They were, on the one hand, pleased that someone wanted to celebrate the great recordings they made, but must have been deeply saddened that their mate was no longer around.

Wonderfully, I was allowed to take Lee's place on some of the photos. I had dressed that morning in a cream jacket, striped shirt and skinny tie to resemble Lee's outfit as closely as I could, anticipating just that situation. I know that sounds a bit weird, but we are talking obsessive fan here. I treasure that picture. Think of an album you held close to your heart in your youth, or a photograph of your favourite football team maybe, and think of how it would feel to have yourself morphed in, like Woody Allen in *Zelig*, in later life. It doesn't get much better than that.

We returned to the Oysterfleet and sat down to dinner. Fig declined, saying he was only in from France for a couple of days and wanted to catch up with family. Wilko dined handsomely and talked openly about the loss of his beloved wife Irene to cancer in 2004. She had been by his side, both personally and handling his booking arrangements, for almost forty years. He was obviously struggling to come to terms with life without her and your heart really went out to him. Eventually, he decided he'd had enough to eat, drink, and of the assembled company, and departed on his own to go back to Southend.

Chris Fenwick, awash with red wine, talked teary-eyed into the night about the band that had been the love of his life.

Last to leave, after everyone else had retired to bed, was John B. Sparks. He sat at a table with Phil and me and his eyes twinkled as he recalled all the gigs, adventures and mishaps of the band's golden age. He was really easy company, and didn't seem in a rush to go anywhere, which was just as well as Wammo and I were reluctant to let him go and for the day to have to end. Gradually though the bar staff retreated, the lights were turned off, and we drained the last of our glasses in a room illuminated only by the street-light glare pouring in through the windows. He couldn't think of anywhere that would still be open, and so we'd no choice but to say our goodbyes.

We shook him by the hand in the car park. I hope he enjoyed the time he spent with us and understood just how much it had all meant to these two middle-aged mates who'd bonded over his band's music so many years before. I don't suppose we could ever fully understand what he felt that day. They were a great, great band that had, like so many other great, great bands, imploded too soon. And with Lee gone, their time could never come again.

John B. Sparks turned, pulled up the collar of his leather coat, and disappeared into the Canvey mist.

Dr.Feelgood

Down By The Jetty

COLLECTORSEDITION

2. THE DAY I TOOK BROS INTO A GOODS YARD

It was 1988 and at number one in the charts was a dreadful group called Bros with a dreadful song called 'I Owe You Nothing'.

Bros consisted of twin brothers Matt and Luke Goss. One of them, I don't remember which, sang and the other one played the drums. The only other member of the group was called Craig. He played bass. That was it. No guitars. No keyboards. No lead instruments at all. Of course, if you had the misfortune to hear the record, and as it was number one it was pretty hard to avoid, all those instruments were there, but if you saw them on the television, it was just vocals, drums and bass. That might suggest it was an interesting experiment in minimalism. But it wasn't. It just made it more obvious that they were miming. Matt and Luke were pretty. Craig wasn't. What he was doing there was a mystery to everyone. Perhaps he had a van.

As Bros mania swept the country like Dutch elm disease with streaked hair, Radio 1 was in the process of switching over to the FM frequency. This was happening gradually across the country as we'd been messing around on Medium Wave up to that point. Medium Wave, with its tinny buzzing sound and constant interference, made it an imperfect frequency for the broadcast of high-fidelity music. It didn't much matter if all you were going to do was use the new clear channels to play Bros records of course, but we marched on to the future regardless.

To mark the switchovers various events were mounted in different parts of the UK to let the local populace know that they could say goodbye to poor signal misery and would henceforth enjoy the music of Bros and the words of our DJ philosophers on crystal-clear FM. What a tonic it must have been.

I produced the switch-on ceremony in Dundee. It involved Ian Botham pulling a small lever to illuminate a sixty-watt light bulb atop a two-foot Meccano tower. You could almost smell the indifference of the shivering Dundonians who witnessed this paltry spectacle.

In Manchester it was decided to hire Matt, Luke and the other one to herald the arrival of FM in the Northwest by making an appearance on the roof of the BBC, and hope that nobody pushed them off.

They flew in by private jet at Manchester airport, and myself and my immediate senior 'Juke Box' John Leonard were despatched in hire cars to meet their motorcade and guide them back past the screaming hordes of underdressed female fans or Brostitutes, as I've just christened them. Why John and I were given this job is unclear as we were allegedly radio producers and not minicab drivers. I imagine there was a cost consideration.

As John's home patch was Yorkshire, which may have had some bearing on that cost consideration, it was decreed, possibly by me, that I should be the lead driver as I knew South Manchester like the back of my head.

The plane landed and the band ambled down the steps. Ooh look, there's Luke. Or is it Matt? And here comes the other one. What's his name again? Ken was it?

They were ushered into their fleet of limousines along

with their retinue of PR people, bouncers, hairdressers and ego masseurs, and the stretch vehicles lined up behind me, crouched like David Coulthard (but with a less square face) at the wheel of a hired Mondeo. John, wearing a Radio 1 bomber jacket and finishing off an egg mayonnaise barm cake, positioned his Vauxhall Cavalier at the rear of the procession. Confident that everyone was present and correct I flashed a 'chocks away' thumbs-up through the open window for the benefit of no one in particular save the gathered paparazzi. I then floored the accelerator and, as Dan Brown might say, gunned the car out of the compound with the precious Bros following in my wake. Speed was of the essence. We were already running late. And there was FM to be switched on. It was a matter of national importance.

On leaving the VIP zone of the airport apron I confidently took the first right. Straight into a small, disused goods yard stacked with rotting pallets and rusting oil drums. If I'd been in there on my own I could perhaps have negotiated my way out within ten minutes by performing a seventeen-point turn. Unfortunately the rest of the motorcade had piled into the dead end behind me, and gridlock ensued. Already a quarter of an hour behind schedule, we were then delayed a further twenty minutes while the consignment of stretch monstrosities reversed gingerly back out onto the busy airport approach road. What Matt, Luke and Baz thought, heaven only knows.

However, we found our way back to the BBC and in scenes reminiscent of *Mission Impossible* managed to throw the all-important fake switch in the nick of time. What a relief to the people of the North.

Today that FM we switched on is still working. So am I. And so is John.

But whatever happened to Bros, eh?

3. THE DAY I LOST SEVERAL PLOTS

My first job in the media was at Piccadilly Radio in Manchester where I started work in September 1979. In those days of idealistic optimism it was perceived that commercial radio stations would rival the BBC in the breadth of programmes they would offer. As a result Piccadilly employed people to look after news, current affairs, sport, drama, specialist music, documentaries, features and community action projects. Not all the programmes they turned out were of top quality, but at least if you were in Manchester for a week and listened to the station's output, you would understand something of the city you found yourself in. It was a wholly noble attempt to create a viable alternative to the BBC establishment and, while not entirely driven by altruism, profit being part of the equation, it seemed for a time that the plan would work. Across the country a network of big town and city stations sprung up offering something that seemed to combine a genuine desire to reflect and add to the cultural life of the locality with a bit of the heady excitement of the pirate stations thrown in.

Sadly the principles were gradually eroded and sacrificed in the pursuit of profit. Once it became evident that you could win more listeners, and therefore more advertising revenue, by playing Whitney Houston and Dire Straits records instead of trying out new magazine programmes, the end was in sight for anyone who worked outside the mainstream. Don't get me wrong, I understand that these enterprises have to turn a profit, but somebody somewhere, the government or the Independent Broadcasting Authority, should have made it impossible for them to go down that road. If they had, we would now have a network of long-established commercial stations giving a vibrant picture of life in their locality. What we've ended up with is a collection of identikit operations all playing whatever you consider to be the current equivalents of Whitney Houston and Dire Straits. Leona Lewis and Coldplay, perhaps. With all due respect to the people who work for these organizations, and I dare say there are lots of talented and hard-working souls involved, my point is that these stations have become interchangeable and that can't be right. Glasgow isn't interchangeable with Edinburgh or Aberdeen or Liverpool or Hull, so why should the radio stations be? It's not the end of the world or anything, but it's one hell of a missed opportunity.

I arrived at Piccadilly when the blueprint for a brave new world of radio was still intact. I was interviewed by a suave and sonorously voiced chap called Tony Hawkins who was head of drama and classical music. His was a pretty good job although slightly compromised by having nobody to be head of. That was where I came in.

I wasn't particularly worried about what might come up in the interview. I had studied English and American literature at university and so I'd read a few plays in my time and could drop names like Ionesco, Wesker and Marlowe into the conversation. I had no idea if Piccadilly were planning a Marlowe season, though it was hard to see how *Dido, Queen of Carthage* might sound if interspersed with adverts for Kwik-Fit exhaust centres, but I figured they might be drawn towards someone who at least knew what a play was to become the assistant (to) head of drama.

Similarly, I had a blagger's knowledge of classical music. My dad worked as a reviewer and critic for several newspapers and I'd been going to concerts by the Hallé Orchestra since I was a toddler. Accordingly I could tell my Sibelius from my Vaughan Williams and knew that Albinoni hadn't been signed by Manchester City on loan from Lazio. That had to put me ahead of most people they were interviewing, surely.

Well, it must have done because I got the job. My career in radio had begun and I'll always be indebted to Tony Hawkins for that.

I was duly installed on a starting salary of two thousand six hundred pounds per annum, which might not sound like much now, and wasn't much back then either. However, it was about five hundred quid more than I was getting on a higher education grant so I felt comparatively well off, especially as I carried on living in the flat I'd been occupying while studying for my degree with Phil and fellow flatmates Carole and Tracey. Pretty soon they began to feel the benefits of my new-found wealth and largesse as we became one of the few student households in West Didsbury to have fresh milk in the fridge at all times and to be able to purchase cider by the demijohn. Heady days indeed.

My new place of employment was located in the heart of Manchester city centre in a monstrosity of concrete obelisks known as Piccadilly Plaza. There were office blocks and a hotel there as well as an open-air piazza on the first floor. The architect's vision of this space was that it would provide a meeting place where stressed office drones could gather together in their breaks to appreciate the Zen-like calming effects of wandering amongst the new brutalist pillars and cubes. There was even a crazy-golf course up there at one

point, and also a duck pond. Unfortunately, on the day of
the grand opening, the specially installed ducks had taken
one look at their proposed new habitat and flown straight off
through the open skylights into the wide blue yonder. It
was hard to blame them. The forlorn deserted pond was
then drained of all liquids save the odd pool of tramps' urine,
and served as a large rubbish bin thereafter. The project was
probably a valiant attempt to reconfigure the urban workplace, but it was wholly misguided. Why would you drift
around a windswept wasteland of quick-set cement in your
lunch hour when you could go to the pub?

Piccadilly Radio was located at one end of this desolate
downtown graveyard, under the tower-block hotel, above
the Olde Englishe Chippie, a greasy eatery with a half-
hearted Tudor theme that was compromised by its being
located in a concrete box. The stench of rancid chip fat rose
up to drift around the corridors of the radio station and you
could begin to feel quite queasy when this was combined
with the lack of natural daylight in there. In fact the overall
feeling was of living in a stuffy space between floors. It was
like being a character in *The Borrowers*.

The great thing about working at a radio station with
limited numbers of staff is that you get involved with making
programmes straight away. I was given the responsibility of
looking after a Sunday morning classical record show called
Square One presented by Richard Sinton. Richard was head
of music at Manchester Grammar from 1965 through to
1993, having also had a spell teaching at several schools even
higher up the educational food chain, including Eton. He
was evidently of wealthy stock and there was talk of the
huge swathes of Derbyshire that fell under his family's
ownership. His voice was a fruity baritone that had been put
to good operatic use earlier in life, and his accent was a
perfect example of received pronunciation. With his warm,

easy delivery and mellifluous tones, he was an ideal radio presenter, especially for a Sunday morning. But it wasn't so much the voice as what he said that registered with me. He absolutely loved the music he was playing with a passion, and desperately wanted to share its joys with everyone listening. His trick was to dig out stories about the composers and musicians involved, and not simply trot out the usual dates and details of the orchestras and conductors. When he talked of Paganini leading the itinerant life with two suits to his name, a scruffy one for everyday wear and a slightly less scruffy one for performing his shows, he made him sound like the leading rock and roll star of his day. This brought the music to life in an accessible and compelling way. I think in some respects he was as much an influence on me as John Peel.

He was also, like all true music lovers, really open-minded. He was of the strong belief that there are only two kinds of music: good and bad, and just because something wasn't to your own taste didn't mean it was the latter. What he loved was to meet someone whose passion was as great as his own, irrespective of what it was you were passionate about. He developed a strong affinity with the ageing greaser Chris Tetley, who lived for heavy metal and produced the rock show. And he developed a similar affinity with me, overlooking my obvious lack of experience in the job because to complain about the mistakes I was making would have been inconsiderate and impolite. Richard would never have been either of those. He knew I was doing my best, and that was good enough for him.

Outside the studio he was lovably colourful and eccentric. He had a range of garish sports jackets that had obviously been purchased from high-end tailoring establishments, but which were all blighted with cigarette burns and stained reminders of a thousand school dinners. His jacket pockets

were so stuffed with cigarette packets, lighters, handker-
chiefs, spectacle cases, fountain pens and bits of paper that
they stuck out almost horizontally from his body like the
fustanella kilt of the Greek Evzone soldier. During the
summer months he wore a 'Man from Del Monte' light,
linen suit that was well travelled, though had never visited
the dry cleaners. His greying hair was swept in carefree fashion into an unruly comb-over. Yet he wasn't what you'd
call scruffy. None of his sartorial quirks seemed to disguise
the fact that here was a true gent; the whole package just
seeming to ooze raffish charm.

In truth, I don't think appearance mattered all that much
to Richard. Though he'd clearly been no stranger to money
in his life, he was heroically non-materialistic. His car was a
battered, powder-blue Renault with a dashboard gear stick
that had had to withstand years of the driver's random and
violent pulls and shoves. Every time he finished another
packet of Dunhill fags, which would be about twice a day,
he would throw the empty box over his shoulder into the
rear of the car. When the pile of discarded packs reached
shoulder height and threatened to spill into the front of the
car he would empty them all out, and the whole process
would start over again. You had to love a guy like that.

He also had the mark of someone with real class, by which
I mean basic honesty and goodness, in that he refused to
judge people on the basis of class, by which I mean rank or
background. He knew that, like music, there were only two
kinds of people: good and bad, and if you were stupid
enough not to engage with good people who weren't from
your own perceived social world then the loss was entirely
yours. He loved people, music, wine, cigarettes, cricket and
curry. And what more is there to life than that, eh?

Richard Sinton died in March 2006. Not only did he
inspire me in so many ways, in his urgings to follow your

passions and treat everyone you met as a potential new best
friend, but it's gratifying to know that he inspired countless
others during his extended tenure at Manchester Grammar.
If, when I look back over my life, I can feel that I was half the
man he was, I'll think I did all right.

And so my life at Piccadilly Radio drifted on as Richard
waited patiently while I tried to push the right buttons, and
I worked hard to reciprocate that patience while he tried to
find a mislaid foolscap sheet of scrawled notes about
Canteloube's 'Songs of the Auvergne'. I would then take the
tapes and retire to an airless broom cupboard with a tape
machine in it to make any necessary edits. How clearly I
recall being in there late one Saturday night and watching in
horror as the spooling tape snapped and became mangled in
the metal reels, rendering the programme unbroadcastable. I
think I panicked for about two or three hours trying to
untangle the spaghetti before, close to tears, realizing the job
was futile. In desperation I phoned Richard, who simply got
in his car, hauled his load of Dunhill packets in from the Peak
District, and did the whole show over again.

I did work on more general areas of programming as well
and this is where a place like that used to provide excellent
grounding. If someone was on holiday you could find yourself putting features together, or manning the phone lines or
operating the radio car as your mate Julian Bellerby, dressed
in full armour as St George, attempted to create memorable
radio by soliciting opinions on the patron saint of England's
designated day from some bemused female assistants in a pie
shop.

The other really great thing about working at a radio station was that it became apparent you could get free records.
Representatives from all the major record companies used to
visit on a weekly basis, and they were all happy to give you
copies of their stock if you expressed an interest, even if you

didn't have your own show. I suppose they thought you
might be able to share your enthusiasm with someone who
did have access to the airwaves. I also imagine that the stuff I
was enquiring about was the gear that was hard to get rid off,
and they figured it was better for someone who liked it to
have it than for it to roll around the back of the car until it
got slung into a skip several months later.

   Another way of getting records was to sift through a plastic dustbin in the record library. Here, the disc jockeys
chucked away the tunes they didn't want and it was while
rummaging in this receptacle that I met my other kindred
spirit from those days. His name was Stuart James and he was
employed in the engineering department, and later went on
to work with The Smiths and The Chemical Brothers. We
soon discovered that we shared a voracious appetite for new
sounds, and attended the same clubs that formed the thriving Manchester scene, notably the Russell Club, or The
Factory, immortalized in the film *24 Hour Party People*. We
thought it insane that the city's foremost radio station should
be without a programme that reflected the pulsating local
music scene. Everyone else, with the exception of Richard
Sinton and Chris Tetley, seemed to be content to wallow in
the musical mainstream and some seemed actively resistant
to anything new disturbing the status quo, and indeed the
Status Quo. Certainly punk records were viewed with utter
disdain. I remember one plugger telling me how the sight of
a seven-inch single in a picture sleeve, a tradition that the
punk and independent labels had revived, was enough to
ensure that that disc would be despatched to the plastic rubbish bin straight away. Accordingly he would sit outside the
station taking the records out of their picture bags and
inserting them into plain white ones. When local boys Joy
Division made the national charts with 'Love Will Tear Us
Apart' the ruffled head of music, a large suntanned man in

Cuban heels, approached me and asked if he could borrow my copy of 'that record by this girl from Manchester called Joy Davidson'. I mean, honestly.

Stuart and I thought it ludicrous that the station didn't have a programme that reflected the wealth of local talent operating in the area. We had Joy Division, A Certain Ratio, Durutti Column, John Cooper Clarke, Jilted John, Buzzcocks and a host of others to whom history has not been as kind such as The Spherical Objects, Biting Tongues and Crispy Ambulance. And nobody was playing any of it.

Stuart and I approached our boss Tony Ingham urging him to let us do 'Manchester's answer to John Peel' kind of show. Astonishingly, and it's hard to imagine the same thing happening in a big city commercial radio station today, he agreed, despite the fact that neither of us had presented a radio show in our lives before. Before the first programme aired Stuart had decided that he preferred the anonymity of production, which left me to front the show alone. We were given a two-hour slot between four and six on Saturday afternoons, but only during the summer while there was no football. The only stipulation the station made was that we had to put out the local cricket scores. This meant we would follow the first play of the new Buzzcocks single with an update on how Rishton were going on batting against Oswaldtwistle. I had no problem with that. The programme was named *Transmission* in honour of the majestic Joy Division single, and my career as a DJ had begun.

Looking back, the strange thing about all of this is that though I took to the world of radio easily I'd had no previous desire to get into it. I'd love to be able to tell you that I spent my childhood tinkering with short-wave sets, seduced by the romance of these voices materializing through the ether, but I didn't. All I wanted to do was to play drums in a successful band and if that wasn't going to happen, to get a job that involved music in some way.

Working at Piccadilly came about because the station, still valiantly attempting to nurture local creativity, had come up with the idea of a short-story competition. Local writers, whether previously published or complete novices, were invited to send their yarns in, the winners to be narrated by seasoned actors and put out on air. The programme controller Colin Walters, a gruff, fearsome individual who once berated me for being late for a meeting even though I'd been interviewing U2, who'd been stuck in traffic, decided that the sackloads of stories needed sifting before the good ones were sent on to the panel of judges. He asked my dad, who had written a book entitled *The Piccadilly Radio Story*, which had failed to appear in the bestseller lists, whether he could find a 'couple of students' who could read and weed out the dross. As I was a literature student on summer vacation, it was clear that I was the man for the job.

I recruited a fellow student, the blonde and beautiful Susan Nightingale, and together we sat for days on end in the Piccadilly boardroom scanning the hordes of entries. It was thrilling being inside an actual radio station, and equally exciting to not have to compete with several other pustulous undergraduates for the attentions of the decorous and serene Ms Nightingale. But the experience soon began to pall. With every new delivery of post a fresh mail sack would be slung into the room and, even worse, Susan began to talk about her boyfriend a lot. She'd kept that quiet when I offered her the gig!

One bright August day Susan had announced she was unable to come in as she had a prior engagement. That left me alone, my head filled with images of her strolling through some wooded glade hand in hand with a Sean Bean-alike, the sun adding radiance and lustre to her already radiant and lustrous hair. It was more than I could stand to be cooped up in there all day and so I asked if I could take a batch of stories home and read through them in a deckchair in the garden. No one had any objections, so I put a large pile of stories under my arm, and walked across town to where I'd parked my mum's car. Opening the car door proved difficult under the weight of paper I was carrying, so I placed the sheaf on the car roof while I fumbled with the keys. Having successfully tackled this onerous task I then climbed happily into the driver's seat and took off, thinking that the council street sweepers were doing a pretty poor job as, in the rear-view mirror, I could see literally hundreds of sheets of paper blowing about in the summer breeze. Of course I realized what I'd done almost immediately. I stopped the car but there wasn't a single page of a single story left on the roof, and trying to pick them all up would be a futile exercise. There were far too many of them, and even if I had managed to get them gathered back together, I'd have never got them into the right order again. Bugger.

One of the proudest days of my life came in 1998 when my first book, *Showbusiness – Diary of a Rock 'n' Roll Nobody*, was published. I went into Manchester on the train that day and as I walked down the platform at Piccadilly station, I could see the book's cover on the shelves in WH Smith's. Me with a real book in the shops! How about that? I can hardly describe the glow it gave me and to think I may have prevented someone else from experiencing that, as their masterpiece lay windblown in the grimy gutter of a side street in the heart of Manchester's crumbling rag trade quarter, bothers me to this day.

Still, at least I had the afternoon off, so it didn't turn out all bad.

4. THE DAY I WAS AN A.R.S.E.

When I went to work for the gloriously named Popular Music Department at the BBC in Manchester in 1986, we had too much time on our hands.

During the winter months we made the odd programme for Radios 1 or 2, but in the summer we did a bit of filing, listened to some records, went to the pub and played Trivial Pursuit in the afternoons.

Tired of losing the game to the girls in the office, my boss John Leonard and I became aware that there was an empty office along the corridor. Here, for our own amusement, we created a fictitious department called Regional Strategic Events.

To kill an afternoon I would send out memos to various people around the country, starting each one with: 'Further to my previous memo . . .', thus instilling a vague sense of panic in the recipient. The memos concerned preliminary plans for fictitious events to promote the regions, and were all copied to heavy-duty management figures who, of course, never actually received their copies. Once a week we would nip to the deserted office to pick up the apologetic replies from the poor souls who'd failed to find any record of our initial memo, read them in fits of giggles, and then put them in the bin before starting all over again.

The BBC has a great love of abbreviations. The controller of Radio 2, for example, would routinely be known as CR2. An engineer in charge of a programme would be the E.I.C. You get the idea.

I appointed myself Assistant, Regional Strategic Events. That made me A.R.S.E. John, as my boss, was therefore Head over A.R.S.E.

We also recruited a chap called Nick as a technician. Obviously he needed to be instructed in all relevant regional strategic events protocols and procedures. That made him technician in training. Or T.I.T. for short. He was answerable to me in theory, which made me A.R.S.E. over T.I.T. John though took ultimate responsibility, which made him Head over A.R.S.E. over T.I.T.

As I say, we had too much time on our hands.

5. THE DAY I GOT MY FIRST GUITAR

I got my first guitar from my granddad Harry Goad. He was the first of my grandparents to die but none of them made it much past seventy, although that was very much looked on as 'a decent innings' in early-seventies England. My grandparents and their generation were proper old people too. They didn't go around saying stuff like 'seventy is the new fifty' or taking up speed-skating, or indeed speed-dating, like old people of today. No, they were content doing things old people were supposed to do, like playing bingo, crown green bowling, trimming privet hedges, smoking Senior Service fags, watching wrestling and keeping daily newspapers under the cushions of the settee. They were the kind of people who watched *Mastermind* religiously without answering one question correctly ever. You knew where you were with old people like that. They didn't like pop music or attend raves or abseil down the Eiffel Tower. That was young people's stuff. Stuff they could shake their heads at while starting conversations with sentences that began: 'Eeh, youngsters of today . . .' They did like *Sing Something Simple* and tea dances and strolls along the promenade. Proper old-people's things. Things that 'youngsters of today' considered boring. It was the natural order of things and everyone was happy with that.

In fact, it seems to me that Harry, Esther, George, Doris and the millions like them were more contented than my own generation has ever been because everything they would ever need could be found within four square miles of where they were born, which for them meant Farnworth, a slightly poorer relative to the great metropolis of Bolton. They weren't stupid people. They knew there was a big wide world out there. People had come halfway across it to live next door and work in the same cotton mills, bus garages and Co-operative stores as them, but that didn't mean they needed to travel themselves. There were no package holidays so it was financially out of reach for the most part, but even if it could have been afforded, what was the point in going abroad? For a start it was rumoured to be 'hot', and the Lancashire summers were too hot as it was.

Then there was the food. My dad's mum Doris had once said that she didn't fancy going to Spain because she wouldn't fancy eating 'all that curry'. Fair enough. What's the point in taking a fortnight off work to do things you don't fancy doing? I don't fancy skiing much, so I don't go. Why experiment if you know what you want to begin with?

I once went with my wife for one night at the splendidly appointed country house hotel the Sharrow Bay on Ullswater in the Lake District. It's a beautiful place, lavishly yet idiosyncratically furnished with myriad objets d'art assembled by someone with a good eye for all that. It was the first time I'd encountered a sommelier. To be truthful I didn't know what a sommelier was and had to ask someone. This would have been less embarrassing if the bloke I asked hadn't turned out to be the sommelier.

I'm not trying to make out that it's anything other than a really well-run, sumptuously appointed, idyllically situated gourmet paradise, but I just didn't have the requisite experience to feel at home there. It's the kind of place that doesn't have a bar because that's a bit vulgar perhaps. Maybe it is, but I like a bar in a hotel. I'm sure it's all terribly grown-up to sit wherever you fancy, click your fingers and order a couple of Kir Royales while pondering the Lakeland landscape, but I wasn't used to it and felt about as relaxed as Doris would have been in Spain. But Doris was smarter than me, because she didn't put herself in that situation. She didn't go to Spain. She went to St Anne's on Sea again. I, on the other hand, found myself perched on a bench in the Sharrow Bay arboretum being accosted by a white-jacketed assassin who'd been loitering in the rhododendrons.

'Yes, sir?'

'What?'

'Can I be of assistance, sir?'

'I'm sitting on a chair. I think I can manage, thanks.'

'No, would sir like something?'

'Like what?'

'Drinks perhaps, sir?'

'Oh, errm, all right then. We could take afternoon tea I suppose.'

'Indeed, sir, though it is only nine-thirty a.m.'

Cobblers. So it was.

'Oh, I don't know. Bring us two pints of bitter shandy then.'

I didn't really ask for bitter shandy, though it would undoubtedly have been served without so much as a knowing smirk, well, not outside the kitchens anyway. The point being that I felt like everything I was going to say there would be the wrong thing.

That night at dinner, with Alan Bleasdale at an adjacent table, I'd somehow recovered enough confidence to walk into the dining room without feeling acute stomach cramps, and even managed a knowing nod to my new mate the wine waiter. Sorry, sommelier. Emboldened by my new-found poise, I decided to mark the occasion by ordering something I'd never had before. I think it was pheasant. Or possibly partridge. Something that had been shot and left to hang in a mouldy barn for a couple of years anyway. Whatever it was, one bite was enough to tell me it was disgusting. It did have a real flavour of the countryside, I suppose, in much the same way that a slice of blacksmith's apron marinated in badger vomit might, but that didn't make it edible. I cut it up into bits and tried to hide it under the parsnips and kale. So there I was, having the most expensive meal of my life, and eating something I found completely repulsive.

Doris would never have found herself in that situation. Dining out was an experience that happened, for her and George, perhaps twice a year. For these occasions they always went with George's cousin Harriet and her escort Charlie, always went to the Pack Horse Hotel in Bolton, and always ate the same thing. And always enjoyed it. They were going for a treat, and so with unarguable logic, they went for something they knew they would like. This wouldn't stop Doris describing the meal in meticulous detail, the first gobbet of information invariably being:

'Well, Harriet had turkey . . .' Harriet always had turkey because turkey was what Harriet liked. If Harriet had won the football pools and gone to the Sharrow Bay, the Dorchester or the Waldorf Astoria, she'd have had turkey. And she'd have been happy.

The other comment that always cropped up during the course-by-course recounting of the Pack Horse banquet was that the food 'covered the whole plate'. These were people who'd known rationing, and so getting what you liked and plenty of it was central to an enjoyable evening. The madness of nouvelle cuisine, and it's two scraps of guinea fowl the size of fifty-pence pieces marooned on a plate the size of Iceland, had yet to be inflicted on the restaurant-going public, and so going for a meal that actually filled you up was still relatively commonplace.

I'm fifty now, and have finally got to the stage in life where I'll go to a nice restaurant and order shepherd's pie if that's what I fancy. I know I don't like seafood and so I don't have it. Not even when I went to Rick Stein's fine establishment in Padstow. I went to the Ivy with my boss and had a mixed grill. It was terrific, and what's more, it covered the whole plate. What's not to like? I'd finally learned the lesson Doris inadvertently taught me all those years ago. If you don't want to try it, then don't. Have what you know you will like and you will not be disappointed.

Pressurized into it against his better judgement, my mum's father Harry once bought a Scandinavian toasted-sandwich maker from a stall on Morecambe promenade. It was pretty much a small bedpan affair that you stuffed with two slices of bread and your chosen filling, and then thrust into the open fire. Anxious to try this revolutionary culinary device on getting back to Farnworth, he searched the pantry and kitchenette for likely fillings before plumping for marmalade. After perhaps fifteen minutes he removed the contraption from the flames, tipped out the small charred delicacy, and bit in hungrily. The bread was toasted to perfection, however the marmalade had become heated to more or less the temperature experienced on Mercury. It was as if nuclear fission had occurred between two slices of Warburton's Milk Roll.

The roof of my granddad's mouth gradually recovered over several months, and the Nordic instrument of torture was banished to the tool shed, but it just confirmed his deepest suspicions about non-English methods of preparing meals. The point here is that my grandparents didn't have a fear of foreign foods, or foreign lands, they just had no need of them. They weren't prejudiced towards 'abroad', in fact Harry and George had been there, though they weren't much impressed. Admittedly there'd been a war on there at the time which might have influenced their opinion, but they had no desire to experience any culture other than their own, and this seems to me rather wonderful.

Of course what they did have, which many people nowadays don't, was the secure knowledge that their jobs and houses were theirs for life, and that the state pension would ensure there was no real drop in living standards in retirement. How many of us can say that now? How marvellous to know that life would stay the same until you died, if you wanted it to. You knew every crack in the pavement in your own little corner of the world, could walk into any of the local pubs and find someone you knew to chat with over a pint, and would be greeted cordially by everyone you happened upon in the street. Those were the cards you'd been dealt, and no one was ever going to take them away from you, which some might say makes for a rather uneventful card game. Perhaps so, but the security of knowing things weren't going to change unless you wanted them to must have seemed like ample compensation. And of course you had the grandchildren.

My grandparents were very good to me and my brother and sister, and were inordinately proud of anything we achieved. Things they'd never done, and never wanted to do, like foreign holidays, A levels, university degrees, playing in bands, they experienced vicariously through us. When I got my first radio show on Piccadilly Radio my dad's stepdad George used to listen to it on his own in the communal lounge of the Laburnum Lodge rest home. I can't imagine he enjoyed the music much, but that was his grandson on the wireless and he was going to listen no matter what.

And in fact, my involvement in music dates pretty much

from an act of grandfatherly generosity. OK, it might have happened anyway, but I really started to believe I might one day be in a band when I got my first guitar.

It was Christmas Day and we were at Harry and Esther's for our dinner, having called in at Doris and George's in the morning. I must have been eight or nine. During the unwrapping of the presents Harry gave me a parcel which contained a guitar strap. I still remember it vividly. It was beige leather with white fluffy padding and silver buckles. The fact that I can still picture it to this day gives you some idea of how momentous an event this was.

'There, a strap for you, for when you get a guitar.'

You might think I was a bit slow not guessing what might come next, but buying a guitar was a big deal in those days, and never in my wildest dreams did I think I'd be getting one. Anyway, at some point Harry must have got up and left me tearing open other presents, hoping for something long and wooden to hit my sister with. A new cricket bat! Ideal.

'Mark.'

'Yes, Mum?'

'I think Granddad's got something else for you.'

I looked up and there was Harry pushing a full-sized guitar case across the parlour. I can honestly still see him mock-struggling to emphasize the size and weight of it. It wasn't wrapped or anything as nothing bigger than a Monopoly set got wrapped because that would have been deemed a waste of paper. (A few years later, while building up a drum kit by getting a single drum every Christmas and birthday, I got a bass drum wrapped in a tablecloth.)

I gently unbuckled the buff canvas bag and slid the precious instrument out. It must have been pretty much as tall as me, and was a natural-wood steel-strung guitar. Not a poxy, ten-a-penny nylon-strung Spanish thing, but a real steel-strung proper one. I immediately put the strap on it, and struck what I considered to be a classic rock-star pose while pulling a face that suggested acute constipation. It just came naturally, being a pain in the arse and a show-off, and I reckon that was the first time I knew that I wanted to be in a famous band. When Harry bought me my first guitar.

Now what would be really great here is if I could wrap this story up by telling you how the songs I wrote on that guitar became million-sellers as I conquered the world as a member of Radiohead. But I didn't. I did get in the charts with The Shirehorses, and I have been in bands my whole life, but I've never been the successful rocker I so desperately wanted to be. I have, though, been lucky enough to earn a decent income doing the next best thing: listening to records and playing them on the radio. Well, it beats working for a living, I can tell you. And when I think how many hours Harry must have worked at the Co-op on Highfield Road to pay for that guitar, the first guitar I ever held and which made me dream of a life in rock and roll, I wish there was some way of paying him back. In fact, I wish all four of my grandparents were still around so I could pay them all back for the things they did for me. The presents, the trips out, the cakes, the treats, the love. Now I've made a few quid and have got a nice house and car, and even a little place by the sea, I wish they were here so I could treat them the way they treated me. And I keep a photo of each of them on display at home because it strikes me that there aren't many visible signs of them having been here at all, and I don't think that's right; because though they led 'little lives' they lived good lives, lives which had a profound effect on my own.

I still have the guitar. It's even still got the three stickers I stuck on the body of it over the next couple of days: a purple and turquoise pop-art peacock, and two pink and orange flowers. 'Groovy, man', as the beatnik-speak of the time would have had it. It doesn't have a make embossed on the headstock, it's obviously not really a good one or anything, but you can still just about get it in tune and knock out 'Route 66'.

It's one of three things Harry gave me that I've still got. I've got his wedding ring, and also the binoculars he used for watching horse racing. Every time I put them to my eyes to watch the seabirds I know his eyes have touched the same viewfinders, and I feel a bit closer to him somehow. But those things came to me after he died, while the guitar he gave to me himself, and it'll stay with me till I die. Hopefully after I've had 'a decent innings' myself. So far so good.

6. THE DAY I INTRODUCED DAVID BOWIE ON STAGE

'We could be heroes – just for one day'.
(David Bowie – 'Heroes')

I've never allowed myself to have heroes. Hero worship strikes me as an irrational suspension of your critical faculties. Naturally there have been individuals and groups whose work has had a deep and lasting effect on my life, and my admiration and regard is unconfined. But to constantly fawn over a single being, blind to their failings, has got to be a flawed way of thinking. The power of an individual who can use charisma to promote their own dogma to an audience that never questions their wisdom or judgement has been proved repeatedly to be a highly dangerous thing. That's why you can't trust a politician. They may have a deeply and sincerely held desire to serve the community, and possibly a deeply and sincerely held desire to have a new kitchen paid for by the taxpayer, but they also want to control the way you think. They want you to think like they think. Furthermore they are taught to never admit they are wrong. If you met someone like that in real life you wouldn't want them to be your friend, would you?

Perhaps, growing up in a relatively free England, I've had no need for a political messiah. If I'd been born into oppression I would quite possibly have believed with a religious zeal in someone like Nelson Mandela, because I had too. He might have represented the only hope. But I wasn't. So I didn't. You can see why someone like that would become idolized as the figurehead for a revolution that brings about social change and a fairer society, but you couldn't rationally feel the same way about modern politicians in Western society. After all's said and done, they're not really doing anything, are they? They're just going to meetings and shuffling papers. If Gordon Brown nipped round and lent a hand putting together a particularly tricky flat-pack shelving unit, then you'd be more inclined to listen to his views on the prudent running of the economy over PG Tips and bourbon creams. If David Cameron dropped by to do a spot of canvassing and offered to fetch the ladders from his van to check out a couple of loose roof tiles, you might start to think of him as worthy of your vote. But none of them will ever do something as useful as that and neither are they creators or visionaries, and surely if you're going to have a hero they should have those qualities.

So ruling out politicians, who does that leave as potential hero fodder? Sports stars? Hmmm. I can understand why a kid contemplating a sink-estate future might utterly idolize Ricky Hatton. He's determined, likable, very funny, a Manchester City fan and can hit people very hard. I'm not a man of violence myself, and have no love of boxing, but the gladiatorial bearing of the boxer is perhaps the closest thing to heroic in the world of sport. But it's still only having a bit of a scrap at the end of the day, isn't it?

Similarly you couldn't have a hero who was a runner because we can all run. Admittedly Paula Radcliffe is better at it than the rest of us, but that's just because she's practised more than we have. I'm not underestimating the dedication and discipline that that takes, but that's not the issue. I could

work for hours every day on, say, my spitting distance. Given
the right wind conditions I might eventually be able to spit
further than anyone else in the Northwich area – which
might not sound like much but if you visit that town centre
you'll see I'm up against some pretty daunting competition –
but that wouldn't make me a hero, would it? The same unarguable logic applies to motor racing. Lewis Hamilton can
drive a car. So can I. Lewis Hamilton's car is faster than mine.
Big deal.

I'm also put off by swimmers and decathletes who are
always keen to let you know that they have to get up at five
in the morning to run a thousand miles, swim the Channel
and lift weights equivalent to a Pendolino train before breakfast. Well, don't then if you don't like it. Pack it in and lie in
bed of a morning. Don't do it because you want all the glory
and then whinge to the rest of us about it being tough. We
know it's tough. That's why we're not doing it. We understand that all that training is horrible compared to being in
bed. That's why we've decided to stay in bed.

Of sportsmen in the modern era the category regularly
cited as heroes are footballers. Oh, please. All right, we can't
all play football. That aside, though, what is it about the
modern footballer that is the stuff of heroism exactly? The
ability to buy ever more ludicrous cars? The vision to build
an even more ghastly mansion than Prince Andrew? The
sound judgement that allows them to spend fifty thousand
pounds on a wristwatch? Bedazzled by the bling, countless
young lads aspire to this world of home cinemas, gaudy trin-
kets and sharing girls in London hotels. You might reasonably
think that with their levels of income they could afford a girl
each, but I assume that deep down they're all so pleased with
themselves that what they really want to do is sleep with
each other.

Of course these banalities don't have a bearing on how

blessed they are with the ability to play football, but it's hard to feel deep-rooted admiration for people who choose to live in a world like that. The fact that Steven Gerrard's wife's handbag has had Botox doesn't change the fact that he is a genius of the modern game, but it does make you like him a bit less somehow. And you couldn't easily trust a man with a one-inch forehead, could you? I recently met someone who told me that their hero was Roy Keane. This is a man who not only demolished the leg of Manchester City's Alf-Inge Håland with a gruesome, leg-shattering tackle during a Manchester derby match, but who subsequently admitted as much and profited from the admission by including it in his autobiography. How in the world can you hero-worship someone like that? You can respect his gifts as a player but it's impossible to idolize an individual you find repugnant. And if you don't find someone who has acted like that morally repugnant then you should be asking yourself why.

I think it's also difficult to put any sportsperson on the ultimate pedestal because there's no original thought or intellectual impulsion to what they do. I'm not suggesting that these people shouldn't be admired, amply rewarded and congratulated, with the exception of Roy Keane obviously, but if we're going to have heroes, they must surely have the ability to create something unique. Writers and artists have this, but we rarely feel we know them well enough to bestow hero status upon them. You might well adore the work of David Hockney or Ian McEwan, but they are limited figures publicly because of the essentially private nature of the way they have to work. You may idolize them for what they have created, but can you feel you know enough of them for it to go beyond that? Simple logic must also rule out great creatives of the past, as we can know even less of them. I adore the novels of Thomas Hardy but he can't be my hero as I've no way of beginning to understand him as a human being.

Now I'm as aware as anyone else that there are soldiers, nurses, carers, firefighters and countless others who richly deserve being described as heroic whose daily triumphs never get anywhere near the papers. But if we're talking about famous people who might be dubbed heroes we've already ruled out politicians, sportsmen and women, writers and artists. Actors and dancers can be discounted as well. I'm not denigrating their art, but they are essentially interpreters of someone else's vision. The qualities deemed essential to earning the title seem to be the ability to fashion a unique creative tangible something that most people wouldn't think of, and to allow and admit to the possibility that you might not have got it quite right. The work of all geniuses is littered with absolute rubbish as they strive and edge ever nearer to their own particular perfection. So who are we left with?

Musicians.

I'm sure there are classical musicians whom some find heroic, although we come back to the interpretive argument here. Being, once again, careful not to disrespect the breathtaking skill and artistry of the classical soloist, they're not, for the most part, writing their own material and, for me, a hero has to do that.

So that leads us to rock and roll. The best rock stars make great heroes because they are creative mavericks and iconoclasts, have musical skill and imagination, and are figures of glamour and desire. They've got it all. Wasn't Eric Clapton christened 'God' back there for a while? Some, quite possibly Eric included, might think this overstates Clapton's significance somewhat. God created the world, Eric created one of the ten best riffs in the world with 'Layla'. And yet the greatness of God hinges on pure belief in the absence of conclusive empirical evidence. To really feel that God is great, you have to decide to start from that same point. God is great because those of you who choose to follow believe he is. That's what you're saying, and fair enough if that works for you. But the existence of 'Layla' is not a matter of faith. It exists, categorically. So Eric's act of creation is more tangible than God's as it's available to anybody with seventy-nine pence to spend on iTunes. Maybe Lennon knew what he was on about after all when he said The Beatles were bigger than Jesus.

So if rock and roll is where the true acts of creation occur, if I was to allow myself a hero, which I don't, then it would be a rock star. And that rock star would be David Bowie.

I first saw David Bowie on *Top of the Pops* doing 'Starman' in his tinsel and tat with his arm around the shoulder of the equally otherworldly, though less convincingly androgynous, guitar 'hero' Mick Ronson. To the adolescent Boltonian grammar school boy in 1972 they appeared to have arrived from another planet where men flirted with each other, made exhilarating music and wore Lurex knee socks. I had no idea where this planet was, and wasn't sure I wanted to flirt with men, but it certainly seemed like a world that was worth visiting.

I discovered that the single 'Starman' was taken from an album called *The Rise and Fall of Ziggy Stardust and the Spiders from Mars*, which I bought from a shop called Tracks the next day.

Putting it on in my bedroom in the family home on Albert Road in Bolton it became clear from the opening bars of the first track 'Five Years' that the future I'd been waiting for had arrived. That album is not only packed with really great melodies and beguiling words, but also covers all moods from the reflective, piano-led lament of 'Lady Stardust' to the full-on, glam-rock throb of 'Suffragette City'; from the nightmare dystopian vision of the future on the aforementioned 'Five Years' to the portrait of the doomed rock icon on the soaring title track with its epoch-defining main riff. There was also a vague concept that sought to bind the tracks together into some sort of narrative telling the tale of the eponymous pop superstar who 'took it all too far'. Even more than that though, it had what all great works of art have, the ability to take you somewhere else entirely, to transport you into another world of seemingly limitless pos-sibilities. Lying on my bed in that attic room, gazing at the stars through the open window as the last moments of 'Rock and Roll Suicide' faded away, I felt for the first time that here was an artist talking directly to me.

Then of course there was the whole image thing. The Bowie look was intoxicatingly daring, but presented problems for the pubescent imitator. It was not only nigh-on impossible to find Japanese-print jumpsuits in Bolton but, even if you were lucky enough to stumble across one in some dingy corner of the Market Hall, you were going to run the risk of getting a good kicking if you wore it in Yates's Wine Lodge. Like most other Bowie-ites I had to settle on a compromise of plat-form shoes, over-tight jeans and a brightly coloured bomber jacket with the collar turned up. It was an approximation of the style of the master that was as close as we could muster given the sartorial shortcomings of the Bolton Arndale Centre and paying some regard to the issue of personal safety. Disciples of Oasis, in their baggy trousers and sensible wind-jammers, would never understand the struggle. We fought for their right to wear whatever they chose without fear of discrimination and they turned up dressed as landscape gardeners. There's gratitude for you.

The hair was a little easier to assimilate. The Bowie Ziggy cut is one of the most recognizable rock hairstyles of all time, and that was another reason why he was so obviously in the pantheon of the immortals. You can't be a proper rock star without great hair. If Robert Plant had fronted Led Zeppelin with a limp comb-over, there is no way they'd have become the biggest band in the world. If Prince had tried to carry off the *Lovesexy* tour with a curly perm and a bald spot on the crown he'd have been laughed off the stage. If Mark Knopfler had . . . OK, let's move on.

The Ziggy cut was basically a ginger mullet that was spiky on top. I know that there will be those of you who are finding it hard to accept that the coolest hairstyle of the day was something that, from the way I've described it, might usually be found sitting on the head of ebullient Scottish soccer elf Gordon Strachan. Now I think about it, it was a bit like that, but it looked bigger and better on Bowie. School regulations didn't allow for much length at the back but, and here's a phrase you don't hear often, that was the beauty of the mullet. If you had the sides short, you automatically made the back longer. And there was no rule against having your hair spiked up. They may have been able to force you to tow the line on length but they couldn't get you on height. I pulled back from the ginger bit although I think henna may have been involved on special occasions.

My first encounter with Bowie in the flesh was in 1973 when I met him in a club in the Stretford area of Manchester called the Hardrock. It is now a branch of B and Q and I estimate the location of the old stage to be somewhere near vinyl flooring. When I say I met him, I should perhaps mention that there were about two thousand other people there that night who met him as well. Oh, all right then, I went to see him in concert.

Me and my friends, Clive Walker, Dick Mason, Will Watson and Jonathan Eccles, had taken the bus in from Bolton that afternoon and had arrived several hours early as we didn't know our way around Manchester and didn't have enough money to get a taxi. Our timetable, though initially overgenerous seeing as we reached the big city around lunchtime for a gig that wouldn't start until eight o'clock at the earliest, proved not so ill-judged as we trudged the four miles from the bus station to far-off Stretford. I know four miles might not seem a lot for five strapping young lads, but believe you me, in those shoes it was quite a hike.

Eventually we reached the unprepossessing low-rise Hardrock, which had formerly been a ten-pin bowling establishment, in the nick of time. Around half-past three. We took up our places in the already sizable queue and chatted animatedly about the evening in prospect until the doors opened at seven. There was absolutely no need for us to be there that early. There were two kinds of tickets: standing for a pound, or reserved seating for the rather more profligate one pound twenty-five. As it was such a big deal we had decided to throw caution to the wind and buy seats, though we subsequently ran down the front to get a closer look, thereby wasting a full twenty-five new pence each, which doesn't sound like a fortune but could easily buy you three pints of mild.

The support group that night were Stealer's Wheel, who had a big current hit with 'Stuck in the Middle With You'. They were all right, I suppose, though they had all the stage presence of a set of Tupperware picnic boxes. They were basically a folk group who were tentatively flirting with glitter rock, but you could tell their hearts weren't really in it. You can't pull off the glam image with a beard and spectacles. Well, not unless you're Roy Wood.

When Bowie came on it was as if the world had shifted on its axis. He and the band just looked like no living creatures I'd ever seen before. Even Woody Woodmansey was wearing a tin-foil blouse, an elaborate lacquered crash helmet of hair on his head and a demonic resolve etched into his pinched face. And he was just the drummer. Trevor Bolder, the bassist, had a curtain of straight, shoulder-length hair from which emerged a pair of stupendous silver muttonchop sideboards. He was like a Dickensian dandy from the future. The piano player Mike Garson, whose services are retained by Bowie to this day, I now realize looked like Mike Gatting and so was quite rightly banished to the wings.

I couldn't tell you what Bowie and Ronson were wearing as they just seemed to inhabit a sparkling bubble of light. They would have been wearing glittery stuff for sure, but to me, they had an aura that you felt you could reach out and touch. I certainly tried.

They opened with 'Let's Spend the Night Together', a song we'd never heard before and didn't know was by the Rolling Stones until it appeared on the *Aladdin Sane* album later that year, and the whole thing just passed by in a blur of majestic wonder. It was the first big gig I'd been to and I haven't seen anything to surpass it since.

Buzzing on the energy of the show, and replaying it in my head for days afterwards, I went back to Tracks and bought all the earlier Bowie records: *Space Oddity*, his great under-estimated classic, *The Man Who Sold the World* and the masterpiece that is *Hunky Dory*. They're all wonderful and in fact you can make a strong case for him holding that form right up to 1983 and *Let's Dance*, as you will find different fans who, when asked what their favourite is, will choose one of the above or *Diamond Dogs*, *Young Americans*, *Station to Station*, *Low*, *'Heroes'*, *Lodger* or *Scary Monsters*. Truth is, they're all great. Admittedly it gets a bit hit and miss after *Let's Dance*, but as a run of brilliant albums it's as good as anyone has ever achieved. When I later asked David which he thought were the best he said he wavered between *Diamond Dogs* and *Lodger*. For me, though I occasionally flirt with *Hunky Dory*, I always come back to where it all began and if asked, as I occasionally have been, what my favourite album of all time is, I don't hesitate to say *Ziggy Stardust*.

And so, like every other teenage music nut, I found the

artist who I wanted to claim as my own and retreated to the bedroom with the collected works. And that would have been that. I would always buy his new records for evermore, no matter what the critics said, and would go and see him perform whenever he passed through Manchester. He would always be special to me, and I would be one of ten thousand faces somewhere beyond the glare of the spotlights to him.

Except I became a DJ fifteen years later and started to play his records, the same vinyl copies I'd bought with my pocket money, on national radio. I was doing a late-night show on Radio 1 and as my accomplice Marc 'Lard' Riley was just as big a fan as I was we played Bowie a lot. And not just the hit singles either. Given free rein by the benign regime of new controller Matthew Bannister, we indulged ourselves in the dusty corners of his illustrious back catalogue, airing 'An Occasional Dream', 'Win', 'Lady Grinning Soul' or 'Always Crashing in the Same Car' for the first time in years, and possibly ever.

Inevitably, as we occupied that slot for three and a half years, a new Bowie album came around. Titled *Outside*, it was released in 1995 and depicted a nightmare dystopian vision of the future. Now where had I come across a concept like that before?

Marc made all the running. I didn't think that a lowly late-night show, dubbed with an uncertain degree of irony 'The Graveyard Shift', would have a chance of being granted an audience. But Riley was like a vegetarian dog with a meat substitute bone. He just would not let it go and, fair play to him, he got us an interview. In New York. How about that? I was going to America to meet David Bowie.

Now, those of you who've had the welcome opportunity to read my first book, *Showbusiness – Diary of a Rock 'n' Roll Nobody*, have the option of skipping the next few paragraphs as they recall the historic meeting outlined above that was also documented in that heavyweight tome. For those of you who haven't had that pleasure I'll run you through the gist of it, as that glorious literary achievement is out of print now due to the remaining copies having been pulped. Did I say pulped? I meant to say sold out. All copies have been sold. What a triumph.

I met David Bowie in a small studio used by the BBC off Times Square, and this time there were only three other people in the room. Marc Riley, our producer Lis Roberts and an engineer. Bowie was the size I was expecting, compact and slim, and had sparkly eyes and even sparklier teeth. He was incredibly smiley, friendly and seemed to be laughing all the time. He wasn't remotely remote and certainly wasn't putting on any studied act of cool. I suppose he'd been cool for so long it just came naturally. He ordered a turkey sandwich.

Weirdly, on meeting the musician I'd most admired in my whole life, I wasn't aware of feeling overawed or nervous. He was so affable that he defused any tension the moment he walked in the room. We chatted, tested the microphones for level, and then broadcast two hours live by satellite back to the UK.

He was a very easy interviewee as he chatted about his life in New York and Switzerland, his new album, his favourite new bands, his thoughts on his past recordings and his paternal pride in his son Joe.

Afterwards he bade us farewell and we retired to a bar where television screens flickered with highlights of the inexplicably popular sports they have over there: American football, or 'catch' as we know it, baseball, which we call rounders, and basketball, which is a game that seems to hinge entirely on being tall. That's not a sport, is it? That's just having grown. Where's the skill in that? Don't tell me you've got a hero who's a basketball player or I'll start to get cross.

I ordered a drink and remembered that I'd promised to phone my wife Bella to let her know how the interview had gone. I called her up and she wanted to know all about it as we were relatively early in our relationship at that time and she was still interested in what I was doing. That's what you do at the beginning, isn't it? The weird thing was, though, that when I took a sip of beer and tried to tell her all about it, nothing would come out. All the nerves I must have sub-consciously suppressed came flooding out as I let my mask of professional control drop. It finally hit me. I had met David Bowie. And now I was speechless.

I've met David several times since then, I'm glad to say. He played a live set for us at the BBC's Maida Vale studios and also came to chat on our afternoon programme in 2002 on the day he was playing Old Trafford cricket ground. Before the show he whiled away an hour or so sitting in my chair at my desk in my office. He asked me if he could pinch the new album by The Vines and a *Viz* annual, which seemed entirely appropriate given his ever-present enthusiasm for hearing new things and his playfully wacky sense of humour. He seems to take his work a lot more seriously than he takes himself at any rate, and the thought of your actual David Bowie giggling over Biffa Bacon is rather endearing some-how.

That night Marc and I were booked to compère at the Lancashire Cricket Club gig, which meant we would be introducing our teen idol in front of twenty-five thousand fellow fans. It felt like quite an honour, I can tell you.

Turning up late afternoon we were cheerfully informed by the stage manager, a breezy acquaintance of ours called Graham who was also the guitarist in Inspiral Carpets, that no dressing room had been allocated to us. This presented no immediate problem as we weren't planning to change the clothes we were wearing. Taking another outfit to wear on stage when all you're doing is introducing the acts smacks of taking yourself a bit too seriously, and there's always the risk that you'll have a few too many shandies and leave your original outfit behind. However, as torrential rain was forecast, and eventually arrived during Suede's set, Graham had taken pity on us and found us a little bolt-hole where we could hide away from the elements. It wasn't a dressing room as such, but was a closet on the same corridor as the dressing rooms and had been set aside to hold all the booze riders for the rest of the acts on the bill. So it was that Marc and I found ourselves sheltering from the storm in the company of around two thousand cans of lager. Well what would you have done? You'd have tried to drink them, wouldn't you? And being the only natural course of action, we took it.

The bands lower down the bill received introductions from the masters of ceremonies that more or less resembled something in the English language and included the requisite plugs for the sponsor: the *Manchester Evening News*, which, we were told to point out, was now only ten pence on a Friday. As the day wore on though, and The Divine Comedy and Suede took to the stage, the lager mountain in the broom cupboard diminished, the announcements became less easy to decipher, and the plugs for the *Evening News* ever more frequent and faux heartfelt. By the time we ambled uncertainly onto the stage to introduce the headline attraction we could hardly string a sentence together. Of course, fuelled by the ale we were convinced that we could hold an audience in the sweaty palms of our beer-drenched hands and were utterly sure that what all those people who'd stood in the rain wanted was to wait just a few minutes longer for David Bowie while two inebriated tosspots off the radio slid up and down the stage shouting indecipherable messages down distorting radio mics. I have watched this ill-judged display on video since and it goes on for something like eight minutes, which is about seven minutes and forty-five seconds longer than it should have, and at the end of it you are in possession of no more information than you were before it started, except that there can be little doubt that the *Manchester Evening News* is ten pence on a Friday. What David was thinking as he waited to make his entrance heaven only knows. As a *Viz* aficionado you could only hope it appealed to his sense of the absurd.

And I suppose it must have done, as later that same year he invited us to introduce him again. Except this time it was at the Apollo in London and that gave it an even greater piquancy. The Apollo is a fine old theatre with a hint of faded art-deco glamour that made it such an atmospheric venue through the years it was known as Hammersmith Odeon. It was also the location for Bowie's killing off of the Ziggy Stardust character in a legendary gig back in 1973. This was to be the first time David had returned to that famous stage since and as well as performing tracks from his new album *Heathen*, gems from the past were also promised.

Turning up at the stage door the signs were immediately good. At all gigs at that level, as soon as you walk into the dingy backstage corridors you'll be confronted by hastily produced laminated signs stuck with Blu-tack onto the taupe, gloss-painted walls. These direct the tour personnel to a variety of locations including the production office, front of house and, most importantly, catering. And there, amidst the plethora of others, was a sign bearing the *Heathen* artwork and the words: 'Mark and Laid – Dressing Room'. We'd arrived. We not only had our own private quarters, but an official sign showing us the way there and advertising to everyone involved that we were really part of the show.

However, before we got to our billet, one of the greatest moments in my life occurred. As we were sauntering down the gloomy passageways of strip lights and lino, thrilled to be in the bowels of this legendary rock theatre, a door opened revealing bright lights around a wall of mirrors, lending a radiant glow to the small figure in the cream jean jacket who stood at the entrance to the room. David Bowie.

He greeted us as if we were really proper friends of his, and not two drunkards who'd slurred their way through proceedings at Old Trafford, and invited us into his private dressing room. There was no one else there. The room contained some fresh flowers, lots of fruit, some furniture that was smart enough but might have been more at home in the lobby of a mid-priced hotel somewhere off the A1, Marc Riley, me, and the biggest rock star in our world ever.

He indulged in a few moments of his trademark joshing, and then pulled a handwritten list from the pocket of his caramel-coloured trousers.

'I was thinking of doing this tonight. What do you reckon?'

Stunned, Marc and I cast our eyes down the list, which included such classics as 'Life On Mars', 'China Girl', 'Rebel Rebel', 'Absolute Beginners', 'Fame', 'Ziggy Stardust' of course, and 'Heroes' – an onomatopoeic epic sweep of a song which seems to empower the listener even as he or she is listening to it. It may be the greatest pop record ever made and what number did it get to in the UK charts? One? Two? No, twenty-four! How is that possible? How could there have been twenty-three more popular songs in the charts that week when there haven't been twenty-three better songs written in the history of music?

Then David started to ask us what we thought of the order the songs were in, and asked us if we thought 'Changes' should come before 'Starman' or vice versa. It was one of the moments where life seemed just unreal. That the schoolboy from Bolton with his Bowie albums in his bedroom was now sitting in the same Bowie's dressing room discussing the finer points of that night's running order was something I would never have dreamed could happen. Of course we all fantasize about meeting our idols without it ever happening. And if it did it would be a fleeting handshake and scribbled autograph in a melee by some stage door somewhere. To be in the same room, and for him to be genuinely interested in my opinion, was too much to take in.

We didn't go to our dressing room. We went out to a local pub and nursed a pint as we tried to come to terms with it all. We didn't say much. Each knew what it meant to the other.

That night we introduced David Bowie on stage at the Hammersmith Odeon. We didn't say anything worth repeating but we were sober, didn't mention the *Manchester Evening News* or its cover price and, hopefully, managed to articulate the sense of occasion we all felt that night in the place where Ziggy had been laid to rest almost three decades earlier.

And David was on imperious form, possibly spurred on by the echoes and reverberations from the late seventies he must have been feeling himself. I'd have enjoyed every minute of it whatever the circumstances, but being some small part of the show, with my own dressing room and everything, made it seem just magical.

I watched the whole set from the side of the stage, as enraptured as I'd been as a spotty youth at the Hardrock. And for the duration of that concert at Hammersmith, maybe I did finally allow myself a hero. Just for one day.

7. THE DAY I MISSED AN OPEN GOAL AT MAINE ROAD

By rights I should be a Bolton Wanderers supporter. It's my home-town team, and as a boy I did frequent Burnden Park. It has, of course, long been demolished to make way for a supermarket, but even in my time it was something of a crumbling structure. It was one of the old style of football grounds, towering above the narrow streets of terraced houses that surrounded it. All week it would loom silently yet tantalizingly above the neighbourhood as the supporters toiled in the mills, a symbol of pleasures that would be tasted when the week's work had been done. Come Saturday, always Saturday, the men, always the men, would buckle up their gaberdine overcoats, wrap home-knitted black-and-white scarves around their necks, don a flat cap, trilby or bobble hat to match the scarf and walk from all directions towards the ground. Many, including some of the players, went by public bus. If you went in a car you probably owned the club.

It was a ground that had seen great days, but not in my time sadly. Behind one of the goals was the embankment, a gigantic wasteland of brutal concrete terracing. Here tens of thousands once stood waving their rattles as the drama unfolded against Preston North End or Blackpool. At the back of the embankment, tucked under the railway line you can see in the 1962 film *A Kind of Loving* starring Alan Bates, was a shed on stilts. They may well have kept what blokes keep in sheds in there: shovels, rakes, bottles of whisky, stashes of adult magazines maybe, but its primary function was as a half-time scoreboard. After the first forty-five minutes, a shutter would open and a white-coated steward would hang out number cards under the letters of the alphabet. Each letter would correspond to a different match, but your only way of knowing which game it was came from a list that was printed in the programme. If you didn't have a programme, you had no idea what any of it meant.

This shack was about twenty feet wide by about eight deep and yet while watching a rain-lashed battle of attrition against Torquay, I can remember everyone on the embankment being able to huddle under it to hide from the squall. In front lay acres of crumbling ramparts, infested with weeds, where once so many had escaped the drudgery of the working week. They held the FA Cup final replay there in 1901, for heaven's sake.

Not that it pays to get too misty-eyed and romantic about those days. Behind the other goal was the notorious Lever End where packs of marauding skinheads pursued opposing factions. I have no idea if the prevalence of football violence was statistically greater then but it certainly seemed that way. In the all-seated, heavily segregated grounds we visit today, it's more or less impossible to start a fight unless it's by complaining too forcibly in the executive banqueting suite about the temperature of the Côtes du Rhône or the poor filleting job that's been carried out on the sea bass. Back then, rucks used to occur at every game without fail. You began to wonder if the police and the club hadn't colluded in turning a blind eye. At least, come Saturday at three, always three, they knew where every nutter in the town was. It was simple really, if you wanted trouble you went in the Lever End and the shaven-headed, Crombie-overcoated Cro-Magnons would be happy to give you what you were looking for. The only exceptions to this rule were when Bury or Blackburn Rovers came to town, when they would obligingly stand on people's heads in the surrounding streets as well. Evidently there was more local 'business' to be conducted than could possibly be squeezed into match time.

While in no way condoning the abhorrent violence that erupted with a monotonous regularity that almost made you immune to it, everyone understood the nature of the local rivalries. Some of it lingers to this day across football the world over, but in those days it was of a distinctly parochial nature. All of the Bolton players came from the town and there was a palpable sense of shock when, in 1966, they signed the burly, rumbustious centre forward Johnny Byrom. Crikey, our first 'foreigner'. He was from Blackburn.

And so if you lived in Bolton and had an interest in football, you supported the Trotters, a nickname which may have its roots in the local delicacies of tripe, cow heel, chitterlings and pigs' trotters, though I don't recall any of these being available at the ground. Or perhaps they'd just sold out by the time I managed to push my way to the front to get a beef tea.

I started going to the match with my dad and little brother. My dad worked for the local paper and had a small piece of plastic with magical powers called a press card. If you're familiar with the 'golden ticket' concept in *Charlie and the Chocolate Factory* you'll know what I'm on about. My dad's understanding of the press card was that it meant not having to pay to get in anywhere ever again. Everywhere we went, from Morecambe Illuminations in Happy Mount Park to go-karting at Hesham Head, if there was an admission charge, my dad would nonchalantly flash this creased, badly laminated scrap of paper, bark 'Press' at the startled attendant, and usher us all through the turnstile. I don't recall him ever being challenged, except by my mum, who would cringe with embarrassment and tell him to get his hand in his pocket.

And so for the first few years of visiting Burnden we never actually paid to get in although, to be fair, we did have a different card that specifically entitled us to entry. Unfortunately it was signed and authorized by a manager who'd left the club several years earlier. My dad had an ingenious solution to this. He held his thumb over the signature and then just barked 'Press' as usual, and marched his two young sons in. Not content with that however, he then used to take us into the press room at half-time and let us get stuck into the plates of potted-meat fingers and whist pies that had been laid out for the attendant hacks. So we got three free seats and portions of snacks, and he wasn't even reporting on the game. Again, I don't remember anyone asking to take a closer look at his credentials or question why two urchins were rolling around on the floor perilously close to the tea urn.

Eventually I got old enough to want to go to the match with my mates Rog Milne and Rob Redgate, and so our thrifty family outings came to an end, the sense of freedom from being out of parental control only slightly sullied by the realization that the match wasn't free after all.

Towards the end of our freebie days, though, Dad took us to a couple of matches at Manchester City, who coincidentally drew the largest official crowd to a game at Burnden Park when 69,912 blokes in raincoats attended their game at Bolton in 1933.

Why we went to Manchester City and not United I don't know. Perhaps Old Trafford employed overzealous jobsworths who actually checked signatures on press cards and directed you to the ticket office. I wouldn't be surprised. It's the kind of low trick you'd expect from that lot.

Bolton were marooned down the leagues at that time, whereas Manchester City were a real glamour club. Their team included such legends as Colin Bell, Francis Lee, Mike Summerbee, Joe Corrigan and, later, Rodney Marsh. Long-standing City fans regard this as the greatest team the club has ever had, and to see them in full-blooded matches against the likes of a Chelsea side boasting such heroes as Alan Hudson, Charlie Cooke and the Peters Osgood and Bonetti, well, it was the stuff of schoolboy dreams. Not quite as enjoyable as the ones about Pan's People perhaps, but these guys were actually present in the flesh, and that wasn't going to happen with Pan's People. And even if it did it wasn't going to last an hour and a half and involve intense physical grappling and a lot of mud. More's the pity.

So my head was turned by the bright lights of the big-city club, and my fully fledged turncoat status was confirmed when I went to university in 1976, and found myself sta-tioned in hall of residence fifteen minutes' walk from Maine Road. I suppose I could have taken two buses and a train to get back to Bolton, but I felt that I was beginning a new life, and being a full-time supporter of a new club just seemed right somehow. I realize this is still a pretty lame excuse in the eyes of the die-hard fans who will say, with some justi-fication, that changing your allegiance just isn't allowed. When you're young you either choose a club you fancy, whether through family affiliation or because you like the colour of the shirts, or simply pin your colours to the mast of your hometown team, and that's you for life. In truth, I accept that's probably the way it should be, but it's an idea that comes from another age. It's rooted in the supporters living in the streets around the ground and flocking en masse to the game after downing tools on Saturday lunchtime. Crucially, it's also about feeling a degree of empathy and connection with the boys in the team. We still love it when someone from the youth squad breaks through to take his place in the starting line-up alongside the multimillionaire tourists because he's 'one of ours'. In my childhood they were all 'ours' and once players were allowed to be globetrotting mercenaries it seems to me this bond was broken. If the players aren't expected to be loyal to the club, then why should the supporters have to put up with it? Of course most do because they live nearby and it makes little practical sense for a boiler fitter from Sunderland to suddenly transfer his affections to, say, Barcelona. But the players, richer than Croesus though blissfully unaware of who Croesus was unless he was that bloke who played 'in the hole' for Olympiakos, are free to crisscross Europe picking up ever-bigger wads of cash from whichever oligarch has most loose change. Whether that's right or wrong is open to debate, and I accept that working for a club is a very different proposition to supporting it. You can be sacked as a manager or transferred as a player, but you can't be dismissed as a supporter unless you chant vile abuse, invade the pitch or hurl a prawn ciabatta at the back of Roy Keane's head. And at least one of those ought only to involve a gentle ticking-off. Or indeed a pat on the back. But even if they ban you from the ground, they can't stop you being a supporter at heart. And I suppose that's what it comes down to. What you feel in your heart. I felt in my heart that I could walk to Manchester City and still be back in the pub for five, and therefore wouldn't miss anything that was happening with my mates on a Saturday night. If I'd gone to the Wanderers I'd have got back to a darkened corridor in hall, with a hastily scribbled note pinned to my door saying something like:

'Wanker. We've all gone out without you. See you tomorrow lunchtime. Have used all the milk.'

And so I became a proper City supporter at the age of eighteen and have never regretted it. It's been character-building. There have been lows too numerous to list, though losing one–nil at home to Bury in February 1998 probably warrants a mention. We'd already slipped down from the top division and were plummeting towards a relegation spot in the league below. Our manager at the time was the gruff and avuncular Frank Clark, a man who bore a striking resemblance to Boycie from *Only Fools and Horses*. He once, when asked by the press officer about myself and Marc Riley going out to greet the crowd before a game, said words to the effect of 'I don't want those two idiots on the pitch'. We admired him for that, although it was a pity he wasn't as choosy about who he was putting in the team. He seemed a decent enough chap, but it was hard to imagine him giving team talks of Churchillian inspiration, and this defeat really set the alarm bells ringing for the City faithful. What was going on? We were the big boys, and here we were losing at home to, with all due respects, little Bury. To be fair, the visitors had been on a bit of a run before arriving at Maine Road. They'd failed to win in seventeen games.

But if you're a Manchester blue, you learn to take these things on the chin and wait for the highs to return. Sometimes you can be waiting a very long time, but then you'll get a season like 2001–02. With Kevin Keegan installed as manager and such gifted individuals as Ali Benarbia and Eyal Berkovic (an Algerian and an Israeli for the international relations observers), making the team tick, we swept to the top spot scoring 108 goals in the process. All right, it was Nationwide Division One (which used to be Division Two but is now the Championship, what used to be Division Three now having become Division One if you follow), but that didn't matter. I don't own the club so the fact that we weren't getting as much television and sponsorship money as the top clubs in the land didn't bother me. The crowds were down a bit too, which was brilliant as it saved you a good half-hour getting out of the car park. And we played really attractive, attacking football and scored three or four goals in each game. What more do you want? Every week I would get home and when asked by my wife if we'd won would happily say, 'Yes, three–nil,' and she would just say, 'Oh, good.' She never asked who we'd been playing so I never had to say, again with all due respect, Grimsby or Rotherham, which would have made it sound like less of an achievement than if it had been Liverpool or the other Manchester team. It was probably the most enjoyable season as a spectator I've had in my whole life.

And then of course there was the memorable play-off at Wembley against Gillingham. This game is firmly ensconced in City folklore, not only because of the dramatic events that unfolded that day, but because we all knew it was a turning point. The winners would get out of Division Two and would be in sight of the top level of English football once again. Lose and you were stuck in the mire for the foreseeable future. Look, I'm not denigrating the proud clubs who operate in the lower leagues, but we were Manchester City, and we wanted to be back where we thought we belonged. Hubristic maybe, but we had to win this game to convince us that being 'down there' was a temporary blip in our glorious history.

It was 30 May 1999, and I wasn't at the game. I know what you're thinking. Not only is he a turncoat, he doesn't even turn up when his adopted team play at Wembley. However, in my defence I was honouring a long-standing obligation to play with my folk-rock drinking band The Family Mahone at the Chester Folk Festival. I could have pulled the gig, but that would have been unfair not only on the organizers but also the rest of the guys in the group. In addition it would have let down all the punters who'd booked their tickets for the weekend specifically because we were appearing. I mean, how could you let down five people like that and have a clear conscience?

Initially we were booked to play in the evening, which was ideal. If we won, I could crow about it in front of a sizable crowd, and if we lost, I could drown my sorrows with the guys and take my mind off the result by knocking out a few songs. It then emerged that the committee wanted us to appear in the afternoon as well. I agreed only on the understanding that I could watch the game in the pub before being called to the stage. Accordingly we were scheduled to appear immediately after the match ended. No problem.

So it was that those of us who were interested took our seats in front of the television in the snug of the Morris Dancer, and readied ourselves for an afternoon of high drama. This was the game on which the whole future of the club depended. Or that's what it felt like anyway.

Half-time, nil–nil. We weren't ahead as we'd expected, but at least we hadn't let one in. It was all there for the taking.

'Who's round is it? Mine again? Are you sure? Well, you'll have to go to the bar. I'm staying here.'

The hour mark came and went, no score. Seventy minutes and no goals. Come on, City! And then, disaster struck. In the eightieth minute Carl Asaba put Gillingham ahead. Bugger.

The members of the group who didn't follow City glanced at the score and began to make preparations for getting on stage in the marquee adjacent to the pub. We were due on about five minutes ago, the match having kicked off slightly late.

'Mark, we should get moving.'

'Oh, come on, guys. I said I wouldn't go on until the game had finished and there's still ten minutes to go. Anything could happen.'

Looks were exchanged but it was clear I wasn't going anywhere, and I felt quite safe in the knowledge that I was sticking to my side of the bargain. As soon as the game was over, I would be straight on stage. But the festival crowd were getting restless apparently.

It was at this point that a foolproof plan was hatched. There were seven of us in the band: me on drums and lead vocals, Christy on mandolin, Rusty on accordion, Doc on fiddle and banjo, Don on guitar and new boy bassist Charlie, for whom this would turn out to be a memorable first gig. The seventh member was Jock the van driver, who wasn't likely to be of much use in the present circumstances unless it was by keeping the engine warm to ensure a swift getaway.

Still eight minutes to go, and we only need one goal.

'Tell you what, some of you go on and start and I'll follow you the second the final whistle goes.'

It being a folk festival, this was a perfectly reasonable idea. It's not like a football team starting without all their players. Christy (Chester City) and Rusty (Northampton Town) were quite capable of ploughing through some traditional tunes to keep the stage warm until the rest of us could get there. Charlie (Stockport County) was keen to get his first gig over with and so decided to go with them. Sorted.

And then, nightmare scenario. In the eighty-seventh minute the solidly named and built Bob Taylor makes it two–nil to Gillingham. Bob bloody Taylor. He looked more like a greengrocer than a footballer, and subsequently signed for City where he played like one. Well, that was that then. Doc (Liverpool) gave a shrug and followed the others leaving just Don, fellow City sufferer, and me behind.

'See you in a minute, then.'

'Yes, all right, Doc. We're not going to score twice in three minutes, are we? You go ahead, and we'll be right there.'

So with a heavy heart and an empty pint glass, never a good combination, I pushed back my chair and prepared to slope over to the backstage area.

And then, a lifeline. In the eighty-ninth minute the redoubtable Kevin Horlock struck for City. Two–one, with one minute to go. Or was it?

'Come on, Mark. We're on.'

'OK, OK, give me a minute.'

The referee, Mark Halsey God bless him, then indicated a minimum of five added minutes.

'Errm, actually, give me six minutes.'

By this time Christy and Rusty had taken the stage and announced why they were slightly late and a couple of men down. Christy, never short of a gadget, had a portable radio with an earpiece so he could keep abreast of the concluding stages of the game. Perhaps it was because they were distracted by events at Wembley, or simply that they wanted to make Charlie's debut as traumatic as possible for him out of sheer malevolence, that he and Rusty decided to start the set with 'Green and Yellow', which we hadn't rehearsed and Charlie didn't know. Nice one, lads. If that wasn't going to keep the crowd happy, then nothing would. Evidently Doc sidled on somewhere around verse fourteen.

Meanwhile in the back bar Don and I were glued to the screen. This really was gripping stuff. Four minutes to take it to extra time. But this was City we were watching. Things like that never happened to us. Ninety-one minutes, ninety-two, and you could feel the disappointment welling up in your stomach. Ninety-three minutes played. Well, we might as well go, I suppose. And then, in the ninety-fourth minute, the impossible happened. The pugnacious Paul Dickov scored to make it two–all. In celebration he skidded across the turf on his knees and, with both fists clenched and pent-up frustration escaping, grimaced towards the heavens.

Wembley, and the pub, erupted. Don and I leaped up and down in a manly embrace. We'd done it. We'd taken it to extra time. We were ecstatic.

Christy and his earpiece on stage were considerably less ecstatic. Extra time. That meant they had to fill another half-hour, and they were fast running out of tunes that Charlie didn't know. And to make matters even more uncomfortable for the debutant, our previous bass player Bootsy, a.k.a. Sickly Rob, had decided to make an appearance and sit in the front row.

As is often the case after a compelling ninety, sorry ninety-five, minutes, extra time proved to be something of an anticlimax with no further goals being scored.

'Bloody hell,' moaned Christy, marooned on stage.

'What now?'

'It's only gone to penalties.'

Some of the audience were enjoying this spectacle unfold, others, notably certain members of the organizing commit-tee, thought it less amusing. I was still being true to my word though. When matters were concluded at Wembley, I would be on directly.

Thanks to the heroics of goalkeeper Nicky Weaver, we won the penalty shoot out three–one, and our journey back to the upper echelons of football had begun. Don and I eventually joined the rest of the band only the small matter of about fifty minutes late, and played about three songs before our allotted time was up. We played a full set in the evening though, which went down a storm. Or so I'm told. I don't remember a lot about it if I'm being honest.

My association with the Chester Folk Festival ended that day, although they have invited me back recently, but my Manchester City affiliation continued with renewed vigour.

The club had built a third tier on top of the Kippax stand, which ran down one side of the pitch. Not being in the top division at that point, attendances were respectable but there were plenty of spaces for the casual observer. Graciously the club allowed Marc Riley and I two seats each on the top deck. At first it seemed perilously high, and you couldn't always easily detect the trajectory of the ball. After a while though I got to really like it up there as you could follow the pattern of play, if there was one that week.

In return for these free tickets, rather neatly reviving the Radcliffe family tradition of not paying to get in, we were asked to perform occasional duties on the pitch. These turned out not to be menial tasks with garden forks and buckets of sand, though Lord knows I'd have preferred that, but menial tasks befitting the low-rent 'celebrity'.

Every club likes to have its 'famous' followers and be able to trot them out from time to time. City were fortunate in being able to produce Ricky Hatton on a fairly regular basis, but on the odd occasions he was needed elsewhere to do a bit of boxing they looked around for someone else. First choice would be Noel and Liam Gallagher of Oasis. They would oblige occasionally, but lived in London and were taking too many drugs to get on a train at short notice. Next port of call would be rotund, bird's-nest-coiffured alleged comedian Eddie Large, and then Curly Watts or Les Battersby from *Coronation Street*. Genial pomp-rock keyboard wizard Rick Wakeman might also have to be ready with a good excuse.

Eventually, with all other alternatives exhausted, they might reluctantly call Radio 1's under-performing breakfast-show wrecking squad Mark and Lard.

I have to confess, I always dreaded those calls. If only Frank Clark hadn't been replaced with the chummy Joe Royle.

I know a lot of fans dream of walking on the hallowed turf at their beloved club, but not me. For a social inadequate used to the sanctuary of the radio studio, the walls of people rising up on all sides in the stands were utterly daunting. In a way it was a relief to go on at half-time and find that a good proportion of the crowd had gone off to queue for pints and pasties, but that also made it even more embarrassing. When the dreaded announcement echoed from the PA system: 'Maine Road, will you welcome the hosts of the Radio 1 breakfast show, Mark and Lard,' the reaction was distinctly underwhelming. And fair enough. Who cared that two tin-pot DJs were on the pitch to draw a raffle? I certainly didn't and I was one of them!

However, it got even more toe-curling than that. I was once invited to play in a 'celebrity' match before a local derby between City and the other Manchester team. The game was a testimonial for Paul Lake, a young City and England player whose career had been cruelly cut short by a knee injury. He was a player I admired enormously and it was for that reason alone that I agreed to play. It certainly wasn't because I wanted to play football. I didn't mind playing foot-ball, it was just that I was no good at it. I finished up playing hockey at school as that was where you were put if you weren't good enough to make the third eleven at soccer.

On the day of the game I felt absolutely mortified. Especially as it became clear that local businessmen had bid at a charity auction for the chance to take part. These guys were seriously competitive and, in the dressing room, began to use phrases like 'get stuck in', 'a good hiding' and 'get what's coming to them'. Blimey! I'd rather hoped for a gentle trot round the pitch, ideally only touching the ball when it had gone out of play. And then only to toss it to someone else to take the actual throw-in. I wasn't planning to give anybody what was coming to them unless it was a firm hand-shake and a strip of Juicy Fruit.

Invited to choose which position I'd like to play in I said I'd be a full back because I thought that was the spot in which you were least likely to come into contact with the ball. As everybody else wanted to be centre forward or midfield dynamo, this went down quite well. Honestly, it was like being back at school except this was worse as I was in the team.

The game kicked off, I imagine, though I couldn't be sure from the position I'd taken up a yard from the corner flag. Lots of rough stuff went on, and some goals might have been scored. I remember looking up into the City-blue sky and thinking it was a lovely day for Lakey, as those of us who'd never met him referred to him. Suddenly, there was a shout. Bugger. The ball was coming towards me and at this point I realized that playing at the edge of the pitch is a bit of a mixed blessing. You don't have to do very much, but when you do, the crowd are right there watching you make a mess of it.

The ball bounced a couple of feet in front of me, and more or less rolled to a standstill by my right instep. It was then that I became aware of someone from the opposing side coming towards me. I later found out that, on the opposing touchline, the relatively handy Marc Riley and Les Battersby, the actor Bruce Jones, had struck a deal. To make themselves look good, each would allow the other to dribble daintily down the wing without taking their legs from under them. Good plan. Unfortunately I had omitted to make any such arrangements with Billy Boswell out of *Bread*, played by Nick Conway, who was by now standing in front of me. Taking the only sensible option open to someone who could barely kick a ball straight, I decided to knock it out for a throw-in, because that way I wasn't risking anything catastrophic. Sadly, under the watchful glare of three levels of the Kippax, I scuffed it and presented the ball straight to my opponent. Fortunately, startled to be confronted with this level of ineptitude, young Boswell failed to control the ball

and put it out for a throw to us. Brilliant. That was more of
a result than I'd expected. I'd actually done something of
benefit to the team. Knowing that this was as good as it was
going to get, I bent down and rubbed my hamstring, despite
not knowing where a hamstring was, signalled to the bench,
and trotted off to be replaced by Corrie's Nicky Tilsley
(Adam Rickitt). This proved a popular move with the crowd,
especially the girls on that side of the pitch.

I would gladly never have touched a football again after
that, but unfortunately, duty called twice more.

At half-time some bright spark had concocted a spectacle
called 'Kicks for Cash'. As you might have guessed, this
involved taking shots at goal, and those successfully con-
verted raised money for charity. Well, you can't say no, can
you? And it didn't sound like it was that difficult, even for
me.

Even so, I spent the first half of the match dreading the referee's whistle to signal the end of the first period of play.
When it came I dragged my feet slowly down to the players'
tunnel knowing it would be over with relatively quickly. The
following words, or similar, drifted over the speakers:

'Maine Road, or those of you who haven't gone for a
wee or a chicken balti pie, please be no less hostile than
absolutely necessary to Radio 1 failing breakfast-show
chancers Mark and Lard.'

We trudged out to the centre of the pitch to someone
with a microphone who shook my hand, and then placed the
ball on the penalty spot. It was only when I looked up that I
saw what appeared to be a large rubber ring dangling from
the crossbar.

'Errm, excuse me, mate, what's that inner tube doing
there?'

'You have to get the ball through the middle of it.'

'You are joking, right?'

I mean honestly, most of the players in the City side would have struggled to do that, possibly even the Bermudian gentleman striker Shaun Goater. Christiano Ronaldo might have considered it tricky.

I took a few steps back and looked up. Behind the goal, the North stand was filling up again as punters returned to their seats with cartons of chips and fizzy Vimto. I swallowed hard, ran towards the ball and, as far as I could tell, chipped it hopefully rather than deftly in the general direction of the yellow plastic doughnut. Wouldn't it be lovely to say that the crowd stopped, watched, held their breath and then cast their bobble hats into the air in their thousands to celebrate the ball popping straight through the hole? Predictably, that didn't happen. Less predictably, I not only missed the rubber ring, but the entire goal. That's right. In front of perhaps ten thousand hands gleefully conjoined in sarcastic applause, I failed to find the open goal.

Unbelievably, I subsequently agreed to do 'Kicks for Cash' once again. This time though, I had a plan. Running up to the ball I made no attempt to hit the rubber ring, and simply side-footed into the empty net. There was a general air of bemusement at this, but at least I hadn't suffered the indignity of missing the goal completely. That was enough for me. In my own mind I had 'scored' at Maine Road.

I haven't kicked a football since.

8. THE DAY I LEFT RADIO 1 AFTER EIGHTEEN YEARS

The day I left Radio 1 after eighteen years they gave me a plastic carriage clock.

Unsure if this gesture was ironic, and knowing it would be something I'd wonder about whenever I checked the time, I put it in the wheelie bin the next morning.

At 11.37.

9. THE DAY I MET TONY BLAIR'S TEETH

Wherever possible I've tried to avoid what are known as 'team building' initiatives. For disc jockeys, a term which it's hard to say out loud without it sounding like a term of derision, this is all too understandable, as everyone expects them to be selfish egomaniacs anyway. In my experience there are some for whom this is a perfectly fair description. Even some of the DJs I've become friendly with, and there aren't that many, fall into this category. I'd like to think I don't, but I may well be fooling myself, as I'm sure I've had my moments.

The truth is that you can't really go on air and front a radio programme unless you've got a relatively high opinion of yourself, a basic belief that what you are going to say is worth hearing. This is an entirely different personality trait than being a well-adjusted social animal, however. I know national radio presenters who are almost painfully shy, and I personally find walking into a room of about twenty people to be far more nerve-racking than doing a live show to several million.

There have also been several high-profile DJs who are just as egomaniacal as everyone else, but have chosen to disguise themselves as people with no ego at all. I'm not going to name names here, but I think if I'm honest this is a trick I've occasionally tried to pull off myself. So there you go. I am going to name names after all. Or one name anyway. Me. And I think you can probably work out some of the others for yourself.

However, I would like to think that I'm a pretty solid 'team player' when it comes to working with the rest of the people engaged in getting the programmes I'm presenting made. Then again, as presenter, your role is ultimately different to everyone else on the crew. You can all work closely putting the thing together, but when the red light goes on, everyone else sits in the other room while you sit on your own on the opposite side of the glass, open your mouth and talk. I sometimes liken it to being on board the space shuttle, but only one of you is on the end of a lifeline doing the space-walk. That analogy is not, by the way, intended to imply that what I do or say is remotely important or risky. I'm only playing pop records and talking in between them. It's not rocket science, is it? Mind you, it would also be disingenuous to pretend that I don't think there's some value to what I do. People need to be 'entertained' and given the chance to hear new music chosen by someone who's spent his or her life doing just that. It's all very well being able to download any track in the universe, but there has to be someone pointing you in a certain direction or where do you begin?

The space shuttle on the other hand *is* rocket science, but what have they done for us, eh? I know they've messed about with crystals and alloys and geophysical flow cells, but you'd have to say that palls into insignificance next to me playing you the new Arctic Monkeys album. And I'm cheaper.

Occasionally managers will attempt to create bonding exercises amongst presenters. Good managers realize this is futile as the whole point of employing these people is that they are wildly opinionated and, essentially, mavericks, loners and social inadequates. And I think this is rather wonderful.

That a radio station should be home to all these interesting, knowledgeable, passionate but very different people is a far more seductive notion than it being a hostel for blow-dried clones in matching bomber jackets.

In my experience teams build themselves if people are happy doing the job they're doing and get paid a fair whack for doing it. If you feel underpaid and undervalued, then firing a paintball into the temple of the finance director on an 'away-day' might make you feel better in the short term, but you're still going to be struggling to pay the credit card bill at the end of the month. If you hate your job, then having Will Carling instructing you to walk across a plank in some godforsaken conference room in a motel off the M25 while lashed with a rope around your waist to Big Julie from HR is unlikely to make much difference. There may well be benefits to being lashed to Big Julie from HR in the privacy of one of the bedrooms, but that's a different matter.

The point is that what your boss describes as a team-bonding initiative is sometimes exactly the opposite of that. It's a way of making you do things the way he or she says they should be done, and to brand people who disagree as not being 'team players'. Well, that's my theory anyway.

Having said all of that, I can honestly say that in all my years in radio, I have only had serious disagreements, to the point of arguing, with three or perhaps four people. And that's in a career that began in 1979. I do think we've become far too obsessed with the idea of workplace friendships; you don't have to be someone's best mate to work successfully alongside them, but the vast majority of people I've encountered have been a privilege to know. Even the DJs.

When I was at Radio 1 there were mercifully few attempts at cementing team unity, but the annual DJ photo was pretty much a three-line whip. Outside of a close relative dying or contracting bird flu, you were expected to be there.

My only problem with this was what to wear. I know that sounds a bit pathetic, but the thing is that Radio 1, by its very nature, attracts and employs a lot of highly fashionable people wearing just the right cut of jean and this season's must-have trainers. I'm not one of those people. I would hope that I don't look like I've been caught in the picture by mistake, having actually come to fix the waste-disposal unit, but I was painfully aware that I couldn't compete with the in-house fashionistas. I can basically either wear the anorak, jumper, just the wrong cut of jean and last season's reduced trainers that I've just walked the dog in, or I can put a wedding suit on. I don't really have anything in between, and maybe it shouldn't really matter, but I never felt that looking like you were on your way to a wedding or coming back from walking the dog was the right look. I felt self-conscious. All the female DJs looked effortlessly chic, and most of the male ones had the latest in what I understand you might call 'urban' wear. This seemed principally to consist of the right jeans and trainers, obviously, a gaudy mayoral chain affair, and what my eldest daughter Holly told me was a 'puffa jacket'. Fabio and Grooverider's puffa jackets appeared to have been stuffed with king-sized duvets. They must have been boiling. In fact, there did seem to be some kind of competition going on to see who could have the most ridiculously voluminous puffa in . . . errm . . . da house. Tim Westwood, an utterly charming bloke, but, to me, occasionally difficult to understand – his jacket came into the room five minutes before he did.

There were one or two 'dressed down' souls. I think Steve Lamacq viewed trendy clobber as a betrayal of his indie roots. Chris Moyles tended to dress in black, and it may have been pricey but, fond of him as I am, he was no male model. The blessed John Peel always cut a binman-esque figure, but he was John Peel, wasn't he?

Myself and my then on-air partner Marc Riley hatched a plan to overcome our discomfort. We would dress up in something ridiculous, inappropriate and, above all, cheap, so that it didn't matter when beer got spilled on it later in the evening. Genius.

The first year we bought matching pastel-grey, single-breasted, two-button suits from our favourite gents' outfitters Halon Menswear, which had branches in Shrewsbury and, conveniently, right next door to the BBC in Manchester. While we were in there paying for the suits, a total bill of around ninety-eight English pounds as I recall, roughly the same amount as Pete Tong had paid for his socks I dare say, we noticed seventies-style matching shirts and ties made by the fine brand of Farah. And when I say matching I mean that shirt and tie were both cut from the same swirly-patterned, highly starched cotton. Obviously we'd have preferred a man-made fabric but, with none being available, cotton it had to be.

Suitably emboldened in these dapper get-ups, we muscled centre stage at the photo session to sit either side of Radio 1's head honcho Andy Parfitt. It looked rather as if Andy, worried that he might be hassled by renegade DJ factions, had hired two bouncers from a seventies nightclub in Stockport to protect him. I suppose, if I'm honest, we did want to be noticed, and not just fade into the background. The old ego surfacing again. It worked though. You do notice us in the picture. There's Andy, looking like H from Steps' good-looking older brother, flanked by two burly extras from *Life on Mars*, an island of eccentricity in an ocean of puffa.

So pleased were we with these outfits that we later wore them to meet David Bowie, and also for a photoshoot in *GQ*

magazine, making us easily the thriftiest-dressed models in
that magazine's history I would imagine.

The following year we had the same problem. On this
occasion our sartorial influence came principally from the
sadly defunct Californian band Grandaddy. Formed in
Modesto, California, their music was a compelling blend of
burbling analogue synths and epic, sweeping Neil Young-
ian melodies. It was a new kind of Americana that somehow
acknowledged tradition while taking it somewhere new.
There was an aching melancholy to it as well, not least in the
keening vocals of leader Jason Lytle. Their masterpiece is the
2000 album *The Sophtware Slump*, portraying disenfranchised
Americans marooned in the technological age. They once
told me that Modesto consisted principally of computer firms
and Mexican restaurants, and it was clear that they had spent
a good deal of time in the latter contemplating the effects and
quirks of the former.

As if that wasn't enough, and they were to my mind a truly
great band, they also had heroically unfashionable facial hair.
By this I mean the chin-strap beard – full face fungus on the
lower jaw, clean-shaven in the moustache area. Now normally I'm suspicious of people who go in for any kind of
beard topiary. The only reason for growing a beard is to
avoid the need to shave, unless you've got a ZZ Top audition
coming up, or are a kayak enthusiast from the Northeast
who's faked his own death for the insurance money and
doesn't want to be recognized. If you don't fall into one of
these categories, you've really got to let it grow to full David
Bellamy proportions, to the extent that it might well be possible to film a series of natural-history programmes on the life
forms thriving within it, or stay clean-shaven. The tidy beard
atrocities committed by the likes of Noel Edmonds, Mike
Gatting and Craig David should surely be proof that elabo-
rately trimmed whiskers are to be avoided at all costs. These

days we've become obsessed with not looking our age, and the usual examples of blokes who 'don't look their age', as if this was something to aspire to, are Noel Edmonds and Cliff Richard. Please. Last time I saw Cliff Richard being interviewed I thought at first that he was wearing a badly knitted maroon tam-o'-shanter. It turned out to be his hair. It was as if an auburn chapatti had fallen on his head. Noel Edmonds, mystifyingly released from house arrest and allowed back on television to mess about with some boxes, is regularly congratulated for looking exactly the same as he did last time he was clogging up the idiot lantern. So he had a bad, streaked mullet and meticulously pruned beard then, and looked ridiculous, and he still has it now, and looks ridiculous. Big deal. Or no deal.

Mike Gatting presumably spent hours on far-flung cricket tours boiling his own water to whip up enough lather to ensure his weird goatee with filigree attachments was immaculate at all times. One can only wonder what was going through his head: 'Blimey, it's a lot of trouble is this, but at least I know when I've done it, it's going to look great.'

Grandaddy's beards seemed somehow different. They weren't trying to look attractive but wilfully confirmed their outsider status, while making it clear they belonged together. Whether or not they were influenced by the facial hairstyle of the Amish people, I don't know. I know very little of the ways of the Amish, though I have seen Harrison Ford in *Witness*, but it's hard to see why you'd keep the chin-strap beard tradition going. Bonnets, horses and carts, not joining the military, having no telephone, fair enough. But to force all your young men to grow beards like that. Well, it's going to be contentious, isn't it? If I'd been born into an Amish community I'd have gone along with most of it quite happily I think, but not the beard. I mean, what would your already reduced chances of pulling have been like with a beard like that at the Nocturne nightspot in Bolton?

Enraptured and influenced by Grandaddy then, Marc and I visited a costumiers and purchased theatrical beards, which we sat in the hotel room trimming to shape, before attaching them with spirit glue. Goodness it was itchy, but rather like Mike Gatting slaving over his shaving mirror in his bathroom pod in some Sri Lankan Ibis, we knew it was going to be worth it. Especially when combined with multi-patterned cable jumpers from Halon tucked into stonewashed jeans. And if you've been tipped off and are reading this Noel, I've still got the jumpers if you want to make me an offer. They're very much your kind of thing.

Ridiculously excited and pleased with ourselves, we then set off down Regent Street to the venue, jumping uninvited into a black cab occupied by Annie Nightingale who briefly thought she was under attack from Muslim fundamentalists with a penchant for gaudy pullovers.

So, year by year, ever more elaborate looks were called for to the extent that the last Radio 1 DJ photo we appeared in, we went as goth Victorian undertakers. Look, I have no idea, all right? We wore black suits, big black boots, black ties, white shirts, stovepipe hats and ghoulish black and white face paints. I don't know what we were thinking, though we were confident of getting there and not finding that Jo Whiley had gone for the same theme.

The evening, however, became more surreal from there. While we were lining up for the picture it became apparent that there was an unusually high level of security that night. Normally security wasn't really an issue because the event was held at a 'secret' location, and also, we were just a bunch of DJs. It's not as if we were important like the Royal Family or Girls Aloud or anything. So what were all these furtive guys talking into their cufflinks doing there?

The answer became apparent when Andy Parfitt made his annual rallying call to the fearless disc-jockey elite forces serving on the front line of pop radio. His big surprise, and it was a big surprise, was that here to press the flesh was Mr Cool Britannia himself, the prime minister Tony Blair. Blimey, we'd heard there might be a special guest but we thought it was going to be someone like Dave Grohl or Ronnie Corbett or someone, but here was your actual premier hanging out with DJs when he had a country to run. Well, there was an audible intake of breath and it was hard not to be impressed. It's not every day you meet the prime minister, is it? Furthermore, and I was only told this after he'd gone, he'd expressed a particular wish to meet John Peel and Mark and Lard. Now it's possible that everyone got told this to make them feel important, but when he reached us on his hand-shaking trip along the line, he did stop and chat about the show and in particular our band The Shirehorses. I'm pretty sure Marc said we could find a place for him if he wanted to be rhythm guitarist to Marc's lead. And all this dressed as I've described above. The day you meet the leader of your own country, it just so happens you've dressed as a zombie bodysnatcher.

Blair close up was an extraordinary proposition. He was pretty tall, and had the most piercing eyes I'd encountered since interviewing Geoffrey Boycott years earlier. Perhaps you've met people with eyes like that, but if you haven't, it's hard to describe the effect it has. I was actually a bit scared. You feel like they can see right through you, and know everything you're thinking. An MP of my acquaintance told me that Blair is a decent bloke and a good listener, but if you lose that penetrating eye contact, the moment has gone. Even if he's still standing there.

More than the eyes, though, I remember the teeth. Do you remember the velociraptors who wreaked havoc in the kitchens at Jurassic Park? Well the dental arrangements of the PM were just like that. A smile even bigger and more alarming than the one depicted in a thousand newspaper cartoons. It was like the prow of a cruise liner lined with teeth. He was ever so friendly, but intimidating at the same time.

Sadly for El Presidente, only one of his ambitions was realized that night. Immediately Tony appeared, John Peel had made himself scarce. Talking to him later in the pub he said that as a Labour supporter he considered it would be hypocritical to shake the hand of the man who he felt had betrayed so many socialist principles. Not having a party political allegiance I felt no such crisis of conscience, but I respected John for the stand he took. The rest of us, whatever reservations we might have had, just shook the right honourable member for Sedgefield's hand so we could say we'd done it. So he didn't meet Peel, and I doubt he remembers meeting us, but I do wonder if Blair has a recurring dream of being in conversation with two un-dead pall-bearers, and wakes up in a cold sweat wondering what it can all mean.

10. THE DAY I RUINED A PERFECTLY GOOD SUIT

I'm a strong believer in school uniform. I think it's a really good way of trying to make sure that no one feels like they don't fit in. If everyone dresses the same, no one feels left out. And when you're a kid, you don't want to stand out, at least, not for the way you look. Unless you're a girl possibly, though you'll understand why this isn't something I'll be dwelling on. I have occasionally wondered what it must be like to walk down the street and have builders turn and admire your bottom, while you insouciantly toss a meticulously dishevelled 'Timotei' mane, but these are not experiences I'm likely to go through. My point is that most of us will never stand out due to our sheer, rampant attractiveness and therefore we'd rather not stand out physically at all.

Certainly when we're young we follow tribal dress codes. We identify our clan, and dress accordingly. Punk, head-banger, mosher, Sea Scout, mod, bloke who works in electrical retailers and wears suit trousers with shirt and tie with a fleece when he goes out to Subway at lunchtime, crusty, folkie, orange-skinned girl who'd ideally like to enjoy carnal knowledge of Peter Crouch, skateboarder, goth. We choose our team, and wear their colours. Minute personalizations are acceptable, little idiosyncratic details that proclaim that though a pack animal, we are still individuals, but the basic dress code is unchanging.

Some of these looks are easier to maintain than others and it's worth pausing, briefly, to consider the plight of the goth. The inspiration for the goth look is a flesh-eating zombie gravedigger who's found a discarded leather coat and cowboy hat while working for a firm of frontier funeral directors in a one-horse-trough town during the Klondike gold rush. This may have worked fine if you were a flesh-eating zombie gravedigger working for a firm of frontier funeral directors during the Klondike gold rush. It may also work fine if you are going to see The Sisters of Mercy at Whitley Bay ice rink. It may also work perfectly well when hanging round suburban shopping centres with like-minded friends having a 'who's got the whitest face' contest.

Where it doesn't work so well is on family holidays. Have you ever seen a teenage goth on a package holiday in Lloret de Mar? Hilarious. Unable to accept that heavy black clothes and pancake make-up are not the ideal attire for sipping pina coladas around a rectangular pit filled with murky water, a splash of Domestos and toddler urine, they persist in attempting to maintain the look. This means voluminous black Victorian bathing suits worn with long black and purple stripey socks and wide-brimmed black leather hats. Their dedication to the cause is admirable, if ultimately misguided. My advice to the adolescent goth on the dreaded family holiday is this: why not treat it as a holiday from being a goth? Stay out of the sun to protect your carefully cultivated deathly pallor by all means, but give yourself a week off and wear something white other than your complexion.

(I have to confess a degree of self-interest here as I'm look-ing into setting up a chain of 'whitening parlours' loosely based on 'tanning salons' but aimed at the bronzed goth market. I'm not sure exactly how to do it yet but I think it involves flour. Or possibly lead.)

So the mores of dress are an accepted part of our lives. From the colour-coded crew of the starship *Enterprise* to the gullible, shrink-wrapped-in-nylon perspiring football hordes, we dress alike to feel like we fit in, and school uniform is no different.

Bolton School's uniform was pretty standard I guess. Knickerbockers, frock coat, tricorn hat. You know the kind of thing. However, in the sixth form we were allowed to wear 'our own clothes'. Obviously, though, there were still limits. Own clothes didn't mean anything you liked. If it had there would have been those who'd taken things too far. Danny Little was a burly redhead who'd demonstrated a penchant for dressing up like David Bowie. David Bowie had, at that time, demonstrated a penchant for dressing in tight, Lurex leotards with suspiciously skimpy crotch areas. Without some enforce-able dress code . . . well, you can anticipate the problem. And the prospect of the Little ginger nuts slipping loose of the span-dex gusset would have been enough to put even the heartiest of eaters off their dumplings. Which sort of brings me to the point.

My first day in sixth form in 1974 meant I could choose an outfit for school after eleven years of being told what to wear. A momentous occasion indeed. I'd picked out a beige three-piece suit purchased at Harry Fenton's in Bolton, which, this being the mid-seventies, had flared trousers that covered the platform shoes, and jacket lapels on which it would have been perfectly feasible to land light aircraft. With my blow-dried mullet as crowning glory, I breezed round the corridors that morning safe in the knowledge that I was the envy of admiring fifth-formers, trapped in their blazer strait-jackets. I had found freedom, and all for £29.99 with a shirt and chunky-knit tie thrown in. I felt sure that if Marc Bolan happened to be in the tuck shop that break-time, which was a long shot as he was two hundred miles away in London and probably had someone to go and get his Vimto and crisps for him, he would have signed me up for T. Rex on the spot.

Lunch at school was served in a large hall filled with polished oak tables seating twelve boys, six to a bench on each side, and a teacher in a ladder-backed chair at the head of each one. There was also a 'top table' on a raised dais where the headmaster dined with a gaggle of hand-picked victims. In retrospect I can see that this platform was to reinforce his status and afford him an uninterrupted view of his personal empire. At the time I thought it odd that they'd gone to the trouble of putting a stage in just so we could more easily see a shrivelled sexagenarian dribble gravy down his front.

Having resisted all invitations to school reunions, on the basis that if you were that bothered you'd have kept in touch with people anyway and would turn up to find a room full of blokes you'd erased from your memory or didn't like much in the first place, I eventually went back in 2006 to mark the thirtieth anniversary of my leaving. The smell of that refectory hadn't really crossed my mind in those intervening years, but walking back in, an aroma I hadn't experienced in three decades became as familiar as if I'd been in there for cheese pie the day before. I couldn't honestly say what the olfactory ingredients were, though cabbage, polish and disinfectant may have been involved, but it was a smell I remembered instantly despite being unaware I'd forgotten it for all those years.

There were, perhaps, fifty tables in all, one designated for vegetarians. This might seem a very small non-meat-eating quotient of the overall assembly, but you have to remember that it was the early seventies and vegetarians, like homosexuals, might well have existed, but nobody really knew any. I'd seen a picture of Quentin Crisp in the paper, but assumed he was a character on *The Dick Emery Show*. Sudip Sen had told me he was a vegetarian, which I took to mean that he was really big on cauliflower. I just presumed Julian Goodkin had a sausage allergy.

Playing a game of brinkmanship, myself, Rob Redgate and Rog Milne left it as late as we could before entering the hall, in order that the maximum number of uniformed oiks would watch and admire as we strolled nonchalantly to our places, dreaming of the day when they too would be able to model the finest tailoring Bolton town centre had to offer. Fortunately our designated table was at the far end of the hall, affording practically the full room down which to promenade. And promenade we did. Strutting would be another way of describing it. If that odd-looking woman with big sunglasses and the 1960s haircut who edits *American Vogue* had been sitting at the high table that day, unlikely I concede, I felt sure she would have seen us as catwalk material. And not just building it.

Eventually, the artful amble having taken some time, we arrived at our destination to find 'Greasy' Marsden, one of the deputy heads who'd long ago fallen out of love with teaching but not Brylcreem, already doling out the portions of breaded cod, mash and mushy peas. Slotting in at the far end of the bench I accepted a plate with casual disdain, despite being starving. No wonder models are thin, all that strutting up and down had given me a hell of an appetite.

Once everyone on the table had been served, a two-pint jug of parsley sauce was passed down so we could garnish our food individually. Being at the top of the table, the jug was full to the brim when I took it from Barry Henderson. Or rather attempted to take it. To this day I don't know who was at fault, but the upshot was that he released said ewer before I had fully grasped it. The consequence of this being that a litre of viscous, lumpy, piping-hot, green-flecked gloop was deposited right down the front of the Harry Fenton special. Initially my reaction was one of shock as I felt the temperature of the sauce through the suit. The secondary reaction was annoyance at the gales of laughter coming from around the table. The third was to smack Baz Henderson on the back of the head and call him a wanker. However, it was only then that the full scale of my plight dawned on me. Having ponced my way down the full length of the hall like Beau Brummel on his way to a ball, I would now have to scuttle back out like a shop-soiled bovine artificial-insemination specialist.

'Greasy' Marsden, attempting to retain his schoolmasterly poise but evidently thrilled to have his mundane day brightened by the embarrassment and misfortune of a pupil, peered over his glasses.

'I think perhaps you'd better go and clean yourself up, Radcliffe.'

It was the only logical thing to do of course, though I was sorely tempted to sit there with the savoury mucus seeping through my trousers and waistcoat until every last person had left the hall. I might have needed skin grafts, but that was a breeze compared to the alternative. However, common sense prevailed and I slowly rose, dripping residue down the full length of the trousers, and pausing only to elbow Henderson in the temple.

And so to the long walk of shame. Naturally my progress was considerably speedier than the outward journey, but you'd be surprised by how long ten seconds can feel. Within two or three steps the jeers and catcalls had begun, and by the time I reached the doorway the whole room was filled with gales of adolescent laughter and bile-filled ripostes. I can't remember what was said, I've tried to shut it out, but you know bile when it comes your way. And who could blame them? Had I been a lowly fourth-former in a threadbare blazer, I'd have been just the same. How gratifying to see one of the posturing dandies of the lower sixth reduced to such shame.

Fortunately my family lived a ten-minute walk from school and, it being the middle of the day, there weren't many people about. There were a few perplexed biddies with shopping trolleys who perhaps momentarily thought it strange that a wallpaper-paste salesman was so intent on advertising his wares, but I made it home without further ridicule in about twenty-five minutes. Yes, I know I said we lived ten minutes away but I had to take a detour. I wasn't going to walk past the girls' school, was I?

In retrospect I don't really know why I didn't take the afternoon off. Especially as I had to suffer the indignity of wearing my old uniform and being the only sixth-former in a blazer. Perhaps I thought it was better to just go straight back and get it over with. And, anyway, I knew there'd be no chance of getting another suit before the weekend, at the earliest. So I went back. And it was hellish. But it got it over with.

I did get another suit the following weekend, but it was a cheaper one. From Hepworths. The lapels were smaller, the flares narrower, and there was no waistcoat. It was green.

One of my long-held ambitions is to get a made-to-measure suit from one of the fine emporia on Savile Row. I have the feeling that it's something every Englishman should do once in a lifetime. I know full well that you can get a bespoke outfit much cheaper from tailoring establishments that aren't located on that iconic street, but that's not the point. That's like saying you can walk up a television mast and feel the same as if you're up the Eiffel Tower. Sometimes, only the real thing will do, no matter what the cost. And yet I know when I eventually get round to being fitted for the most expensive clothes of my life, they will struggle to mean as much to me as that besmirched three-piece from Harry Fenton's. It went to the dry-cleaners of course, but in a certain light there was an unmistakable tidemark. You could still see where a bull elephant with a heavy cold had sneezed on me, and I knew that if I wore it, I'd never be able to promenade or strut with the same confidence as before. Perhaps ultimately that was a good thing and some of my pride disappeared forever that day, preparing me for the later years when I would have to hold my head up in public despite everyone knowing that I was a DJ.

Oh, and when I emerge from Norton and Sons and stride down Savile Row in my resplendent hand-made threads, I won't be heading for a celebratory dinner awash with creamy sauce. Just in case.

11. THE DAY I REACHED THE COAST (ON THE OTHER SIDE)

I love being outdoors, although I'm not what you'd call the 'outdoor type'. This phrase is taken to mean someone who is a keen participant in organized outdoor activities such as windsurfing, sailing or mass games of rounders played in an overcompetitive manner on what might otherwise be a tranquil beach. I don't really get involved in things like that as I've no aptitude for sports and am fiercely non-competitive to a degree that competitive people can find quite upsetting.

This approach to alfresco communal pastimes also ties in with my need to spend regular time on my own. I've often taken myself out of the house to get away from people, who are usually only too glad to see the back of me, for a few hours. Or days. Or weeks. I think the venerable doyen of fell walkers Alfred Wainwright was on to something when he said that the wonders of Lakeland were best appreciated in solitude. When he finally relented and allowed his wife to accompany him it was only on condition she didn't speak, and while I wouldn't go that far, you certainly don't want to stride across the ridges and moors to the accompaniment of mindless prattle, which is worth bearing in mind when choosing companions for a walk of any distance.

When I was growing up in Bolton we spent days on end out in the countryside above the town. Enjoying a freedom that my own kids rarely experience, we would take to our bikes after breakfast and head up the steep incline of Old Kiln Lane and make for the lost worlds of Walker Fold, the exotically named yet black and icily cold Blue Lagoon, and Cigarette Tunnel. This was so called because it was a circular passageway that ran under Scout Road, and not because it was somewhere we gathered to share a packet of five Park Drive fags. Honest, Mum. Down the centre of this brick cylinder ran a babbling stream, and by running up first one wall and then hopping over the flow to gallop up the other, it was possible to negotiate the tunnel's length without getting wet. Unless of course you encountered a patch of sodden moss on which you lost your footing, thereby resulting in a thorough dowsing, to the amusement of your gang. Not that being wet was anything to get upset about. You dried off quickly enough as it was always sunny back then. Or so it seems to me now. And in any case, the discomfort of mere water was nothing compared to what Pip McCrosty must have felt when he found himself tumbling down the side of the glade and only coming to a halt when seated neatly in a fresh cowpat. That made him less than popular as the afternoon sun reached its zenith.

But through that tunnel, in those copses, over those outcrops of millstone grit, we became adventurers, explorers, spies and pirates, often staying out until it was too dark to see or the stench of Pip's soiled shorts became unbearable. We would then pelt home, back down Old Kiln Lane without bothering with anything so sissy as bicycle lights, and would only get in trouble if our tea was burned. There was no suggestion that a group of ten-year-olds shouldn't be miles from home all day, as it was generally accepted that the school holidays were spent outside.

As adults we may have less desire or ability to live through our imaginations, but we have just as much need of escapism, and walking for several hours over unspoiled countryside is the easiest way to achieve this. Well, apart from drinking several pints of Coniston Bluebird that is, though most rambling expeditions will allow for this at the end of the day anyway. But it's extraordinary how you achieve a new perspective on any problems or worries you might have as you get out and feel dwarfed by the landscape.

There's also something incredibly satisfying about covering a substantial distance by doing something as simple as putting one foot in front of the other. I once read an interview with Philip Pullman, the celebrated author of the *His Dark Materials* trilogy. He explained how he sat in his summerhouse at the bottom of his garden in Oxford and wrote three pages a day. That doesn't seem very much but, as he explained, it soon builds up. In a hundred days or so you've written a book. It's very much the same with walking. If you climb up the side of the valley and walk along the crest of the hill for an hour or two, when you turn around you'll be amazed how far you've come. And all under your own steam. How great is that? And there's something marvellously appropriate about public rights of way in this respect. In a sense, as it's owned by the nation, we all have a share in, say, Helvellyn in the Lake District, and if you've walked it you really feel like you're claiming your little piece of it.

It's also thrilling to stride out and not know exactly what you might come across that day. You might well have planned your route meticulously but there will always be something that you couldn't allow for that takes you on a different tack. It might be the weather, it might be a change in the topography since the map was drawn, it could be a mistake you make in your route finding, but that's often what brings that childlike sense of adventure, a feeling that – like Laurie Lee in *As I Walked Out One Midsummer Morning* – you're walking towards a future you can't entirely predict or control.

Between leaving Radio 1 and joining Radio 2 in 2004 I
was afforded the luxury of two months off. This gave me the
perfect opportunity to do something I'd always wanted to do:
the Wainwright coast-to-coast walk from St Bees on the
Cumbrian coast to Robin Hood's Bay, 192 miles away on the
other side. Years earlier I'd bought the distinctive little
Wainwright guide to the route and had leafed through it
often, fascinated by the lovingly reproduced handwritten
font, the meticulous line drawings, the personalized maps
and intriguing place names like Black Sail, Clay Bank Top
and Danby Wiske. As the years went by, and family commitments grew, I began to wonder if the right time would ever
present itself, but here it was.

Before setting out there was the issue of who might join
me on the trip. Though happy to spend time on my own,
and with the greatest of respect and deference to Wainwright,
I didn't fancy two weeks' walking alone, not least because I
was worried I might get lost on a daily basis. The first recruit
was an on-line bicycle trader called Roger who I'd met in the
sauna at my local health club, which is in no way a veiled way
of saying we were regular visitors to a swingers massage parlour. Roger was a no-nonsense, cheery, solid sort of a chap
and was desperately keen on undertaking a lengthy walk. He
also had some experience of Outward Bound activities and
talked of things like survival blankets, which I suppose was
wise, though I was thinking more of bed-and-breakfast
accommodation myself.

My university friend Jamie was next to sign up. He was a
seasoned long-distance hiker and was also very keen to spend
as much of the money he'd made in advertising as possible on
every conceivable map from a specialist shop in London.
This would lead to problems before too long.

Last to join our merry band was Mark. He had become a
pal of mine after marrying a close friend of my wife's and was

a lofty, dryly humorous former telecoms analyst. Even now I'm not quite sure what one of those is, but he seemed as glad to have left it behind as he was about the lifestyle it had brought him. A keen cook, he had a healthy appetite, which would also have consequences.

We began on Sunday 28 March. That morning the weather was bright and clear, and in fact we would be blessed with favourable conditions for the major part of our crossing, if that doesn't sound a bit like we were traversing the Polar icecap.

The traditional way to begin the trek is to walk down to the wide, windswept beach at St Bees, wet your boots in the Irish Sea, and pick up a pebble that you pop in your pocket and carry all the way across to the North Sea. Naturally, someone, Mark I think, made the equally traditional joke of picking up a boulder the size of a watermelon for this purpose. Though well worn it was a moderately funny gag as the weight of our packs began to dawn on us. I had selected my kit very carefully so as to minimize what I had to carry. It's amazing how small a load you can end up with if you really think it through. For example, and relax ladies, the bulk of two weeks' worth of boxer shorts can be reduced massively if you just wear Speedo swimming trunks which can be rinsed through and dried on a radiator overnight. Similarly, if you wear thin liner socks under your hiking socks, these too can be easily refreshed during a night's stay somewhere. Even so, once you begin to walk with everything you need on your back, the weight seems to double as you contemplate lugging it for almost two hundred miles. Especially when you add the not insubstantial load of a packed lunch.

Mark took a keen interest in this area of the mission and a standard day's rations might include sufficient quantities of fluid, a couple of large filled baps, a pie or two, some Scotch eggs, several flapjacks, a selection of fruit, biscuits, slices of fruit cake, energy bars, cereal bars, standard chocolate bars and maybe a few tomatoes. If this really felt too much to carry we would thin it out slightly. By leaving behind the tomatoes. Roger's Outward Bound training was invaluable here as he pointed out that we would need plenty of provisions if we had an accident and had to wait to be rescued. By the looks of what we were carrying we could have been lost after a plane crash in the Andes and not have to start eating each other for a month.

On the first day we walked about fourteen miles to reach the Shepherd's Arms at Ennerdale Bridge. For reasons that escape me now we had booked two twin rooms for each night. I think that because some of the locations where we needed to stay were fairly remote, there weren't four separate rooms available, though we would occasionally wish there had been. That first night in Ennerdale I shared a warm, chintzy room with Roger. Once you got both of us in there, with our sizable rucksacks and swimming trunks and socks steaming on the storage heater, it felt slightly claustrophobic if I'm honest. Still, after the day's exertions and a couple of pints, a good night's sleep was surely guaranteed.

The food at the pub was hearty and home-cooked and so it seemed discourteous not to show our appreciation by sampling as much of the menu as possible. One of the great things about having walked all day is that when you order a large meal spanning several courses at night you do so without the slightest shred of guilt, knowing full well that you have earned it. And so, after afternoon tea and a hot bath, I followed Mark's lead and plumped for deep-fried brie, steak and ale pie, rhubarb crumble with custard, a selection of choice farmhouse cheeses, a bottle or two of Merlot and several pints of the local hand-pulled bitter. To steal a gag from the late Boltonian poet and philosopher Hovis Presley, it was a meal in itself really.

As I lay in my single bed that night, unable to sleep as the feast and my intestines fought a particularly gurglesome war, the end of the journey seemed a long, long way away. I was also aware of the fact that when sleep is proving elusive, you become doubly conscious of noises around you. This wouldn't have been so bad if it had been the shrieks of a lone tawny owl or restless windhover. Unfortunately it was Roger in the other bed eighteen inches away, snoring like Henry VIII after a particularly fulsome banquet. I must have dropped off at some point as when I awoke the following morning it was to a bleary-eyed Roger saying, 'Blimey, you can snore a bit can't you?'

Evidently the accommodation was going to need looking at.

The next day the weather was again perfect. Bright, dry and not too warm. Around nine miles from Ennerdale we reached the youth hostel at Black Sail, one of the most spectacular settings we would encounter on the whole trip. A small timber bunkhouse at the bottom of Loft Beck, it is surrounded by towering peaks and crags, including the celebrated Haystacks. Sitting outside on the rustic benches, where generations of hikers had sat before us, and gazing at the wonder of the fells in spring sunshine was just one of those feelings and moments you never forget. I think it was here that I finally realized what I was doing. Before I'd set out I'd talked about it not being a routemarch and if the weather was bad and I didn't fancy it on any particular day, I'd just get a bus or cab to the next overnight port of call. Now the realization dawned that whatever the weather, whatever the pain, I was going to go every step of the way. The wonderful thing about a journey of this kind is that you begin to exist in your own private world, and nothing matters except what you see that day, and reaching the next leg of the journey, and it is this total absorption that completely frees the mind.

The interlude at Black Sail I also recall for two other significant reasons. It was here that it became clear we were going to have to enlist the services of one of the Sherpa services after all. Initially we had decided to forgo this idea as we considered ourselves to be carrying light packs, especially as we had no camping equipment on board. However, tackling the steep fells of Lakeland in the sunshine soon began to take its toll. We had banked on an average speed of three miles an hour, but on the more arduous ascents this could easily slow to just one, which would mean that our itinerary, and all the bijou twin rooms we'd booked, would go completely out of the window. Jamie, though an experienced walker, was really struggling. This was because he had selected a pair of mountain-climbing boots last seen on the feet of Frankenstein's monster. These, though ideal for ascending the Eiger, offered little flexibility and therefore removed substantial pads of skin from his feet. He was also carrying about twenty Ordnance Survey maps, which weighed a considerable amount. We could, I suppose, have offered to take some of that bulk from him but that would have meant reducing the size of our packed lunches, and that was obviously out of the question. We enlisted the services of one of the many relay bag-drop providers the next day.

Black Sail was also memorable because of the warden of the hostel. He had thick glasses and long greasy hair and was wearing a Fair Isle pullover, jogging bottoms and slippers. It was difficult to glean a great deal of information from him as he was a man of few words for whom the word 'loner' could have been specially invented. We did manage to establish that he lived alone here for the season, never quite sure who was going to arrive to utilize the utilitarian bunks, and then returned home to his mother for the winter. A fascinating character, we took our leave from him and this breathtakingly beautiful spot reluctantly, but not before Mark and he shared a memorable exchange:

'So is this the remotest youth hostel then?'

Pause.

'Naah.'

'Right. So where is then?'

Longer pause.

'Skiddaw.'

'Hmmm. So where is that exactly?'

Even longer pause.

'Skiddaw.'

The next few days passed easily as we crossed the Lake District calling at Borrowdale, where we were summoned to dinner in the hotel by a large South African woman beating a brass gong; Grasmere, where the six-foot-four Mark attempted to sleep in a single bed that was a good eight inches shorter than he was; and Patterdale, where Roger and I found well-thumbed pornographic magazines in our bedside melamine bureaus. A touch of class and no mistake.

Friday 2 April was a strange day because it was going to mark the end of our time as a foursome. Mark was due at a stag weekend in Leeds, and Roger had to return to his online cycling empire due to some crisis in the internet bike-bell business or something. Walking the nigh-on twenty miles from Shap to Kirkby Stephen, the first eight or nine in the drizzle, was therefore a muted affair. It was remarkable how close everyone had become in just a few short days. Before we set out the only common bond between the other three was that they were friends of mine, which you may hardly think much of a recommendation; they didn't know each other at all. It was intriguing to see how the group broke up into every conceivable pairing as different conversations sprang up. It was also apparent that though everyone was reasonably fit, we had very different body clocks. Mark was pretty steady, Jamie was often slower because of his shredded feet, Roger found it tricky to get going in the morning, and I got grumpy if we weren't having tea and scones by around four. Whatever the struggle at whatever time of day though, there was always someone who would walk with you and spur you on. The only exception to this was when Mark misread a map somewhere along the High Stile Ridge and took us over a substantial peak that wasn't meant to be on our route. No one fell out over it, but we did walk in well-spaced single file for an hour or two after that.

Reaching the Cumbrian market town of Kirkby Stephen in the late afternoon, Mark was picked up by his brother more or less immediately. Roger stayed on to have a last four- or five-course dinner with us before being picked up by his family the following morning. When it finally came time for him to leave he was on the edge of tears, so great was his desire to carry on to the end. As a bluff, straightforward guy I hadn't expected that but it really did underline what an amazing experience a journey like that can be and how important seeing it through becomes in your mind. He phoned us on a daily basis for the following week and later said he'd found it almost impossible to concentrate on work as he thought of us somewhere out there on the North Yorkshire Moors as the hail drilled against his office window.

The Saturday was also an odd one for Jamie and me. We were easy and relaxed in each other's company, as friends of long standing are, but it was certainly different without the other two. It was quieter without Roger, and after Mark left we carried noticeably less cake.

We were heading for Keld, which was more or less the mid-point of the march, and a mere eleven miles away over relatively unchallenging moorland. Or so we thought. We reached one of the key landmarks of the route with ease. The Nine Standards are cairns perched on top of a ridge, staring out like sentinels on the watershed of England. From here the waters flow west back to the Irish Sea, and east into the North Sea. Their existence is probably due to their location on the former border between Westmorland and the North Riding of Yorkshire, but stranger tales remain. One such is that they were built to create the illusion of an army encampment, which might have been just enough to put off the odd band of marauding Scots. Whatever their purpose they afforded Jamie and I some much-needed cover from the horizontal squall that was, by now, accompanying our every step. Spending two weeks exposed to the elements in England you have to expect a couple of days like that, and we bore it with reasonable grace as we squatted in a muddy hollow and tried to eat sandwiches without them getting overly soggy.

The afternoon proved taxing, though, as there was no path to speak of, just a series of marker posts emerging from the damp mist across the peaty moors. Walking on peat in dry weather is a delight as it is spongy and soft, but once it becomes sodden, there is no way of preventing your feet from sinking in above the ankles. I don't know what it is about having wet feet, but it really tests your resolve. At one point we lingered for about half an hour in a lonely telephone box, just to be out of the rain. Some time that afternoon we came across a stony track, and even though our map advised against it, we set off down it just to experience the luxury of firm footing once again.

To make matters worse, once we reached Keld we discovered that the farmhouse we had booked for the night was a further two miles up a steep road from the hamlet itself. When we finally staggered up the driveway the owner, a russet-faced woman in a floral-print apron, gesticulated from the window with a kettle and a teapot and I wanted to weep with gratitude and relief. I've never been so glad of a cup of tea in all my life.

We had hot baths, rinsed the browny peat from our socks, and hung them on the Aga to dry before enjoying both sweet and savoury home-made pies with mountains of mashed potatoes and huge jugs of custard, though not all at once you understand. We then sat with the couple who lived there and chatted over a couple of beers as they flicked through the local paper and gossiped about the folk of the neighbour-hood. We would never see them again, but for one night we sat in a room together in front of a log fire as if we were family. We were strangers dropping in on their lives for one night only, yet it felt anything but awkward. That's just what life's like along the trail.

After the exertions of the peat moors the following couple of days strolling through the Yorkshire Dales became a blessed relief, before we left Ingleby Cross and headed up onto the North Yorkshire Moors to complete the final leg. At the steam-railway village of Grosmont our old college pal Phil hooked up with us to accompany us on our final day. He was supposed to be there to make the last stretch that bit easier, although he actually had the opposite effect after discovering that Grosmont boasted a late-night railway drinking club and absolutely forcing us to have more pints than we needed. Well all right, I'm being disingenuous here. The quaffing of the local brews had been a feature of the outing and I didn't take much leading, but by anyone's standards, let alone the comparatively abstemious Jamie, Phil is a black hole where the ale's concerned.

Robin Hood's Bay is a charming and atmospheric fishing village of narrow streets and teetering stone cottages clinging to the steep cliffs between Whitby and Scarborough, leading to a shoreline pockmarked with rock pools at the edge of the brutally cold North Sea. Though nearly forty years had elapsed since I imagined myself as a pirate up at Walker Fold atop Bolton, it was hard for the village not to conjure up images of smuggling and contraband as we made our way down the winding, cobbled main drag to complete the formalities.

Our great friend Julian and his family had booked into the same hotel as us in order to lend a real sense of occasion as we completed our quest. Sadly the establishment in question was a grotty and barely clean fleapit of a dosshouse with delusions of adequacy when it came to being a hotel. The food was practically inedible, the rooms shabbily furnished and unclean. I had carried a toilet roll in my rucksack all the way across but never had cause to use it until now, as no one had considered it necessary to place one in my bathroom. As an act of revenge for their appalling service we later chanced upon their reservations book by the phone in the hallway, and filled in about half a dozen spurious bookings for the Christmas period. I know that sounds petty and mean but believe you me it was better than people booking into that place for the festive period and then turning up and seeing the state of it.

With our phalanx of well-wishers, Jamie and I headed down to the beach and wet our boots in the lapping waves of the North Sea. We then took the pebbles from our pockets, the same fragments of rock we'd carried from St Bees 192 miles away on the opposite coast, and hurled them into the steel-grey waters. The feeling of satisfaction was incredible, so much of the effort and emotion of the previous fortnight compressed into that one little action. The experience is something that has stayed with me vividly and still gives me a greater sense of achievement than I can really explain. The half a stone I gained during the trip, thanks to Mark's approach to ration control, took rather longer to offload than the pebble sadly.

That night, at the final resting place, I lay down feeling exhausted and elated. Finally, in a room on my own, and with the knowledge that I didn't have to walk the following morning, I slept soundly. Or at least I might have done if it hadn't been for the karaoke session going on in the bar below, and the strong feeling that I wasn't the first person to sleep between those sheets since they last saw a washing machine.

12. THE DAY MICK JAGGER WAS TALLER THAN ME

The Rolling Stones are the ultimate rock-and-roll band. There hasn't been one successful white guitar band ever that hasn't been in some way influenced by The Stones, or one fan of white guitar bands who doesn't like some of their singles. The Beatles may well be the ultimate pop band, but in terms of style and attitude, The Stones have always had the edge.

Ironically, though they are the epitome of the white rock band, their influences were mainly black blues players, and in fact the key to their success is that they made black music accessible to the white audience, giving it a real whiff of danger in the process. For the same reasons the hip-swivelling Elvis eclipsed the duck-walking architect of some of rock and roll's essential moments, Chuck Berry.

The Rolling Stones more or less invented what a rock-and-roll band should look like. They had all the elements right from the start. They had the extrovert front man who exuded sexuality; two moody-looking guitarists, one blond, one dark; and two grumpy-looking blokes at the back who didn't say much. Over a period of time this evolved into the even cooler line-up of the extrovert front man who exuded sexuality; the dead-moody-looking guitarist; the should-rightfully-be-dead moody-looking guitarist, and one grumpy-looking one at the back, the other grumpy-looking one having gone off in a grump. The 'new boy', who joined in 1974, is a cheery-looking guitarist who seems to be employed as mate-in-chief to the should-rightfully-be-dead guitarist.

The new boy is called Ronnie, and the grumpy-looking one Charlie, but it's the relationship between the extrovert front man who exudes sexuality and the should-rightfully-be-dead guitarist that's the subject of continued fascination. In fact, people instinctively feel themselves to be drawn to either the Mick or the Keith camp, and for decades, the argument has raged about which of them is the most rock and roll. This is an argument I can now resolve.

If you had to pick one person as a personification of rock and roll it may well be Keith Richards, and you suspect that rather like McCartney's chagrin at Lennon being considered the 'interesting one' in The Beatles, this may be a source of irritation to Mick Jagger. Keith, in the mid-seventies anyway, probably looked as cool as anyone ever has done. He more or less invented the meticulously dishevelled hairstyle that became a prerequisite for all rock guitarists, while Jagger's lustrous barnet couldn't quite escape the thought that it had involved one of those beehive hairdryers you still see in 'blue rinse' salons. Keith also came up with the brilliant idea of taking enough drink and drugs on board to kill you, without actually dying. This is a terrific trick if you can pull it off, and all the more beguiling for quite clearly being fraught with danger, as all really good tricks are. Las Vegas illusionists Siegfried and Roy got mauled by their own tiger, who'd obviously had enough. Why Keith's body hasn't reacted the same way is one of the great mysteries of modern science. Mick, on the other hand, obviously knew when he'd had enough. Which is not very rock and roll. So Keith is more rock and roll.

Except that these days Keith looks like he's been recently exhumed to perform. His skin resembles clay uncovered at the bottom of a reservoir during a severe drought. He seems simultaneously haggard and bloated. His hair, what's left of it, is embellished with all manner of headbands, bits of wire, fishing hooks, toothpicks and leftover slivers of game pie. Mark Ellen, a friend of mine and editor of *Word* magazine, swears that when he met Keith Richards, there was a small teaspoon dangling in his locks. Is that cool? I suppose it's possible that he might need it handy if he wanted to 'cook up', if I understand the lingo, but surely that's going to be tricky if the spoon's attached to your head, isn't it? Keith claims not to have visited a barber for a hundred years or something. As if somehow we should be surprised by this.

'Right sir, what are we having?'

'Well, I thought a little off the sides and top, and a couple of items of cutlery round the back.'

I imagine that Keith uses these decoy techniques in the hope we won't recognize the fact that he's thinning a bit. It's not working, Keith. If it did, every balding bloke in the world would be walking round with pastry forks where their fringe used to be.

Mick's hair – and in rock and roll you need good hair – still looks great. And he's not trying to be rock and roll by plaiting offcuts of fuse wire into it. Which may ultimately be more rock and roll. Because surely being rock and roll has to involve 'not trying too hard'. If Mick Jagger wants to be Sir Mick then let him. The fact that Keith needs to sneer at him for it, vaguely accusing him of selling out to the establishment, seems misguided to me. When Keith walks out on stage in front of two billion people in the baseball arena of the Los Angeles Venture Capitalists, does he really believe he's anti-establishment? You feel that Mick Jagger knows exactly who he is and what he's there for, and has probably kept the band running while Keith was involving himself in his 'hobbies'. Like falling out of coconut trees and shopping for a small enough penknife to tie on his eyebrow.

Also, if you listen to the early Stones records like 'Come On', 'Carol', 'I Wanna Be Your Man', 'It's All Over Now' and a host of others, the really striking thing is the ferocity of Jagger's voice. The band are good, but finding their feet, searching for their sound. You can also make a pretty strong case for the interesting instrumental bits being, for the most part, the work of Brian Jones. But Mick's voice was the finished article at that early stage. It has spunk and spite and snarl and soul, and undoubtedly drags the rest of the band along in its wake. So Mick Jagger is more rock and roll.

Then again Keith retains a certain unpredictability, a sense that things could go very wrong or indeed very right. Mick Jagger is quite possibly the best front man of a rock band ever to have lived, a role I'm sure he takes very seriously. In fact he told me as much in the interview we'll come to shortly. He sees it as his job, his duty, to run up and down and shake the part of his body where his bottom should be at the audience to 'put on a good show'. Everyone who has seen The Stones expresses astonishment at how a man of his age can still keep this up. I've never heard of anyone seeing the band and being disappointed that Mick seemed distracted and did the show on a stool wearing Dunlop slippers. This is commendable, but it's the element of 'accident waiting to happen' that Keith brings that makes it such an absorbing spectacle. Is he going to turn up? Is he going to be off his trolley? Is he actually playing anything? Will he fall over? Is that an egg whisk in his hair?

These uncertainties are essential to visceral rock and roll. Predictability limits how special a moment can be. I imagine you can go and see Bon Jovi anywhere on their world tour and the experience will be pretty much exactly the same.

And fair enough, in a way. If you've paid two hundred quid to sit in a football ground and watch them, you want it to sound like the records so you feel you've got your money's worth. And yet what's the point in that, really? You might as well stay at home and listen to the record and not have to wait four and a half hours to get out of the car park.

A really top live rock show should bring you something that the record can't. A sense of excitement, and tension, and certainly the knowledge that these are human beings making this racket, and it could go off in a completely different direction at any moment.

If you go to see Bob Dylan you'll find yourself surrounded by people who not only know a lot more about Bob Dylan than you, they know a lot more about Bob Dylan than Bob Dylan does. But even they are struggling to work out exactly which song he's doing at any given moment. Not only does he change the set-list every night, he changes the words and tunes to his most famous songs, and while this can be frustrating if you get him on a bad day, how delicious to catch him at the peak of his powers, knowing there will never be another gig quite like the one you've just seen. The ephemeral nature of the perfection, as with the weatherworn artworks of Andy Goldsworthy, makes for a unique and compelling experience. Admittedly, this might mean going to more than one concert on any given tour, but again, it's all the more rewarding for having put the effort in.

Of course, this, while undeniably true, is relatively easy for me to say as I don't normally pay for my own tickets, and if I had shelled out the price of a long weekend in Krakow to see His Bobness mangle 'Leopard-Skin Pill-Box Hat', I might well be standing on my seat shouting, 'Come on, you cowboy-hatted pillock, do some of your good ones!'

But truly great rock and roll has to have that element of

chance to it, and Keith has managed to retain that. So, in summary, the one out of Keith and Mick who's the most rock and roll is Keith. Or possibly Mick.

When you go to meet a big star the procedure is always the same. Unless they're coming to your studio, you'll always be told to turn up at a London hotel at a given time. These hotels are generally so posh they don't have anything to identify them as hotels on the outside. Or indeed on the inside to the initial untutored glance. Discreet might be one way of putting it. Ludicrously priced might be another. Often they're tucked away down side streets or back alleys gentrified with the word 'mews'. They normally look like rather grand town houses and often have names that are simple addresses to put you off the scent even more like Number 1 Palmerston Crescent, 3 Montmorency Terrace or 27A Back Scuttle Street, although obviously I've made these up as I wouldn't want to reveal true locations and have you turning up and bothering Mariah Carey.

Once you get to the hotel you'll be greeted by an attractive woman from the PR company sporting expensive highlights and a clipboard. She will never know who you are, ever, until she has checked you're on the list. Once this formality is out of the way, you will be escorted into the lift and taken up to the rooms where the interview is going to take place. Usually this will be a suite, as otherwise you'd all be lying on the super double-deluxe emperor-sized bed to do the interview. No matter how spacious the rooms, though, this is still a hotel, and there will always be an en suite bathroom in evidence. Occasionally I've been interviewing someone in such a location and been unable to shift the image of the interviewee performing his or her ablutions as the bathroom is in such close proximity. There may be people who might get more than a little excited at this thought, depending on the celebrity in question, but not me. Especially when picturing Van Morrison in there with the *Racing Post*.

Once you've been brought to the suite you'll encounter the expensively casually dressed senior PR man, who, in contrast to the blonde girl, will profess to have known you for years, even if you've never met before. He will make chummy chitchat for a while, before reminding you you've only got twenty minutes. At some time during this period you will be offered a drink. Of tea or water.

After five minutes have passed one of two things will happen. Either you'll be left alone while they go and see if the star turn is ready, or another PR man will arrive who's worked with the band since the sixties. This will always be a very well-preserved, lat-thin, grey-haired gentleman wearing designer spectacles, a pink shirt and brogues. His accent will be that of an officer in the Household Cavalry. He will make some sort of weak joke about the room having been deco rated by a colour-blind homosexual chap, before telling you that whoever you're going to be talking to is on 'good form'. Well of course they are. They may be world-ranked superstars, but they still need to sell records or they wouldn't be here.

So, all in all, it's a bit like being in the queue at the grotto, feeling that it's all taking a long time, but at least you're getting closer to Santa. Or Mick.

When he entered the room, the senior PR man unnecessarily, though rather charmingly I thought, introduced him. Of course he introduced me to Mick, which is fair enough, and so it's only polite to do it the other way round, but is there anyone in the world who doesn't know who Mick Jagger is?

During the course of my radio career I've met lots of people out of famous bands, and though it's nearly always been pleasurable, and mildly exciting, I've rarely been starstruck. I had trouble speaking after I first met David Bowie, as he was the closest thing I had to a hero when I was young, and never in a million years did I think that I would one day be in the same room as him. But other than that, I've taken it all relatively calmly. I think you have to. If people are going to submit to the interview process they want to be confronted with someone who's capable of following a logical line of questioning through a structured conversation, not a gibbering idiot who keeps telling them how great they are. Presumably there are plenty of those on the payroll already.

I have to admit though, when suddenly confronted with the real Mick Jagger, I was momentarily flummoxed. It's quite extraordinary meeting someone that famous in the flesh. This is a face that would have been unforgettable on a washing-machine repairman, let alone on the lead singer of the world's biggest and longest-established rock band. Here was the face that had stared at you from billboards, magazines and record sleeves your whole life, actually moving, forming expressions and talking normal words. I know that sounds ridiculous, but it's such an iconic face it was rather like that poster of Che Guevara or the *Mona Lisa* suddenly chatting away to you.

People have asked me what sort of nick he's in close up, and the truth is, he looks simultaneously about forty and about a hundred. Again, I know that sounds crazy, but while he's lithe and fit with thick healthy hair and clear skin, he's also got deep ravines down his face. Weirdly though, he doesn't have wrinkles, so while the crevasses either side of his mouth indicate a person who's been around a good while, the rest of him seems almost youthful.

He was dressed in a black linen jacket, jeans, black trainers and a plain cotton shirt that looked like it had come from the lost-property department at school, and so presumably cost about three hundred pounds. He was pretty small too, which wasn't a surprise because everyone knows The Stones are tiny. Or at least, tiny by today's standards where everyone over the age of seventeen is six-feet-two. And not just the girls. How did that happen? I know lots of men my age and height, about five-feet-nine or ten, whose sons can't fit through the door without ducking. What have they had that we haven't? Did they start putting growth hormones in cans of cheap cider sometime in the eighties?

The Rolling Stones were probably normal-sized in the early sixties, but they look ridiculously small now. It's a bit like Mini cars. If you see an original Mini on the road now, it looks like a toy, not least because the contemporary Minis are the same size as removal vans were in the late fifties. So The Stones are not small as such, they just date back to a time when five-feet-six was normal for a man. Six-footers were few and far between, and if you were a six-foot woman people pointed at you in the street. Not only that though, it's possible that The Stones have got a bit shorter with age. It's a fault in the original design really. No one expected rock-and-roll bands to be around this long, it was supposed to be a fad that would pass like skiffle and trad jazz. If they'd known they were still going to be going in the twenty-first century they might have tried harder to grow in the sixties. Gone to a stretching parlour or something. Or Mick might have, anyway. Keith would have been too busy with his chemistry set and that's probably why he's smaller than Mick. Also, it's commonly known that all of us are half to three quarters of an inch shorter at night than when we got up that morning. Well, Keith Richards doesn't go to bed, which means he's doing well not to be shrinking by a good three inches a week. By rights he should be the size of a garden gnome by now, as well as having the face of one.

So I was prepared for Mick being a little bit smaller than

me, but what really shocked me was how thin he was. I don't mean he looked anorexic or anything, he looked really, really well. But his shoulders were about as wide as a standard laptop computer. Seriously, I would say about fourteen inches. He had a build unlike any other grown man I've ever met. He was nothing if not affable though. The ostensible reason for our meeting was to talk about a collection of his solo recordings, but he was happy to chat about other things. I asked him if he ever wished he was Charlie Watts, not having to cavort around at the front for two hours to hold the show together. He said that being a born show-off he didn't, except occasionally when it was raining. At those gigs, exposed on the lip of the stage or scampering along a catwalk getting soaked through, he said he sometimes thinks Charlie's got the best job. He'll even shimmy over to the drum riser and say, 'All right, Charlie? Nice and dry are you?'

Watts presumably gives the faintest of nods, an inscrutable smile and just gets on with holding down the beat as he has since 1962. Never having got wet.

On the way to the interview I'd also been musing on how great it must be to be Mick Jagger. The Stones remain universally loved, you need never work again if you don't want to, women still fancy you, blokes probably fancy you too should you be interested, you can have a nice house wherever you like and there's always someone around to do the stuff for you that you can't be bothered doing yourself. It must be terrific to wake up in the morning and think: 'I'm still Mick Jagger. It wasn't a dream. Brilliant.' After listening patiently to my theorizing he said that he really didn't think that way because he was always busy. Often with mundane stuff like 'getting the kids' breakfast'. Well perhaps so, but even while you're scraping the last of the Marmite onto the toast, you must still know you're the singer in the world's biggest rock-and-roll band.

He said he didn't train much to stay in shape, and had to eat like a horse to keep his weight up around the ten-stone mark. He reminisced about the 'Dancing in the Street' duet with David Bowie in the rushed run-up to Live Aid and happily admitted that the accompanying video makes slightly cringeworthy viewing as two incurable extroverts attempt to out dance and out-gurn each other. He was perfectly happy to laugh at himself and his past crimes against showbiz. He talked a bit about cricket, said he felt he had a couple more tours in him yet, and we were falling into easy conversation. I so wanted to ask all about The Stones and their colourful past, but, of course, there wasn't time. I was always aware that there was someone with an eye on the clock in the room, and you wouldn't be allowed to run over your allocated slot by more than a couple of minutes. And that's understandable. He can't be expected to go through his life history every time someone shoves a microphone up his nose.

There was time to get a little glimpse of the relationship between him and Keith though. He admitted that at times Keith's work rate had led to the band progressing at a painfully slow pace and this was something he found irritating. He said there were times when they worked pretty much separately on songs, often Mick doing days and Keith wandering in to clock on for the night shift. He acknowledged that they were a bit like an old married couple, who'd had lots of ups and downs, but had come to accept that they were going to be together forever, however frustrating that sometimes was.

What I really wanted to know about, however, was the shepherd's pie. Rock legend has it that either Mick or Keith demands shepherd's pie before they go on stage, and at one gig in an enormo-dome somewhere in the Midwest, either Mick or Keith had been into catering and eaten the last portion. This meant that when Mick or Keith, whichever one of them really wanted it, went to present their meal ticket, there was no shepherd's pie left. The story goes that the show was then held up for forty-five minutes while another helping was whipped up. True, Sir Mick? Sadly not. However, he did reveal that he didn't eat before a gig, and so if there was a ker-fuffle in the food tent, it must have been Keith that caused it, and he admitted it might have been possible because Keith, the great hedonistic, non-sleeping, chemically infused, drink-addled apothecary of rock-and-roll myth, really does love shepherd's pie. Bless.

We wound the interview up, exchanged a few pleasantries and he agreed to have a photo taken with me. Usually, I look kind of small in photographs with bands, but on this occasion, I knew that I was going to be the tallest one in the picture, or at least equal tallest. But at the precise moment of the photo being taken, Mick Jagger went up on the balls of his feet and stole an extra couple of inches on me. Of course he did. It was exquisitely timed, being a trick he perfected years ago. There was only time for one snap too, so now, when people ask me what he was like and I say, 'A gentleman but smaller than you'd think,' they look at that photo and think, 'Yes, but he's still bigger than you, Mark.'

13. THE DAY I DIDN'T GO TO AYIA NAPA

Back in the days when dance music was king, Radio 1 decamped to Ayia Napa for part of the summer. It's a resort on the south coast of Cyprus which became a Mecca for party-going ravers anxious, and not just because of the drugs, to head for sunnier climes in which to hear 'banging block-rocking beats', if I recall the appropriate vernacular correctly.

Not being trendy enough, or particularly au fait with the, errm, 'phat' tunes, Marc Riley and I weren't invited to participate. I absolutely understood this. It seemed to me an entirely sensible decision. We were woefully underqualified to fly out at the licence-fee payer's expense to attempt to, let me get this right again, 'mix flavas in a area'. By which was meant playing back-to-back records from what I could make out, though I'm sure there must have been more to it than that. Some of our Radio 1 stablemates were being routinely flown out on a weekly basis to do it and you wouldn't go to all that trouble just for someone to spin a few discs, would you? There must be Cypriot mobile discos in the Nicosia Yellow Pages.

So we didn't get to go, which was fine, but it did rather offend our sense of fair play. If everyone else was getting a free trip, why weren't we? Accordingly we hatched a plan to visit one of our favourite holiday destinations and to do a

programme from there. Management, probably rushing to
catch a plane to the sun, surprisingly agreed. Result. So it
was that while the rest of Radio 1 jetted off to Ayia Napa, we
trundled over to Robin Hood's Bay in two Fiat Puntos,
having been let down by the hire company on a people carrier at the last minute.

We chose to do our Friday afternoon show from the
lounge bar of the Bay Hotel with its unrivalled collection of
novelty teapots – the absolute antithesis of what was going on
in Ayia Napa. It was here also that we first met the effervescent and matey lads from Travis, who became such firm
friends that they returned to play on our final Radio 1 show
in March 2004. Perhaps they just wanted to be sure we were
going.

Broadcasting from Ayia Napa presented some technical
problems, of course. Breaks in transmission were not unheard
of and there was the ever-present risk of events down there
not making it to air for a number of reasons. And if that were
to happen, well, it's not the sort of thing you can just repli-
cate back home at the drop of a beanie hat. You can't just
grab someone, throw them into a studio, and get them to
play some records without talking in between, can you? Or
can you?

Ironic, then, that it was the *Mark and Lard Robin Hood's
Bay Holiday Special* that went off-air. Apparently, somewhere
up the hill, a combine harvester ran over a power line and
our programme was prematurely curtailed before our specially constructed 'The Cod is God' quiz, in honour of the
fine fishing tradition in that part of the world, could be heard
by an avidly expectant British population.

The programmes from Ayia Napa went out without a
hitch.

14. THE DAY I HEARD THAT JOHN PEEL HAD DIED

When I got a job as a producer at Radio 1 in 1983, I felt as if I'd won the pools. I was given my own little office, a sunny PA from Catford called Sue, and a pass that allowed me to walk through the front door of Broadcasting House. I was actually stationed in a distinctly unlovely (and now demolished) office block called Egton House right next to BH, as I soon learned to call it, the BBC being very keen on abbreviations, but my recording sessions took place in the main building. To pack up your tapes and records into one of the BBC programme boxes, or BBCPBs as I've just christened them, and stride through those hallowed portals as mere civilians looked on, hoping for a glimpse of the mighty DG (Director-General to you), or even the great DJ (David Jacobs), was utterly thrilling. I'd arrived. If you've got a career in radio, BH is the most recognizable and prestigious building in the world, and being allowed to work in it felt like the most enormous privilege. Like going to university at Oxbridge perhaps, or playing football at Wembley stadium, or WS as it would be called if the BBC owned it.

On top of the sheer delight and surprise at being at the centre of the broadcasting universe there were other factors that made life hugely pleasurable. For a start, people would turn up at your office and give you lots of records. Working at Piccadilly Radio in Manchester I'd received occasional visits from record-company personnel bearing gifts, but at Radio 1 it was more or less an hourly occurrence. And if you wanted something they didn't have, they biked it over the same day. I'd never experienced anything like it. You just mentioned you were a fan of, say, Talking Heads and their back catalogue would arrive by elevenses. You let it drop that you were a Springsteen aficionado and a signed poster to adorn the office wall would be delivered that afternoon. You enthused about the majesty of Kiss and a private mental-health practitioner would pay you a visit later the same day. It was wonderful. And not content with saving you all the money you'd have spent on albums, they also cut down on your food bills by offering to take you out for lunch all the time. On my very first day there I found myself sitting with Adrian from A&M records at a restaurant in Charlotte Street drinking wine I'd never heard of and scoffing something called Chateaubriand, which was carved for you at the table. And we were sitting outside! It was like being on holiday. Not only that, but you had no hands-on boss who would be clock-watching to see what time you staggered back that afternoon. There were guys in Egton House who'd accordingly been 'out to lunch' for years. All that was asked was that you knocked out the programmes you were trusted with. When and how you did it was entirely up to you. The trick then for the old-timers was to get the amount of on-air time you were responsible for down to an absolute minimum, or preferably zero. I did see this trick pulled off by two separate individuals, who shall remain nameless because it would cause upset and embarrassment, and you wouldn't know them anyway.

I will say that one of them 'produced' Jimmy Savile for years. All this entailed was making sure the cotton-wool-headed Godfather of Bling was in the studio and alive, and ensuring there were a few records around for the engineer to stick on when there was a gap in the chat. Once done, the tape would be dropped off with the requisite PA, and that was another gruelling week at the coalface completed.

Another chap, of whom I became immensely fond, produced a programme fronted by the cordial font of all music knowledge Paul Gambaccini. Paul, or Gambo as it was customary to refer to him, presented a rundown of the *Billboard* American charts on a Saturday afternoon. This immediately presented the 'producer' with a problem, as he rather liked boating at the weekends. However, as Paul was choosing all his own records, writing and researching his own scripts, and making sure it all started and finished on time, there was precious little for a producer to do. I suppose he could have gone along to the studio to lend a bit of moral support and fetch the odd cup of tea, but canal boats don't maintain themselves, do they? So the system they ended up with was that Gambo would drop off all the records in the right order during the week, then the PA would time them and print out a running order. The whole thing would then be left in the 'producer's' cupboard under lock and key, waiting for him to find half an hour in which he wasn't detained at the chandlery to check it through, sign the form, and sling it into a BBCPB, as they're not known. Unfortunately, on the first weekend I was working at the station, producing the magazine show *Saturday Live*, a problem with the rack and pinion of a lock somewhere on the Grand Union had prevented Paul's 'producer' from getting in to the office. Well, you can't be in two places at once, can you? Accordingly, I found myself as the new boy having to jemmy the good captain's cupboards open with a coat hanger to get the Hot 100 records out, an act for which the gracious Gambo (GG) has often expressed his gratitude.

The producer, worried that this problem might recur, deftly solved it by issuing Paul with his own key. He also instigated a scheme, as all good bosses should, to give the junior member of the team more experience and responsibility. The newly refined system was that Paul brought in the records, the PA timed the records, signed the form and locked them in the cupboard before Paul unlocked the cupboard to take the records to the studio on Saturday, do the show and return them to the cupboard from whence the PA would retrieve them on Monday morning. Brilliant. It worked seamlessly, and left the week nicely free for water-borne adventure without the pesky interruption of struggling into the West End on a regular basis.

Another producer and boating enthusiast went off cruising for several weeks, despite ostensibly having the odd show to sort out. As he'd made sure all the work was being done by his secretary and the presenter, the smooth running of this operation was only threatened, as usual, by bloody management. Realizing they hadn't seen this chap for a couple of months, his PA would receive a call from one of the big cheeses asking him to 'nip upstairs' for a bit of a chinwag. The admirably primed girl would then follow instructions by saying he was at the dentist, but would pop up tomorrow. She would then fire up the field telephone, make contact with him in dry dock on the Trent and Mersey, and he would simply hop on a train and present himself for executive platitudes the next morning, often wrong-footing the relevant executive by arriving before they did in order to look keen. It was all meticulously planned and kept everyone involved perfectly happy, which must mean that he was one of the very best producers in the BBC.

Radio 1 in those early eighties days was anything but a classless society. The fourth floor was home to the giants of the daytime schedule: Mike Read, Simon Bates, Steve Wright,

Gary Davies and other similarly exalted figures. I didn't see much of them, possibly because they were ferried in and out of the studios by sedan chair, though more probably because they rarely frequented the lower floors. They appeared to keep to their own small groups of trusted accomplices and seemed rather like mafia dons heading up rival families. Not that anyone found a horse's head on their pillow. Well, not unless it was as a *Roadshow* prank in a hotel in Bognor Regis.

Those of us involved with weekend programmes or specialist music were afforded grubby rooms on the third floor. My particular cell boasted a spectacular view of the air-conditioning units and was perhaps nine feet square, though I wasn't complaining. Where I'd come from, Piccadilly Radio, you were taught to count yourself lucky if you had a desk. James H. Reeve, one of the finest broadcasters ever to emerge from the north of England in my view, had to make do with a drawer in a filing cabinet for years. And there were people with smaller drawers who looked at Jim's with some envy, let me tell you. So to have a 'room of one's own' felt extraordinarily grown-up.

Throughout the week this room with a view, albeit primarily of ducting, was plenty big enough as there was only me in it. Unless someone from EMI dropped by to see if I fancied going to the Wimbledon Finals with Kate Bush. Or a good lunch at the very least. Towards the end of the week, though, my personal space would also have to accommodate *Saturday Live*'s presenters, Richard Skinner and Andy Batten-Foster (who is in the photograph at the start of this chapter with me, on stage at Wembley, and who remains one of my closest pals to this day). That's why we always start phone messages with the chummy phrase: 'All right, ya bastard?'

Well, that's what pals do, isn't it?

All the producers on that floor enjoyed a similar 'cellmate' existence with their pet DJs. On a daily basis you could bump into Tommy Vance, Jimmy Savile, Dave Lee Travis, Peter Powell, Paul Gambaccini and, if you were lucky, Annie Nightingale.

Annie was one of the very few radio presenters to have touched my radar before I began working in the business. I used to listen to her Sunday night request show religiously, especially at the start when, instead of babbling inanely over the introduction of the first record as several of her turbo-tongued, blow-dried male counterparts might have done, she simply said 'Hi' in that sultry, honeyed tone just before the vocals started. It was as if all was well with the world when you'd heard Annie say 'Hi'. She played great music too, and seemed to be genuinely enjoying doing so. You didn't get the impression she was passing through pop radio en route to fronting a television quiz show. She gave the impression of being exactly where she wanted to be. Also, to state the obvious, she was a woman in what was, to all intents and purposes, a man's world.

How amazing then that she was one of only two people to knock on my office door that first day to see if I was all right. The other was her producer, a laconic, denim-clad ageing hippy who'd once engineered for Hendrix called Pete Ritzema. Nice one, Pete, but when Annie stuck her head round the door, well, it bordered on the surreal. I'd grown up listening to her and here she was checking if I was all right. I was, but I was even better after that.

The other notable occupants of the third floor were the Johns Peel and Walters, but we'll come to them shortly.

Third-floor life was relatively harmonious. The producers secreted themselves away in their little lairs, unless they were crossing the Llangollen aqueduct, and the PAs sat in a large open-plan space where they could mock record-company pluggers, disc jockeys and producers alike. It was generally good-natured stuff though it became apparent that my office was one of the least desirable, as you had to run the gauntlet of catcalls to get back to it after returning from lunch at around half-past four courtesy of CBS. Longer-serving producers had taken offices immediately adjacent to the lift when they became vacant, as that meant you didn't have to negotiate the 'typing pool' and could sneak back in and get pretty much straight to sleep after someone who wanted you to programme the new Thompson Twins single had plied you with claret.

I know this sounds like there was no one doing any work at all, but that's not strictly true. The girls in the outer office all cracked on with stuff, and some of us producers did manage to knock out what I'd like to think were pretty decent shows. I'm still very proud of the work I did on *Saturday Live*. It was a magazine show and we prided ourselves on putting together guests who might seem like odd bedfellows. The high point of this policy came when we sat teen heart-throb David Cassidy alongside German avant-garde tinkly-bonk composer Karlheinz Stockhausen. They seemed to get along perfectly well. Karlheinz seemed to think he'd hummed along to 'How Can I Be Sure' at some point. David was less sure he'd heard *Mikrophonie II* for twelve singers, Hammond organ, four ring modulators and tape. Certainly if he had chanced upon it, it had exerted little discernible influence on the Cassidy oeuvre.

We would only ever book guests we were genuinely interested in ourselves, which I think is a pretty good rule to follow, as if you're not engaged by the content then there's a fair chance no one else will be either, but occasionally we would bend a little to help mates out. We'd never book someone we detested or thought of as having no artistic merit at all, but we would have people on we were ambivalent about, if it made the life of a record plugger we liked a bit easier that week. Especially if he or she had taken us to Claridge's or a grand prix or something recently.

One such occasion happened when a charming if hyper-active Irishman called Paul White virtually begged us to have this new American disco singer and dancer on for the last ten minutes of the show, as he was having precious little luck in getting her on elsewhere. Evidently he was under severe pressure from his superiors, who had great hopes for this girl. Well, we'd all heard that before, only for the starlet in question to sink without trace within the year. Still, I listened to the record and I thought it was OK, and she seemed to have an interesting story to tell about the club scene in New York so, as a favour to Paul, we booked her.

On the day of the interview we were unable to get a proper studio to record in, so we had to make do with a smelly cellar under Egton House known as 'the pit'. Here we cobbled together our trails under the studio management of the bloke who played 'Mr Angry' on the Steve Wright show. He wasn't angry in real life, he was a very nice and patient man, which was surprising seeing as he'd been sentenced to live this subterranean existence.

We met Paul in reception and initially I thought he'd brought a young niece with him because he was accompanied by a tiny girl with a bad, eighties teenager's curly mullet on her head. I think she was wearing a leather jacket and some moth-eaten-looking leggings. She seemed pleasant enough, and so down the stairs we went to the dank basement where the faint rumbling of the tube trains mingled with the vague whiff of lavatory freshener. Andy talked to her for a while about discotheques in the Big Apple and some other stuff presumably as, to be honest, I wasn't really paying much attention. Anyway, we shook her hand and sent her on her way, stuck the tape out for five minutes the following Saturday, and looked forward to Paul's record company funding a modest helicopter jaunt to Paris for dinner at Regine's on the understanding that we took in a gig by latest no-hoper signings Goth Fiancee or Skiffle Widow or Dog Borstal, whoever it happened to be. And all because we'd agreed to chat to some desperate wannabe who would never be heard of again. Except in this case we did hear from her again. Quite a lot. It was Madonna.

So producing *Saturday Live* took up four days a week, which left one working day that I owed the BBC. It was therefore decided that on Tuesdays I would be despatched to the Maida Vale studios to produce sessions for John Peel. Un-be-lievable. Me, producing bands for John Peel.

In truth, this was as worrying as it was exciting as I'd no actual experience of producing bands in the studio. You might reasonably wonder how someone without any basic knowledge of recording techniques got the job in the first place. The same way everyone else gets jobs they want but are a bit underqualified for. I lied at the interview. I told them I'd produced loads of bands from Joy Division to Echo and the Bunnymen to Freddie and the sodding Dreamers. By the time I'd finished they were under the impression that I was Manchester's answer to Phil Spector. But without the guns. Or wigs.

In truth I had knocked around various studios while bands like these had been recording, but I hadn't had any actual hands-on experience of sorting the sound out or anything like that. I had made tea though, which turned out to be just about the most useful thing a producer could do, although it took me a while to accept this.

Initially, with the naive enthusiasm of relative youth by Radio 1's then standards, I did try and exert some influence on proceedings. One of my early sessions, with an industrial-indie outfit called Tools You Can Trust, was immortalized on film for *The Old Grey Whistle Test*. The band, wearing council haircuts and Oxfam suits, grind away, hitting fire extinguishers and wrestling with a bass guitar in the name of art. The producer, myself, wearing a yellow jumper and what looks suspiciously like a mullet, keeps looking at his watch and encouraging them by telling them their time is fast running out and issuing such comments as: 'It all sounds a bit ragged.'

Well, move over George Martin.

Eventually I realized that the bands were going to do what they were going to do, and the seasoned BBC engineers were more than capable of recording it. Accordingly my working session would involve turning up at lunchtime to see that the band had arrived and then getting the teas while they set up. This being duly done I would hold off going to the pub for long enough to hear the first song, after which I'd say something like: 'Brilliant. That sounds marvellous. Do four more like that and I'll see you later.'

I learned that whether the band sounded 'ragged' or not, and ragged was often the point, particularly when Marc Riley and The Creepers came in, I wasn't going to convince them to do it differently in a single day. Here I'm also reminded of a long and forthright discussion with The Jesus and Mary Chain regarding the acceptable level of feedback on a track. They wanted more, I wanted less. But, in retrospect, what did it have to do with me? Peel wanted to hear them sounding like them. He didn't want him or his audience to hear them mixed by a bloke in a Benetton pullover who'd brewed up for A Certain Ratio. It was their band, not mine. As producer I wasn't responsible for the material. I was just there to make sure everyone was getting on with it, and no bits of BBC equipment got broken or stolen. That might sound like dereliction of duty in a way, but it wasn't. It brought home to me one of the most important things a producer can learn, that if everything's going smoothly, don't be tempted to stick your oar in just to satisfy your own ego. I was delighted to be asked to produce The Pogues, but I think my main contribution was to ask Cait O'Riordan, the bass player, to take her feet off the chairs as she was in danger of stabbing Ted the engineer in the temple with her stiletto heels.

This, then, left me plenty of time to swan around the Maida Vale area, which I discovered to have a charming canal-side area known as Little Venice. If I'd had any money I might have been tempted to buy a boat and take a few leisurely trips around the waterways. That was what producers did when they didn't have a heavy workload, wasn't it? Of course I could never have afforded it so I had to content myself with taking the water-bus through Regent's Park up to Camden Lock, getting back in time to wish Julian Cope adieu and turn the studio lights off.

However, just to be involved with the Peel show felt incredible. Growing up in Bolton I had three ways of experiencing new music. Bolton Institute of Technology promoted gigs on a Saturday night and I would attend religiously to watch Hawkwind or bands on tour from the Low Countries who sounded very like Hawkwind. We also had 'Whispering Bob Harris' and *The Old Grey Whistle Test* on television once a week. The main supply line for the young musical adventurer, though, was the John Peel programme. Night after night I would listen and marvel at the new sounds he'd discovered. I kept a small notebook by the side of my bed to scribble down the names of new bands I would need to investigate. There in that single bed in an attic room in Bolton I first heard Bob Marley, The Ramones, The Clash and countless others.

It wasn't just the music, but the way Peel presented it. Rather like Annie Nightingale, John just had this knack of communicating enthusiasm without getting overexcited. He never thought he was more important than the tunes he was playing and that spoke volumes to me. He also, I think, made the idea viable that you could do a show in that way. That it wasn't necessarily a given that the DJ had to be some wacky celebrity figure. Without John blazing the trail, not that blazing seems quite the right way to describe him, I doubt that anyone like me would ever have been considered for fronting programmes. You may consider that to be a mixed blessing, but there is a generation of us who will always be in debt to Peel, and to some extent Annie, for kicking that door open.

The best part of all this was that I got to know the man personally. It took me quite a while to approach him because, though he would have hated me saying this, I was in awe, but also he was difficult to engage because he was so low key and diffident. Without being remotely menacing, he just didn't seem to invite the casual approach. I know that it wasn't just me who felt this. People were wary of approaching him because he was John Peel and looked like he had things on his mind. I remember being with him at an 'In the City' music conference in Manchester. We had a chat about what we'd heard recently over the customary bottle of red, and talked vaguely of hooking up later in the week. It never happened, because Peel left town early and went home to his beloved Sheila. When I later asked him why, he said, 'Well, I was bored because I had no one to talk to.'

Of course, the truth was that there wasn't any one of the thousands attending the event who wouldn't have been absolutely delighted to have a chat with John Peel, but most tended not to as they respected his privacy and didn't want to bother him.

My route through to Peel came via his long-time producer John Walters. Walters and Peel occupied an office the same size as mine on the third floor of Egton House, but if mine was cluttered, it looked like a bomb had gone off in theirs. In the Tate Modern is a wonderful room containing a single work: *Cold Dark Matter* by Cornelia Parker. To create it the artist has blown up a garden shed packed with paraphernalia, photographed it, then collected up all the bits and hung them where they appear in the photograph. It's not only an astonishing technical achievement, but also incredibly beautiful, particularly in the shadows it casts around the outer walls. John Walters's office looked like Cornelia Parker had mounted just such an installation there, and then Walters, actually a keen observer of modern art, had cut it all down and left it lying around. Amidst piles of books, newspapers, records, cassettes and trays hopefully awaiting a return to the canteen that would never come, there was a small pathway to a chair for Peel, and one the other side of the desk for Walters. When Andy Kershaw later came to share the office they couldn't fit another chair in the room and so Andy made do with perching on a programme box.

Of the two Johns, Walters was by far the most gregarious and communicative. If you hadn't known which was which, you'd have sworn that he was the presenter and Peel the back-room boy. I'd always assumed that they'd been lifelong friends, so perfectly balanced was their relationship. Peel once said they were like a man and his dog, but each thought the other was the dog. Or was it Walters who said that?

In reality the BBC had brought them together, something that Peel was initially less than delighted about. He'd been very close to his previous producer Bernie Andrews. It was considered by management, though, that Bernie was a little under-employed and so they gave him another programme to oversee. They found something that dovetailed perfectly with the work he was doing with Peel: 'Music While You Work'. Inspired. This began to take up a lot of Andrews's time and so a new producer for Peel was sought.

Walters was a large man in a crumpled sports jacket with a scrubby beard. He looked like a dishevelled lecturer and it was in fact whilst wandering the corridors of Newcastle University that John hooked up with Alan Price, joining his band on trumpet.

When I met John Walters, he was unlike anyone I'd met before. He was an unbelievably witty raconteur. You couldn't really say good morning to him without the riposte, 'Well, is it?' This would be followed by a fifteen-minute tidal wave of reasons why it might not be. In departmental meetings this approach didn't meet with unanimous approval. Those of us too young to have experienced music hall relaxed back in our chairs and listened with glee to his meticulously constructed epic grumbles. Longer-serving inmates, particularly management, would raise their eyes and emit long breaths, accepting that the meeting, though to all intents and purposes over, was going to last another twenty minutes. On one occasion I remember the controller asking if anyone had any comments about the lift at Egton House, which had recently been redecorated and branded with the station's colours and logo. And mirrors. Walters launched into a ten-minute tirade on the pointlessness of the whole exercise and saying that it now resembled 'a Maltese businessman's idea of a discotheque'. And he was spot on. You knew exactly what he meant. It was the specific identification of the businessman as Maltese that somehow made it all perfect. They should have given him his own show. Well, in fact, they later did. Not soon enough though.

Coming into contact with Walters made me believe utterly in the BBC. He was the kind of one-off who wouldn't have lasted five minutes in a commercial operation, and therefore it had to follow that the BBC was a wonderful place because it was home to colourful mavericks capable of original thought. That had to be great, didn't it?

Walters, it seemed to me, had it all worked out. He once

told *ZigZag* magazine: 'From what I'd seen of the BBC studios, they seemed full of people doing nothing at all, and it looked like money for old rope.' Wise words, mate.

He regarded his primary function as dealing with all the bullshit and politics so Peel could get on with the programmes uninterrupted. Outside of that, he entertained the rest of the department with limitless anecdotage, got up the noses of the bosses and, on a Friday lunchtime, played his trumpet in a jazz band in a grimy bar owned by the Beeb on the ground floor of what is now the Langham Hotel. It seemed the perfect life really.

John Walters died of a heart attack in 2001, and I'm not sure Peel's life was ever quite the same again. Not at Radio 1 at any rate. They just seemed so perfect together. I often think of a moment early in my London life where I was sitting at a pavement cafe just up from Oxford Circus, having coffee and croissants with the pair of them, watching the world go by and gently taking the piss out of anyone we could think of as a suitable target. It was just another day for them but for me, I felt like I was at the centre of the universe. Or at the centre of the only universe I cared about anyway. They, and Annie, were the people I admired the most, and to be taken into their company was something I'll never forget. It's just one of those moments in your life where nothing truly memorable happens, but you feel you're exactly where you want to be.

I shared many more coffees and bottles of red with Peel over the years, but the time we spent together at the Reading Festival in 1991 I remember perhaps most fondly.

Peel's show was going out from the backstage area as the event wound down on the Sunday night, and I was invited to co-present. I'd been fronting my own shows for the network from Manchester and, to my enormous relief and satisfaction, Peel had publicly given his seal of approval to what I was doing, in particular the eclectic musical mix of 'Out On Blue Six'.

But to appear side by side with John Peel felt like the ultimate accolade really. Because his blessing was so crucial to so many bands, and a clear indication for the listeners that something was worth looking into, his endorsement of me meant so much. As the show began Peel was chatting to Andy Kershaw, host of the previous programme, and said: 'I'm here with Mark Radcliffe and the two of us are going to fill the air for the next three hours with gossip and stories and lots of penetrating interviews with pop stars.'

The key words for me are 'the two of us'. John Peel on Radio 1 said 'the two of us' and it meant me and him.

We talked a lot about the location of our makeshift studio, which I described as resembling a janitor's hut or 'Little House on the Prairie' as it was the only occupied structure amidst the detritus of the festival's end. Peel spoke of us broadcasting to the nation from 'a shed on wheels courtesy of the Radio 1 Roadshow limited-resources division'. It was pure Peel. At the same time enthusing about the music, while debunking any sense of glamour about our own surroundings.

There were two more revealing moments. Early in the proceedings Peel bemoaned the number of bands who felt the need to use the 'f-word' in their stage announcements. He took particular issue with Iggy Pop for not only swearing, but also taking his trousers off. This was pretty much par for the course with Iggy but Peel talked of it as being 'a bit of a disappointment, a bit embarrassing'. And that was a part of John. He was always scrupulously polite to everyone and hated rudeness of any kind. I don't know whether it came primarily from his family or his schooling, but somebody had instilled in him the importance of manners. He was certainly always very nice to me.

He also played a request for Steve the stage manager, who

wanted Peel to greet his family back home. Steve had evidently asked John to do this as he made preparations for The Sisters of Mercy's set, and Peel had obliged. But then he would have done. Having promised, it would have been impolite not to and he wouldn't have wanted to let Steve or his family down. Family meant more than anything to Peel. He played 'Teenage Kicks' by The Undertones for Steve's family and said afterwards that he considered it 'the finest record ever made. Where do you stand on this, Mark?'

Blimey, John, you're asking me?

Of course the music meant a lot too, and the programme was littered with the names of bands we'd seen, most of whom never appeared at such a big event again: Babes in Toyland, Pooh Sticks, Ned's Atomic Dustbin, Pop Will Eat Itself, Swervedriver and Chapterhouse.

The Fall also appeared, a band John explained he followed like Liverpool FC with 'a blind, unreasoning passion'. He told of how he was prevented from filming the band during their performance and complained that though he doesn't expect people to fawn all over him, you would have thought that given their relationship, he would have been allowed to catch a couple of numbers. I pointed out to him that apparently the group had a new American manager who didn't know who John Peel was. Cheekily, I accused him of narcissism for assuming he would do. Peel, chuckling, conceded I may have a point.

The interaction between the two of us I found pretty endearing, to be honest. I didn't sound uncomfortable in the presence of the master, but fitted easily into that good-natured, bumbling style that was Peel's trademark. He was nothing if not generous to me. He talked of wandering up to the Mean Fiddler tent and seeing me introduce some long-forgotten band with some long-forgotten witticism and wondering 'why I hadn't thought of saying that'. He announced that we'd recorded interviews and that 'Mark's done some of them – probably the better ones'. Which was untrue. They were all rubbish. I mentioned how impressed I was that he'd managed to time a record to finish exactly on the hour for the news and quipped that 'I'm picking up tips.' I didn't need to. I'd picked them up listening in my bedroom, years before. We talked of Nirvana appearing well down the bill on the first day and the subject of stage passes came up. Peel had 'Access All Areas' and watched from the stage. Evidently I didn't.

'Maybe next year, Mark,' he deadpanned.

I'm pleased that you can hear the genuine affection and respect that there was between us without it sounding like I was trying to impress him, as John would never have been impressed by someone trying too hard to do that.

Whenever I can I escape to Anglesey with my family. It may well be my favourite place on earth, with its windswept coastal paths above the cliffs and wide stretches of sculpted sand. I really feel like I'm away from the world down there, not least because I can't get much of a signal on my phone. Well, not unless I stand on the headland and hold my Nokia into the prevailing wind like a portly Statue of Liberty wearing an anorak. Once a day, usually around teatime, I'll switch the phone on, scan the skies for a signal, and check my messages. Normally there won't be any, as everyone I work with knows I'm away, and also, being a bloke, I don't really do social calls.

I went through this ritual late one afternoon in October 2004 and discovered, to my astonishment, that I had about a dozen new messages. This was more than I'd had in my entire life, so I knew something must have happened. I began playing the messages back and they were from a variety of radio stations, television news programmes, magazines and daily papers asking me if I could 'say something about John'. As I hadn't heard any news throughout that day, I initially had no idea what they were talking about. None of the callers actually told me what had happened, presuming I would already have known. And so, in a stiff breeze overlooking Cemaes Bay, I pieced together the awful news from the babbled fragments of chatter.

John Peel had died of a heart attack on a trip to the Inca city of Cuzco in Peru. He was sixty-five.

I did agree to talk to Five Live that evening because I wanted to express just how much I thought of him, and what a profound influence he had on me. After a while though, as the interview requests continued to flood in, I started to turn them down because I felt I'd said what I wanted to say, and to keep talking about it, or repeating it, was unnecessary.

Of course I discussed it quite a lot in private with other people who'd known him. He had contracted diabetes and wasn't perhaps in the very best of health, but no one had expected anything like this.

He left a big hole. For me, as listener, fan and later colleague, he'd just always been there and I suppose I assumed he always would be. He was like a cricketer holding up one end while wickets tumbled at the other.

I think I felt his passing most keenly at Glastonbury. I'd presented the TV coverage of the festival in the early nineties for Channel 4 before being jettisoned for someone prettier. I was surprised then to be asked, ten years later, to resume my duties for BBC2, who pretty much admitted I was there as cover in case Peel got fed up and wanted to go home. I found myself perched on a hay bale with John and Jo Whiley, filling the gaps between the bands with tales of toilets, mud and torchlit scenes of debauchery in the fields of Avalon. So to take our positions for the first time without John was really very strange. Jo and I talked quite a lot about this and while I wouldn't start to say stuff about 'feeling his presence' and all that nonsense, we really did find it hard to accept that he wasn't there and that he wasn't going to come shambling in wearing shorts, a waterproof and sun-hat, grumbling about not being able to get close enough to the stage to watch Misty in Roots.

In the hallway of our house hangs an exquisite limited-edition portrait of Peel by the great British pop artist Peter Blake. Often when passing I'll look up and say 'Morning, John', or 'Goodnight, John', or sometimes 'What do you think, John?' Because I always did care what he thought. When he said kind things about my programmes it made me glow. It meant so much to me to feel that John Peel thought I was doing all right, and wherever he is, I hope he's doing all right too.

Goodnight, John.

15. THE DAY I WASN'T SCOTTISH

It was Wednesday 10 June 1998. The football World Cup was starting that day in Paris with the opening match between Brazil and Scotland being staged at the magnificent Stade de France. Marc Riley and I had been despatched to the Continent to broadcast several of our afternoon shows to tie in with fixtures of particular interest to the audience back home. When these plans were first mooted we were delighted. We were going to the World Cup at someone else's expense, all our travel, accommodation and match tickets would be sorted out for us, and all we had to do was turn in a couple of radio programmes. Doddle.

It was a bright and sunny morning as we unpacked our programme boxes and scripted our ad-libs on the stage of the Radio 1 Roadshow vehicle that had been parked in the main square of St Denis. The roadshow was for many years a familiar sight over the summer months as it toured the UK providing free shows at a succession of seaside resorts. In the past it had been a rather gruesome spectacle as oversized men in undersized white shorts and monogrammed satin bomber jackets mounted feeble stunts before introducing the latest B-list popettes and polluted the district with throbbing disco music. On the other hand, it was free, and if you were on holiday with four kids I imagine it was a blessed hiatus from the haemorrhaging of cash. So, well worth a big Cleethorpes cheer after all.

I never really took to the roadshow, though I did produce a few, notably one in a park in Nottingham that opened with Mike Read and Cliff Richard lobbing tennis balls into the crowd while wearing skimpy sportswear. It rather went downhill from there. I blame the production.

Presenting roadshows I always found a bit embarrassing to be honest. All our usual work was done in darkened studios with scraps of paper, and it wasn't what you'd call an exhilarating visual experience. You could also argue that for a great deal of the time it wasn't exactly an exhilarating aural spectacle either. On stage, where you could actually see the whites of the audience's eyes, I felt wholly out of my comfort zone. Both Marc and I had spent a lot of time on stage, but always playing in bands where you can more or less ignore a crowd's indifference, or hostility, by performing all the songs at high volume with no gaps in between. That way, even if they are trying to boo you off, you can't really hear it, and anyway you've got safety in numbers with the guys in the group. You might get hit on the head by the odd flying bottle or can, of course, but with a bit of luck it might be a full one and you can pick it up and drink it. That really annoys them.

As a DJ, you don't really have that sort of protection. It's just you and a microphone. It's also very difficult with a big open-air crowd to get any semblance of complicated wordplay across, as no one can really be sure of what you're saying. As a result you just find yourself resorting to the time-honoured clichés like: 'Are you feeling all right?', 'Come on, Prestatyn, make some noise' and 'Are there any Honeyz fans out there?' This tends to keep the assembled throng happy, as everyone knows what they're doing and will confirm through collective cheering that they are feeling all right, will make some noise and are prepared to be fans of The Honeyz for the day even if they're not quite sure who The Honeyz are. It doesn't make for satisfying listening back home, though, which I imagine is why it was stopped in the end. Well, that and the shorts.

The occasional roadshow wasn't too bad. We did one in Ipswich with the unfeasibly tall and good-looking Jamie Theakston. Because he was a big TV star and everything, people were genuinely excited to see him and so we contentedly played the support act to his headline. We also made sure that we stood next to him quite a lot, as rather like Paul Simonon of The Clash, who was so handsome in their press photos that he made the rest of the band look handsome too, we were hoping some of Jamie's beefcake appeal would rub off on us. A long shot, but worth a try.

On this occasion in St Denis, though, it was just us, with a special guest co-presenter in the shape of former Everton and Wales captain Barry Horne, who'd become a bit of mate of ours. Two Englishmen and a Welsh bloke doing a roadshow for Scotland fans. What could possibly go wrong?

The show we'd planned featured quite a few of our regular items, plus two specially inserted additions. There was going to be a big singalong of the Scotland team's World Cup song, the fate-temptingly titled 'Don't Come Home Too Soon', led by Caledonian country rockers Del Amitri. There was also a 'Name That Tune'-style quiz where the rogue melodies were performed on a range of the kind of hooters you routinely hear at Continental football matches called, with an ingenuity that bore the mark of Marc, 'Barry's Air Horn(e) Orchestra'. These bastardized songs had been carefully recorded before we crossed the Channel, but we had still transported an elaborate steel frame onto which were clipped a variety of horns so that the tousle-haired Horne could look like he was performing this task live and with great dexterity, like Jean-Michel Jarre but with hooters.

We had also decided to wear Scotland World Cup team shirts. Truly we did this in the spirit of *Solidarność*, as we genuinely wanted them to win against Brazil that day. I know there are a lot of Scottish fans who hate England with a vengeance, and will support any team we're playing in the hope that we will be defeated. I also know there are some Scottish fans who are happy for England to win as long as it's not at their expense, but it sometimes seems like they're the minority. There certainly didn't seem to be many of them staggering from bar to bar round St Denis that day.

The crowd that gathered for this great radio occasion was a good deal sparser than anticipated, although I can't say I was surprised. Those who were in possession of precious tickets had already started to make their way to the ground to soak up the atmosphere. Others had opted to stay in bars so they could get a good position in front of a television screen. That left us with four groups of people. Scots without tickets who were disgruntled because they'd been to the ground hoping to get some off touts only to be disappointed. Disgruntled Scots without tickets who weren't sure where the ground was. Drunken disgruntled Scots without tickets who'd been thrown out of bars and couldn't find anywhere to watch the match. And drunken, disgruntled Scots who had no idea where they were or who these wankers on the back of a truck with some bicycle horns were. It was the biggest gathering of disgruntled Scottish football fans in a municipal square right up until the big screen in Manchester's Piccadilly Gardens failed shortly before the 2008 UEFA cup final between Zenit St Petersburg and Glasgow Rangers.

As soon as we went on air the torrent of abuse began to rain down on us.

'Ye fucking bunch of English dicks. Get those shirts off

now,' came one memorable expostulation, though not all the comments thrown at us were that good-natured. To make matters worse, it is customary on these occasions to direct a couple of microphones at the audience to relay their enthusiasm to those listening at home. Unfortunately, until you belatedly realize what is happening, a less-enthusiastic reaction is broadcast with equal clarity. As most of our assailants were absolutely hammered, the full wealth of their vocabulary was lost in a sea of slurring, but you'd be amazed how the f-word sticks out even under those circumstances.

Minutes into the show it was painfully clear that our choice of shirts was controversial, as the front few rows made it abundantly clear, through an impressive range of shouts and hand gestures, that we were not fit to wear the Scotland strip. Now in the strictest sense I could see what they were driving at, as we weren't actually Scottish. But we weren't pretending to be. We were only trying to support them as underdogs on this great footballing occasion. Would I have been offended if Scots had donned England tops to lend moral support if such were needed? Absolutely not. Then again, I don't regard Scotland as the enemy, and it was clear that they saw us as just that. I think this was just because we were convenient Englishmen wearing Scotland shirts placed on a big open stage. We couldn't have been more vulnerable if we'd been clamped in the stocks wearing comedy tam-o'-shanters and Russ Abbot comedy ginger wigs. At least I think that was the root of their antipathy, though it is possible that they were familiar with our work and had developed their aversion over several years. In which case, absolutely fair enough.

Contemplating the events of that day, I've since wondered if I would mind if Manchester United fans put on City jerseys if we were in the Champions' League Final. Well, that situation is beyond hypothetical because they wouldn't, and we're not going to be, but the honest answer is probably yes. So, with the benefit of hindsight I can see that the dress code we adopted was well intentioned, but woefully misjudged.

'Bloody hell, mate,' hissed Lard, 'this looks like being a long two hours.'

'Yes, and not just for the listeners,' I replied, glancing at my watch and wishing away the next 120 minutes of my life. I know you should never do that as it's time you will never have again, but that was OK because I didn't even want it once, let alone again.

It became clear early on that we had no chance of delivering our links from anywhere near the front of the stage, as there was a risk of us being physically attacked or hit by a flying bottle, and also further verbal abuse would be audible on our microphones and relayed to the millions listening back home. To make matters worse, Del Amitri turned up and had clearly been on the ale for several days and nights without bothering about details like sleep. Lead vocalist Justin Currie made a valiant attempt to perform an acoustic version accompanied by a plainly sozzled band-mate who had a melodica in his mouth, though it looked liked touch-and-go whether he played it or vomited into it.

Having no choice but to yield the front of the stage to the opposing forces, we retreated and regrouped in a new base camp at the rear of the stage, where we were afforded cover by the console containing the record decks and tape machines. Here we crouched and cowered as we managed to get the links out that would keep the show running as a broadcast, if not as a stage show. Barry, wisely, made no pretence of miming his way through the air-horn orchestra medley, preferring to sit in the shadows at the side of the stage watching the streams of warm lager rain down on his specially transported apparatus. I felt for him. It wasn't his fault he was Welsh.

Thankfully, one of the stalwarts of the roadshow crew, the redoubtable driver and fixer-in-chief Richard Greaves, had seen what was happening and had made a mercy dash to the French equivalent of Matalan, returning with two safer shirts of plain blue and grey.

'Here boys, get these on,' he advised.

'Do you mean get changed in front of everyone?' I enquired.

'What, like you've got any dignity left to worry about in the eyes of this lot?' he fired back. It was a fair point.

We ducked down behind the decks and re-emerged in neutral garb. The mood seemed generally calmer, though that may have had something to do with half the crowd having drifted away in search of big screens or fresh victims, and the other half having drunk so much that they had become incapable of sustaining the DJ baiting. In a final attempted act of reconciliation we returned to the security barriers and offered our removed Scotland shirts to the few punters at the front who were still capable of seeing clearly enough to reach out for them. We apologized if we'd caused any offence and tried to explain that we just wanted to get behind their team for the day. Those who deigned to talk to us began to gruffly accept our excuses and even shook hands while telling us not to take it too personally.

Of course, we had the last laugh because as we left them to their mutterings in the town square, we hopped in a cab and entered the hallowed stadium with our VIP tickets.

The game finished two–one to Brazil after a calamitous own goal conceded by the unfortunate Tommy Boyd. Poor chap. He started the day hoping that he would please the travelling fans, and ended up cruelly disappointing them. Well, we knew how he felt, although his mishap was balanced against the regard in which he was held as an all-round Scottish soccer legend. No one knew us from two Adams. I imagine that leaves our account still in the red.

Oh, and at the game I sat immediately behind the cherished, tartan-clad, sandpaper-throated, 'hedgehog with highlights'-headed, Scottish mascot Rod Stewart. Who was born in Highgate.

16. THE DAY I BOUGHT FLOWERS
FOR KYLIE

Not liking Kylie Minogue is more or less impossible really. You might not be the biggest fan of her acting or music, though I think if you listen to a Greatest Hits album you'll be surprised at how many good tunes you find, but she's just so utterly likable that to go out of your way not to seems slightly perverse somehow.

I first met her when I was co-presenting the *Radio 1 Breakfast Show* with Marc Riley, though I can't imagine she remembers it as a pivotal moment in her career. She was totally charming, preposterously pretty – as if she'd stood in the queue when they were handing out looks long enough to be given someone else's helping of prettiness as well as her own – and absolutely tiny. I knew beforehand she was around five feet tall, but meeting her in the flesh was still a shock. She was almost doll-like in her slightness. Beautiful, funny, smart, but beyond petite. Or do I mean less than petite? Look, small, all right?

She'd also agreed to sing live on the show at seven in the morning which, understandably, was something not all singers wanted to do. At that time of day most of us struggle to even speak. I know I did, which may have been a contributory factor to the spectacular failure of that show.

Kylie was a real professional though. She'd had a sensibly

abstemious early night given that there was a six o'clock call
the following morning. The prospect of this had seen her
band take refuge in the bar, forgoing bed altogether. This
reminded me of my friend Noddy Holder's memory of being
tapped on the shoulder one morning in a hotel bar by a
waiter who asked, 'Mr Holder?'

'Yes?'

'Your earlymorning call, sir.'

It's hard to imagine now, but there was a time when Kylie,
Queen of Showbiz, was struggling a bit career-wise. Perhaps
she'd never have agreed to come on our show if she hadn't
been. True, it was the *Radio 1 Breakfast Show*, which was a
big deal in theory, but it was getting much less big by the day
thanks to us. The previously 'most listened to radio programme in the EU' was witnessing a mass exodus of
proportions that Europe wouldn't experience again until fifteen years later when hotel workers and plumbers deserted
the Baltic States. And at least that meant you could get your
heating fixed. There was no positive side to our migrant
crisis.

Back in 1997, Kylie had just released an album originally
called 'Impossible Princess', a title that was changed to *Kylie
Minogue* following the death of Diana, Princess of Wales.
The record saw her hook up with, amongst others, The
Manic Street Preachers. This might look a strange move
now, but it was following on from her collaboration with
Nick Cave in 1995 on the murder ballad 'Where the Wild
Roses Grow' in which she took the part of the lover's
victim. In retrospect, this might not have been the greatest
career move on her part, as it was certainly something of a
shock for the Minogue-ophiles who were used to seeing
her with permed hair tinkering with cars in *Neighbours* or
hearing her sing 'The Locomotion'. Naturally, we thought
this unexpected career turn was wonderful, as it hinted at

something more interesting going on than we'd originally thought. She got up at a poetry slam at the Royal Albert Hall, at the suggestion of Cave evidently, to recite the lyrics to 'I Should Be So Lucky'. Brilliant. She invited Nick to perform the duet with her live on stage. For Kylie fans who had no idea who he was, and there must have been plenty, it was as if some randy, drunken old funeral director had given security the slip, and was mauling the blessed Antipodean sex thimble in front of their very eyes. Genius. There was clearly more to her than 'Especially For You', her duet with Jason Donovan, who, ironically, would later turn out to be doing nearly as many drugs as Nick Cave. Who'd have thought it, eh?

But her new direction left some of her old fans confused and underwhelmed. Conversely, people like us, who'd always had an affection for her but never taken particular notice, became intrigued. Unfortunately for Kylie, there weren't enough of us, and it wasn't until she squeezed her microscopic posterior into a pair of gold lamé, doll's hot-pants in 2001 for 'Spinning Around' that she re-established herself as a chart-topping artist.

So Kylie came on our show and sang, chatted, giggled and entranced, and we got on well enough for us to feel like it wasn't going too far to subsequently ask her to be the voice of the jingles on our Radio 1 afternoon show, which was to prove considerably less catastrophic in terms of audience figures. At regular intervals she would record a bunch of phrases and slogans such as: 'Mark and Lard – skinning the competition alive', '– bog-trotting playboys', '– multimedia metrosexuals' and, rather wonderfully in an Irish accent, '– are you looking at their pint, Michael?'

At a later meeting, ostensibly to discuss the 2003 album *Body Language*, which includes the great underrated Kylie single 'Slow', co-written by the beguiling Italian–Icelandic singer-songwriter Emiliana Torrini, she thanked us for choosing her to do those jingles, which had kept her voice on the air, and in the minds of the public, when she wasn't having big hit records. That's the kind of person she is. So, all very lovely and cosy, eh? Well, not quite.

Somewhere back there is a programme called 'An Audience with Kylie'. I've tried to blank it out, but I think it might have been in 2001, when she was emphatically back on top.

The audiences for these things are, of course, invited and have to have a fair proportion of at least vaguely familiar faces. The bigger the star, the higher grade of celebrity you tend to get in the audience, and Kylie's guest list included the generally expected smattering of soap starlets and TV regulars. There was Cat Deeley the game-show host, Pete Waterman the pop svengali, Julian Clary the exquisitely made-up camp comic, Emma Forbes the decorous and charming presenter, Melinda Messenger the pneumatic former double-glazing salesperson, and Boy George the enormous homosexual community servant. From various soap operas I don't watch came Claire Sweeney, Tracy Shaw, Patsy Palmer and someone called Jennifer Ellison. But not everyone was as 'A' list as that. From the darkest bowels of radio came me and Lard.

So it was that we turned up at some godforsaken concrete box on a windswept corner somewhere south of the river early one Sunday evening. Our producer 'Genial' Joe Graham had been keen to come with us, professing himself something of a Kylie aficionado. This surprised us until we saw the manner in which he clapped his hands to the music, at which point we realized he was gay and everything fell into place.

Showing our gold-embossed invitations we were ushered into a lift and turfed out into a large room with polystyrene ceiling tiles and a small bar being besieged by famous people I didn't recognize.

Immediately I had the feeling that we shouldn't have been there, a sudden realization that we were fish out of water. I tend to go out of my way to avoid large social gatherings, and many of my closest friends have helped me with this by not inviting me anywhere. I once forewent the conference catering backslap-othon that is The Brits in favour of a pub quiz at the Railway. So what was I doing quaffing warm Chardonnay here, having to skulk in the shadows to avoid catching the eye of Lisa Riley, who we'd referred to many times on air as 'that fat lass from *Emmerdale*'?

Feeling awkward, we took the only logical course of action open to us by drinking heavily. During this period we thought it was odd that no one had approached us to give us the question we were going to ask Kylie. We'd let someone with a clipboard, headphones, blonde hair and a short skirt know we were there, news she seemed particularly unimpressed to receive. We then just assumed a researcher would track us down and give us our instructions. After all, we were practically family, though not quite like Kylie's brother Brendan and sister Dannii, who were also present.

Eventually we were encouraged by some histrionic goon in an undersized designer sports jacket to take our seats for the performance. We still hadn't received one of the rather ostentatious-looking question cards but by then we were past caring. Having discovered a hitherto unknown love of tepid cava, we just assumed they had more would-be inquisitors than slots available and had passed over us in favour of someone people might recognize when the show went out. If I'd been in charge I think I'd have probably made the same decision.

I think she did 'Spinning Around' first, and as the show unravelled it became clear that here was a first look at what was to become the glitzy 'Showgirl' spectacle. There were lots of costume changes, big chorus-line numbers and dazzling lighting and sets. Marc and I loved it and we weren't even gay.

Between the songs, as expected, the fragrant Kylie would look over the assembled congregation and hand-pick the next questioner, who would oblige with the prearranged enquiry. Obviously this is the way these things have to be done because Kylie, who had evidently been struggling with the flu on top of everything else, couldn't be expected to remember all the words, all the moves and have to field questions she hadn't had time to think about. Even smart-arse politicians on *Question Time* get to see the questions beforehand, and they don't have to vogue in a Lycra leotard, which must come as a relief to Alistair Darling.

About halfway through the recording, a slightly breathless Kylie strolled across the stage and stopped in front of us, although we were, if memory serves, about six or seven rows back from the front and so it was hard to work out exactly who she was looking at. She then uttered the words I remember to this day: 'Well, I can see two gentlemen there looking down at me.'

Assuming Hale and Pace had snuck in behind us we craned our necks round to catch a glimpse of the burly twosome, although knowing what they looked like already, I can't really think why. At this point a ripple of laughter began to spread amongst the audience which, had we not partaken too liberally of the hospitality, would have told us that Hale and Pace weren't in the house after all. Suitably bemused we turned back to face the front, which was when we noticed the camera. We couldn't really miss it as it was pointing right at us.

At that point a harassed floor manager leaped into view, gesticulating wildly.

'Mark and Lard, Mark and Lard.'

'What?' we replied, being genuinely unaware of what he wanted. Were we in someone else's seats? Had someone from *Hollyoaks* arrived late? Was there a problem with the bar tab?

'Mark and Lard, Mark and Lard.'

'What?'

'Have you got a question for Kylie?'

Again, and I promise you this is true, we replied with complete honesty.

'Have you got a question for Kylie?'

'No.'

Well we hadn't. We knew they meant one of the questions on the special cards, and we hadn't been given one, so the answer to what we were being asked was simple. No. That had to be the right answer, and yet it didn't seem to be. Generally, at school or in a pub quiz, when you get a question right people are quite pleased with you. Nobody seemed that chuffed with us here, though.

I don't know how much time passed during this increasingly heated exchange, but it became apparent that the camera was still directed at us and, somewhere out there, a bemused Kylie was still waiting. She must have asked us if we had something we wanted to know, which we did. Where was the dullard who was supposed to have given us our card, and would it be possible to inflict some act of torture on them in a dimly lit private room afterwards?

I must confess that I froze at this point, but Lard, God bless him, realized that nothing was going to get resolved until we'd asked Kylie a question.

'So, Kylie,' he stumbled, 'you played the part of a mechanic in *Neighbours*. Do you have your City and Guilds qualifications and can you really drain the sump oil from a Triumph Dolomite?'

What a man. He'd gotten us out of that fine mess and no mistake.

Kylie, however, seemed slightly nonplussed. Clearly the pre-cleared question, whatever it was, had little or nothing to do with the intricacies of the Triumph Dolomite. Trooper that she is, she moulded the question into some vague answer about what she did study at college, before announcing there would be a short break and hurrying into the wings. Must be another costume change, I thought.

Somewhat ruffled we slumped back in our seats only to have crumple-faced, foul-mouthed TV chef Gordon Ramsay, who was sitting directly in front of us, turn round and say, 'Brilliant, lads. Well done.'

'How d'you mean?'

'Well, that was all a set-up, right?'

'No.'

So, two things. If it had been a set-up, there's no way we'd have pulled it off so effectively. But also it became apparent that from Kylie's point of view, two loose acquaintances who were there at her own invitation had tried to make her look foolish by concocting some puerile jape for their own amusement. Bastards. And I believe, though I have no concrete proof of this, that she called us considerably worse than that back in the sanctity of the dressing room.

This was all gruesome enough without the added difficulty of her being booked to appear on our programme the next day.

I believe it was touch and go whether she showed up the next day, but show up she dutifully did. Helena, the record-company executive who was accompanying Kylie on her promotional outings, knew us pretty well and took at face value our protestations that it had all been a horrible misunderstanding.

When she came she was nothing if not professional, and we apologized as profusely as we could, but was it my paranoia or had a little of her warmth towards us gone? Perhaps she was just exhausted, or maybe she couldn't be one hundred per cent sure that we hadn't hatched the plan, only to try and deny it after it had gone so disastrously wrong.

We spent a lot of money on flowers that day. I never thought that I would be in the position of giving Kylie Minogue flowers, but when it happened I couldn't help thinking that it would have been much nicer if it was to wish her happy birthday or something and not to make up for having made an idiot of myself in her presence. I've also wondered, in retrospect, whether the size of the bouquet wasn't a bit excessive, especially for such a diminutive injured party. Did it look like we were protesting too much?

If you ever get the chance to see the finished programme, then don't sit there rubbing your hands in glee waiting for this TV nightmare to appear. It was, of course, left on the cutting-room floor. But Kylie, I swear to you on my kids' lives that it was an honest mistake, and somewhere, the card with our question on it sits at the bottom of a landfill site, having been furtively disposed of by a guilt-racked researcher.

17. THE DAY I WAS THE PIED PIPER

I only really enjoyed three subjects at school: art, music and English.

Geography was OK too, I suppose, as it not only involved lots of coloured pencils but also enabled you to recognize physical things around you, and who doesn't like to know a limestone escarpment when they see one? Who couldn't help but feel inadequate going through life without knowing how an oxbow lake was formed? How satisfying it is to know what a pipkrake is, even if it's not a piece of information you need every day. Or indeed ever. That's not the point. It's just comforting to know that you know.

History was tolerable, though to me it seemed obsessed with committing lists to memory. I'm not an ardent republican for the most part, but why would you need to know which monarch followed which? I still have no idea if Edward VII came before or after George V or William IV. I can see it's probably sensible to know vaguely what happened in the world wars, and why Stonehenge was built, even though they don't seem entirely sure on that one, but I fail to see what use it is to know that Henry VII succeeded Richard III. Or was that William the Conqueror?

In any pub quiz there will be a question about monarchs and there will always be some spod in a zipped-up cardigan

who, when confronted with the poser 'who succeeded
Henry II?' will not only know the answer, which is annoying
enough, but will use the opportunity to show that he's in
possession of a bit of biographical detail.

'Hmmm yes, Henry II, who co-ruled with Henry the
young king. I think he produced an heir with Eleanor of
Aquitaine who went on to rule from 1189 to 1199 which
must mean it was Richard the Lionheart, mustn't it?'

There is absolutely no point clogging up your brain with
information that you can just check in a book or online. It's
like committing the phone book to memory just in case
anyone should ask if you happen to know the number of a
local plumber, drain-rodder, prostitute or just Arnold and
Trixie-belle Butterworth of 13 Glebe Meadows, Mickle
Trafford. Why fill your head with stuff that's readily available
when you could be using it for thinking? It doesn't make any
sense and I know this because my head is full of the most
pointless music trivia imaginable, though if you happen to
find yourself on *Who Wants to Be a Millionaire?* and you're
faced with the question: 'Who was the original drummer in
Curved Air?', you might be grateful to have me as a 'phone
a friend'. To save you the bother I'll just tell you it was
Florian Pilkington Miksa. One hundred per cent sure. Go get
your money.

So history didn't interest me greatly, though I approached
it with more enthusiasm than languages. I tried French, Latin
and Russian without ever really getting to grips with any of
them, though I did perform a scene from Soviet peasant life
one school open day. This involved my entering a classroom
packed with parents who were keen to see what academic
rigours might await their offspring, dressed as a particularly
scruffy dung-shoveller from Omsk. I was hand in hand with
my friend Simon Holt who, it being an establishment for
boys, was dressed in a housecoat and headscarf to resemble

the particularly scruffy wife of that same particularly scruffy dung-shoveller from Omsk. With acne. Shuffling into a space that had been cleared in the centre of the room, crippled with embarrassment, we then proceeded to act out an hilarious scene in hesitant Russian. The basic plot involved the imaginary dung-shovelling couple going into an imaginary cafe, and getting their own actual food out of an actual rancid old shopping bag instead of ordering from the imaginary menu. Unfortunately we had forgotten to put the actual food in the actual bag so the extent of imaginary elements was increased still further when we sliced and chomped on an imaginary turnip. Or was it a beetroot? Well, it was hard to tell, what with it being imaginary and everything. Now if that wasn't going to convince people to send their precious sons to Bolton School, what would?

'I thought it was marvellous, Mary. If young Oliver ever finds himself wondering how to behave in a snack bar in Murmansk while accompanied by a lady Hobbit, this sort of thing could be invaluable. Let's get his name down right away.'

Even so, I managed to pass O levels in all the above, which is more than you could say for the sciences. Don't get me started on science. Well, no one ever did, which is why I don't have a single scientific qualification to my name. I did sit physics at sixteen but sadly failed to achieve a pass despite watching back-to-back episodes of *Star Trek* the night before the exam. Well, you've got to be selective in your revision, haven't you? You can't learn everything and it was just bad luck that there was no transporter-beam question on that year's paper.

Then there were the activities that were misleadingly grouped under the heading 'games'. Now I don't know about you, but the word game implies that there's an element of fun involved. Not here, there wasn't. Let me give you an example. One 'game' might involve queuing up in under-sized shorts and skimpy singlets to take a run at a stuffed leather sack on ridiculously high legs, in the hope of clearing it and landing on the other side. I mean, come on, it's not only pointless, it's downright dangerous. Sometimes, lest this should be deemed not insane enough, they would position this thing sideways on! It was about three feet wide. How were you supposed to get over that without dislocating both hips? And if school purports to prepare you for life in the world outside, exactly what eventuality was this activity laying the groundwork for? Needing to negotiate a stray, though oddly static, hippopotamus that had wandered across your path in Moss Bank Park? And if that unlikely scenario were to occur, wouldn't it be easier just to walk round it? I did put forward this theory to the laughably humourless head of games Mr Morrison. If, I posited, the object of the exercise was to reach the other side of the apparatus safely, why not just jog up and then neatly swerve around it? That way there was less wear and tear on school equipment, which represented a net saving to please the governors, and less strain placed on the already overstretched staff at the A & E department of Bolton Royal Infirmary, who wouldn't have to deal with any more boys whose legs protruded from their torsos in floppy horizontal fashion.

The strange thing was that several of my classmates delighted in participating in this systematic torture. The resultant injuries came to be seen as badges of honour. If you hadn't broken something in the first couple of terms, you were seen as being a bit of a wimp. Dale Brotherton was on crutches for most of his adolescence thanks to the ongoing lunacy of 'games'. What was wrong with dominoes? There was no end to the hazardous and yet utterly meritless activities they'd dreamed up in their sick heads. Swinging on ropes against wall bars, balancing on thin beams several feet above

hard wooden floors, dangling from rings until your arms fell
out to match the legs you'd already lost on that vaulting
thing. It was madness, and yet you could always find knuck-
leheads who would throw themselves into it with scant
regard for personal safety, or perhaps hoping they would lose
an eye so they could look tough in the playground. Maybe I
did look fey reading the poetry of Gerard Manley Hopkins in
the cloisters, but at least I had two eyes to read it with and
both arms available to hold the book. Honestly, if they'd got
us into that gym and said that this week's chosen apparatus
was the rack, Trevor Tyldesley and Ivan Mason would have
been injured in the rush to have their spine stretched first.

So that left only the three oases of sanity in the turbulent
ocean of curriculum. Art was blissfully contemplative and
non-competitive under the benign stewardship of 'Granny'
Penrice. You could spend whole afternoons creating abstract,
amorphous shapes in the hope that it would mean something
when you'd finished. And even if it didn't the saintly Mrs P.
would find something to cherish in it.

'Look at the way the colours have seeped together to
create a Turner-esque quality.'

'That's where the water pot got spilled on it Miss.'

As for music, we had rumbustious band sessions marshalled
by the excitable and eccentric Mr Mace. He was like the
Magnus Pike of the school orchestra, leaping from foot to
foot, one hand constantly sweeping his grey fringe back over
his bald pate. He absolutely refused to accept that any pupil
was without musical ability and made sure everyone had a
role in the cacophony. Even if it was triangle. We spent hours
up in the music room hitting things in random fashion to the
continued delight of the effervescent Mace.

I also tried my hand at a more structured approach to
learning music by tackling first the violin, and subsequently
the trumpet. The violin didn't last long obviously, but I

persevered with the trumpet for a while. This was somewhat against my better judgement because it didn't seem like
a good instrument to impress girls with, which was surely the
only reason to learn something as far as I could see. Trumpet
players tend to be red of face, bulbous of cheek and moist of
skin, which doesn't often result in a queue of eager groupies.
I mean, I daresay Dizzy Gillespie was a top bloke, but when
he puffed his cheeks out like a giant, perspiring bullfrog,
well you'd have a quick look at the rest of the band before
you plumped for him, wouldn't you?

   In truth, there are really only two instruments worth playing in this life, unless you're planning to work in a
professional symphony orchestra, and those are the piano and
the guitar. You can go anywhere and do anything with those.
You can join a band, play classical stuff or just entertain
people at social gatherings. You can't lose. Even if you're not
very good, if you restrict yourself to three or four songs you
know inside out, you can fool all of the people all of the
time. Especially when people are too drunk to notice the
bum notes. But what happens when you've completed your
limited repertoire and people are clamouring for more, I
hear you ask. Well, this is the really good bit. You then make
self-deprecating remarks about 'letting someone else have a
go', or 'everyone's had enough of me, I think', before wandering off to the kitchen. That way everyone thinks you're
really talented but modest with it. You can't go wrong.
Nobody likes a show-off, do they? Except for Debbie
McGee, evidently. And possibly David Beckham.

   The only other instrument that comes close to these two
is the saxophone, and even then it's lagging some way
behind, not least because you can't do a song on your own
with one as it's impossible to sing and play it at the same time.
In its favour you can play with almost any group of musicians, but here's the thing: they don't really want you to. Sax

is all right for an eight-bar solo every half-hour or so, but that makes a saxophonist a bit of a waste of a wage. You're much better giving that share of the money to a van driver who will at least get you home at the end of the night. I mean, look at that gigantic gentleman Clarence Clemons, who is a member of Bruce Springsteen's E Street Band. He spends at least 75 per cent of his time on stage absent-mindedly shaking a tambourine and he'll be on the same money as the poor sods who are playing bass and drums all the way through. It makes no financial sense, does it?

So I tried the guitar, and am still trying to this day, but I found my calling when I sat behind a drum kit. To my everlasting surprise and gratitude I found that my arms and legs seemed to know exactly what to do from the very first moment I played. This was amazing, as there'd been no hint of that sort of coordination when I'd tried to play sport of any kind, and it felt great to be hitting something other than my sister. Playing drums in a never-ending succession of dodgy bands has been a constant feature of my life and has brought me lasting friendships, lots of adventures, plenty of excitement and precious little cash. But being in a group is the best hobby in the world. You go out with your mates, play the music you love, attract the attention of girls, receive free drinks and get dropped off home again afterwards. If you're lucky you might get fifty quid as well. Where's the catch, eh?

So I had music and art to keep me happy, but English was my overriding passion. From as long ago as I can remember I had a voracious appetite for reading. Life felt incomplete unless you were in the middle of an absorbing work of literature. I tended to go for long books for just that reason. I didn't want it to be over too quickly. I wanted to live in that world for as long as I could. The novels of Thomas Hardy became something of an obsession, his Wessex having been created so meticulously, you couldn't help but lose yourself somewhere on the road to Casterbridge or in the quadrangles of Christminster. In fact the depiction of Egdon Heath in the opening of *The Return of the Native*, is the greatest single piece of literary landscape painting ever written in my view. Night after night I hurried to bed to roam those lanes and byways, eager to see who I would meet around the next bend. I was about five or six at this time, moving on to more complex works after I passed the eleven-plus. Not that I'm trying to imply that I was especially gifted in this department. If I'm being honest, I don't think I really appreciated all the nuances of James Joyce's *Ulysses* until I was fully twelve.

I had a great English teacher too, which helped a lot. His name was Charles Winder and he had an infectious love of language and appreciation of literature I found intoxicating. At the time of writing, he's still involved with the same school, which makes me glad that so many others had the chance to be captivated by his zeal.

There was another guy called Mr Sharples. He was nick-named, somewhat inevitably, Ena after the hair-netted, milk-stout-drinking harridan who stalked the snug bar of the Rover's Return in *Coronation Street*. Mr Sharples had a more laissez-faire attitude to the tutelage of the mother tongue, and indeed to the marking of homework. I vividly remember him being asked if he'd looked at our essays yet. He replied in the negative, to which my friend Ross Warburton, lounging on a chair at the back of the class, muttered, 'Lazy bastard.'

Unfortunately he hadn't muttered quietly enough and, hearing what he'd said, Ena was provoked into uncharacteristically speedy action. Striding to the back of the classroom he immediately smacked Ross in the face with a hardback copy of *The Pickwick Papers*. The startled victim was unable to evade the full force of the blow, or even to effectively shield

his face with his hands for three reasons. Firstly, not anticipating Mr Sharples having heard his insult, and guessing that
even if he had he wouldn't be bothered enough to actually
get off his backside, Ross wasn't looking in the master's direction, and therefore wasn't anticipating the attack. Secondly,
he had one of his hands on the wall behind him, enabling
him to tilt his chair back at a precarious angle. In theory that
still left one hand to ward off blows, but the third hampering
factor in mounting his defence was that this 'spare' hand was
otherwise engaged down the front of his trousers where a
feverish frame of pocket billiards was taking place. Fatally
weakened, the helpless Warburton took the full force of the
Dickens on the end of his nose before sliding down the wall
where the back of his head might have taken a nasty crack on
the parquet flooring had his fall not been broken by a cast-
iron heating pipe. Laugh? I nearly passed my fags round.
Though that would have been stupid, as then I would have
had no Consulate Menthol left for behind the cricket pavil-
ion at lunchtime.

Having recounted all that, I do feel rather guilty at having
singled out that one episode of our time with Mr Sharples
because he was a thoroughly nice guy. He had a more infor-
mal approach to the subject than Charlie Winder, but no less
basic enthusiasm for the core material. However, where his
looser approach came into its own was in our weekly drama
periods.

These were held in a little theatre in the basement called,
not unreasonably, the Little Theatre. It was a fairly traditional space with a proper stage, curtains and lights with
seating for around 150 people. Every week we would be
encouraged to split up into groups and construct theatrical
scenes of an experimental nature. I'm quite sure this was a
valuable exercise in firing up the imagination of the slothful
teenager. I'm equally sure it was attractive to the equally

slothful Ena, as it involved no preparation other than getting us there and switching the lights on. After that, all he had to do was sit in the middle of the auditorium and watch, which I imagine was much harder than it ought to have been given the level of performance on stage. I remember one piece involving Gary Adshead and me walking backwards across the stage, with our blazers on the wrong way round, one trouser leg rolled up and dragging fire extinguishers. It was either a comment on the drudgery of modern life, and how we conform to restrictive dress codes that label us to others, or a re-enactment of recruiting night at the local Masonic lodge. I forget which.

On another occasion Roger Milne, Rob Redgate, Jez Mather and me formed a fictitious freeform musical group from the Indian subcontinent called the Kubjar Rhandi Band. The essence of this key work of the avant-garde was the expression of feeling without necessarily understanding the language. Accordingly Rog, Jez and myself would howl and shriek in fluent gibberish while the unflappable Redgate translated in a clipped Bolton monotone. It turned out to be quite a prescient piece, as we were very much trying to present the idea that there could be an Indian pop star to rival the big heart-throb of the day, Donny Osmond, and in this respect we anticipated the growth of world music about ten years ahead of anyone else. If Nusrat Fateh Ali Khan were alive today I'm sure he'd tell you the same. So our creative works, though superficially the aimless messing about of schoolboys who'd watched too much *Monty Python's Flying Circus*, actually had a deeper purpose. Or perhaps not. The deflated Mr Sharples was by now pre-sumably wondering whether improvisation had been a worthwhile addition to the syllabus after all, while simulta-neously tapping his wristwatch to make sure it hadn't stopped.

Those lessons did give me a genuine taste of the thrill of performance though, and I was involved in several 'proper' productions, with real words and everything, that were mounted by the drama club. The same club that had once boasted Sir Ian McKellen in the ranks. I was 'Banquo' in *Macbeth*, and used the method preparation I'd adopted for that role to bring a certain macho presence to the part of Squire Blackheart in *The Thwarting of Baron Bolligrew* by Robert Bolt, who also wrote *A Man For All Seasons*. However, the role I remember most vividly is that of the Pied Piper.

That the Pied Piper is a great part is not in doubt. Everybody knows who he is and you always get a really terrific costume. Brightly coloured tunics are a given, a really cool velveteen pointy hat with raffish tassels is essential, and the outfit will be finished off with some snug tights and groovy brocade slippers. Freddie Mercury was probably the Pied Piper in a production at Zanzibar High.

The production we were doing wasn't the familiar tale of the infestation of Hamelin, though. I don't remember what the actual play was called, as I was only in a few scenes and so didn't get bogged down in the detail. Like title or plot. I was just happy in my extravagant apparel and keen to impress while treading the boards.

Another keen interest of mine at the time was puppetry, and that's not a euphemism. I was fascinated by the marionette programmes on television created by Gerry Anderson, and even things like the 'lonely goat-herd' scene in *The Sound of Music*. Puppets were actually a pretty commonplace toy back then, thanks principally to the craftsmen at a company called Pelham. Based in Wiltshire, and founded by Bob Pelham who'd started carving little animals out of wood for his own amusement while serving in the Second World War, Pelham made beautifully hand-turned and dressed character marionettes at realistic prices. My own figure of a small boy, with his rosy cheeks, jaunty peaked cap and little patterned shirt, still hangs from the ceiling at home today, alongside my sister's bedraggled, gap-toothed witch. Make of that what you will.

There were quite a few of us who shared this love of bringing figures to life by pulling the strings, and so a puppet club was formed. It was then decided that this august society should provide an opening act on the night of the play in which I was giving my Pied Piper. I was aglow with pride as I was the only one who was involved in both productions, which made me feel even more self-important than usual.

Come the day of the shows, run-throughs went without a hitch and it was only at dress rehearsal that a problem emerged. Or perhaps 'battle of wills' would be a better description. There was a slight tension between Mr Lomax, the pugnacious head of the puppet posse, and the statuesque, flaxen-haired Miss Wood, the director of the main event. Each was very protective of their cast, and neither was happy that I had a foot in both camps. The snag was that there wasn't enough time between the end of the puppet show and curtain up of the play proper to get fully tarted up as the Pied Piper. Miss Wood, flouncing around in a haze of cigarette smoke and chiffon scarves, insisted that I be made ready before the marionette spectacle got under way. Grudgingly, Mr Lomax agreed, but only on the condition that I would lose my conical hat and voluminous cloak lest it should interfere with the operation of my wooden charge. So, a happy compromise then. Well not quite.

The audience, including my mother and father, duly filed in, bracing themselves for what was to come, and hoping it wasn't a work devised by the cast under the auspices of Mr Sharples again. Reading their programmes, they would have seen that the opening diversion was to be provided by members of the Marionette Society, which explained the appearance of a tiny stage amidst blackout curtains in the centre of the stage. They would also have seen the title of the main play, but without a list of characters, as things were always chopping and changing as people dropped out or beat each other up in the hope of getting a better part. They would have had no idea that the Pied Piper was set to make an appearance.

Taking my place with my fellow puppeteers it occurred to me for the first time that while they were all wearing grey trousers and black polo-neck sweaters, I might have lost the cape and hat, but was still wearing a velvet blouse and a pair of tights. This wouldn't have mattered in the slightest were it not for the fact that as the teeny curtain went down on our humble show, the proud Lomax ushered us from behind the scenes to take a bow in full view of the audience.

What the bemused applauding spectators then saw was a group of bashful lads attired in modest black and grey, and one idiot, who for no apparent reason had come dressed as Vaslav Nijinsky. What a pillock, eh?

My anguish, though acute, was relatively short-lived, as all became clear as the evening unfolded, and I was also proud to play a character who represents one of the few examples in history of a pipe player actually doing something useful. I'm no expert on woodwind and brass, but anything that involves blowing into a tube while wiggling your fingers up and down over some holes or keys amounts to the same thing, doesn't it? This means that the Pied Piper roughly equates to being the Clarence Clemons of his day, except without having eaten all the pies, and with better dress sense. However, instead of hanging around looking gormless with a tambourine while waiting for the next bit of piping or saxophoning to come along, the Pied Piper had actually learned a trade to fall back on. If Clarence had done the same thing I think we'd respect him more. And how great to be able to hand out business cards that read:

Clarence Clemons – Saxophone and Pest Control.
No job too small. Distance no object.
Call New Jersey 3756 and ask for Bruce.

18. THE DAY I WAS ON *STARS IN THEIR EYES*

I don't watch television very much. I know it's often said that there's nothing much worth watching these days, but that implies there was a golden age of TV when everything on the small screen was truly excellent. There wasn't. There has always been rubbish on television interspersed with the odd oasis of quality. From my childhood I recall adult programmes of merit such as *The Forsyte Saga*, *Civilisation* and *Horizon*, but you also had *Opportunity Knocks*, *General Hospital* and *Crossroads*. Having said that, if I could bring just one of those programmes back it would be *Opportunity Knocks*, but that says more about me than it does about television. Mind you, I was a kid at the time and you wouldn't want to be one of those weird brats who actually watched *Civilisation*.

Quite how the television set has come to dominate our lives is a bit of a mystery, as it's been so relentlessly awful for so long. When I was a child the highlight of Saturday nights was a goofy Irishman in unforgivable knitwear called Val Doonican crooning soporifically from a creaking rocking chair. I mean, honestly. Fancy having a rocking chair as your trademark. You might as well come on stage on a Stannah stairlift wearing a colostomy bag. No offence, Val, who, remarkably, at time of writing is still alive despite having appeared to be ninety years old in the early seventies. Perhaps there's a lesson to be learned there. Val, though seeming ancient to the young me, must only have been middle-aged back then, but as his act consisted of being half asleep on a chair, the target audience being people who were fully asleep on theirs, he's lived to be two hundred years old or thereabouts. Way to go, Val.

So the idea that there are lots of very poor programmes on television is not a new one. However, since we decided that it was essential to have daytime TV, the situation has got a great deal worse, by which I mean that the bad programmes aren't any less bad than they were in the past, but just that there's a whole lot more of them. The very idea of daytime television seems irresponsible to me. Aren't you inviting sad inadequates to spend all day watching this bilge? Surely there are legions of suggestible people who could actually be doing something useful if they weren't hooked on seeing someone botch the renovation of a maisonette in Bridport or buy a salt cellar at an antiques fair in Lincolnshire only to lose a pound on it at auction ten minutes later. And though the words bottom, barrel and scraping spring readily to mind when considering those programmes, they are the stuff of Bafta nomination when pitted against the fully realized vision of hell on earth that is *The Jeremy Kyle Show*.

For those of you who have yet to pass through the gates of Hades into Beelzebub Kyle's inferno, it's probably worth watching it just once because no matter how dreadful your life seems to be, it will be a hundred million times better than the existence eked out by the specimens wheeled out on that show. Perhaps that's the idea and I'm doing the programme a disservice. Maybe it really is therapy on a mass scale as we all laugh and point at the inmates of this cathode-ray Bedlam in order to feel slightly better about ourselves. We're also clearly one up on the hapless turkeys who have voted for this televisual Christmas as we haven't had to meet Jeremy Kyle, and even if we're hitting rock bottom, that's got to be something to cling on to.

Broadly though, watching daytime television, rather like purchasing the elasticated-waist trouser, is a sure sign that you have given up on yourself.

'Reality television', alongside the plastic carrier bag apparently, is generally accepted as the great curse of our age. Most of the blame for this infestation can be laid at the door of the creators of *Big Brother*. So virulent is this epidemic strain that it has eaten into the fabric of the nation in a way that foot and mouth and bird flu can only dream of. If you have managed to avoid any knowledge of this curse then well done you.

Saturday nights on television these days are riddled with combination reality and variety shows with inappropriate titles. You have *The X Factor*, where karaoke singers without it compete to have a solitary chart hit. There is *The One and Only*, in which feeble impersonators strive to be slightly like their idol, thereby defeating the feeble impersonators who are nothing like their idol. Even if they win and attain the title of the show, they can't be 'the one and only' as they're already feebly impersonating someone else. So they can only be one of 'the two and only' at best. And get this. There's a show for people desperate for fame competing for roles in *Oliver!* called *I'd Do Anything*. Well, quite.

I'm prepared to let *Britain's Got Talent* go. Rather like *Opportunity Knocks* it doesn't just exist on a diet of jumped-up pub singers. The May 2008 final featured a shy sixteen-year-old girl and her dog Gin dancing in perfect unity, and if that doesn't gladden the soul slightly then you're a harder person than me. There were also toddlers doing the cha-cha, disco-dancing Sikhs and a young lad from Warrington body-popping in the rain. I don't want to give the impression that I got wrapped up in all this, you understand. I only voted for the extraordinary twelve-year-old contralto Faryl Smith because my kids were all voting for someone and wanted me to get involved. I wasn't connected to the show on an emotional level at all. Though Faryl was quite clearly robbed.

Top of the pile of this type of show is quite clearly *Stars In Their Eyes*. Defunct now, it was until recently pretty much the only prime-time entertainment show you could watch without feeling that your brain was slowly melting. Here genuine civilians were transformed into their pop idols to sing on national television. Presented with great charm by the lofty Matthew Kelly and subsequently the toothsome Cat Deeley, this was a show where the contestants weren't just fuel for the egos of the host or judges. For one night they were the big guns and not the cannon fodder, and in reality-TV-land that's practically unheard of. The brand gradually wore itself out as the public's appetite for seeing yet more precise but predictable Madonnas and Elvises waned, and failed to be replenished by a new desire to see Britneys and Robbies to the same degree.

As a sideshow to the main event, and also to make use of otherwise expensive dormant studio time, they occasionally put together celebrity versions of the show. These would throw up inspired moments like Harry Hill doing Morrissey and Jarvis Cocker's gleeful facsimile of Rolf Harris. Replacing members of the public with well-known personalities is clearly a risky tactic. Watching at home we urge on the plucky shop assistants and gas fitters as they try and conquer the nerves in front of an audience of millions. With famous people, we want to see them suffer misfortune. It's the British way. How funny was it when the news carried the story that Jimmy Krankie had been injured during panto when he/she fell out of a beanstalk? I mean, we don't really wish him/her serious harm, but that's just much, much funnier than you're ever likely to find The Krankies' act. Similarly I remember there being mass stifled giggles at the BBC in Manchester when Bobby Davro, a comedian allegedly, was strapped into a set of stocks for a jape and toppled forward, landing nose first on the stage. Again, I've no wish to see Bobby Davro with a broken nose, but you can't deny the pure comedy of that scenario.

But the celebrities taking part in *Stars In Their Eyes* seemed to share the same sense of glee as the members of the general public who took part, and so the whole thing seemed to radiate a similar warmth.

I don't get asked to participate in celebrity reality shows very often and when I do I always say no for a variety of reasons. Firstly I don't consider myself to be a celebrity, on the basis that the vast majority of the viewing public has never heard of me. I'm also of the opinion that anyone who agrees to take part in these things has a flagging career, which is something I'd like to think I don't have, and a desperate desire to do more of the same kind of small-screen schlock, which I'm absolutely sure I don't have.

Occasionally I get offered a show that's well up the food chain, but is quite clearly unsuitable. Despite the creaking jokes and limbs of the walnut-skinned Bruce Forsyth, a man whose head seems to be adorned with half a coconut in some perpetual Robinson Crusoe makeover, *Strictly Come Dancing* is good, wholesome, family fun. So when I got asked to be a contestant I couldn't help but smile and feel a little bit pleased with myself at having received the invitation. Clearly I was never going to do it though. For a start, I don't dance. I'm also far too antisocial to get along for weeks on end with the same group of pathologically cheery people. And there is absolutely no way on this earth that I could wear those Latin American outfits and stick my posterior out like that without looking like a burst sausage. It's not natural, is it? I'm a

heterosexual married man with a paunch, for heaven's sake.
How's that going to look when I thrust my satin-clad arse
cheeks in the general direction of Craig Revel Horwood
during the Paso Doble? Unconvincing and ungainly, that's
how.

So that was an easy decision to make, but I did accept the
invitation to go on *Celebrity Fame Academy*, as it was for
charity and involves singing, which I like to do a lot with
my group The Family Mahone. Having agreed, they then
sent me a lengthy filming and rehearsal schedule that
entailed being away from home for weeks on end. I looked
at it and wondered whether I'd made the right call. Then
one night in a hotel in Brighton, where I was producing the
genius that is *Count Arthur Strong's Radio Show*, I awoke in a
cold sweat and knew that I couldn't go through with it. I felt
really bad about letting everyone down, not least because I
was going to raise loads of money for needy poor people,
and so I felt sheepishly pathetic when I phoned them the
next day to say there was no way I could do it. I explained
that I'd made a mistake and didn't want to be stuck in hotels
for that length of time, trying to balance the requirements of
the programme with my radio commitments. I think they
understood. That I was a bit of a whelp. And an indecisive
one at that.

When I got the call enquiring if I'd be interested in being
on *Stars In Their Eyes*, though, it was different. For a start, it
was a one-off, so I wouldn't need to be there for more than
a day. Two at the most. It was also shot in Manchester at
Granada studios, and so wouldn't require being away from
home. Not only that but my wife used to work on the show
as production coordinator and quite fancied looking up a
few old faces. So I said I'd do it.

Then I had to decide who to be. My first thoughts were
David Bowie or Bryan Ferry. They were both artists I

admired with voices I thought I might be vaguely able to re-create. They were both snappy dressers and there seemed little point in having the full weight of the Granada hair and make-up departments at your disposal and not going for a bit of glamour and glitz. I mean, I could have given them my celebrated Van Morrison, but that would have meant going through the doors looking squat and grumpy in my own shapeless clothes, and then coming back out again through the smoke looking squat and grumpy in some of their shapeless clothes. However, it was my wife's idea to 'do' Shane MacGowan as she quite rightly pointed out that every time I did a gig as lead singer of The Family Mahone, I was more or less doing a Shane anyway, and was therefore well versed in the part.

I first heard Shane MacGowan and The Pogues when I produced them for a John Peel session at Maida Vale in 1984. They had recently released their debut single 'Dark Streets of London' as Pogue Mahone, but had been obliged to drop half the name when it was discovered that it was Gaelic for 'kiss my arses'. Wisely they became The Kisses, or Pogues, leaving my band to become a family of arses many years down the line.

From the very first breakneck strum through one of Shane's ragged-trousered, boozed-up lullabies, I thought they were absolutely wonderful. They were a Celtic folk band with a punk attitude, which seemed to be a perfect combination that no one had tried before. The sheer bravado of their performance made it unimportant that they weren't the best players in the world, which was very punk, but they also had a deep-rooted connection with Irish rebel music that displayed itself not only in the covers they chose, but infused the original MacGowan songs, which was very folk.

Two of them, Shane and bassist Cait O'Riordan, were too inebriated to play very much. In fact Cait would be sent to

the pub later in the day while another member of the group
put the bass part down again. I imagine when the session was
aired she was quietly pleased with her performance. Jem
Finer seemed older, slightly less pissed, played rudimentary
tenor banjo and was the most approachable of the bunch.
Any moderately tricky bits of melody were handled by the
chipper penny-whistler Spider Stacy and reserved accor-
dionist James Fearnley, who seemed to struggle with his
instrument as if wrestling a live octopus. Andrew Ranken,
purple-faced and rheumy-eyed, kept a marching band beat
on a rusting snare and chipped floor tom-tom. They made a
wonderful racket.

Their first three albums, *Red Roses for Me*, *Rum, Sodomy
and the Lash* and *If I Should Fall from Grace with God* stand as
testament to their greatness. They learned to play a bit better
over time, and hired in a couple of proven instrumentalists to
beef up the sound without ever compromising their early joie
de vivre. And staggering, stumbling and slurring his way
through the fug was the unique Shane MacGowan. His songs
combine gritty poetry of life in London streets and boozers
with haunting melodies that seem to have been around for a
hundred years, yet seeing the often shambolic individual
clinging on to the mic stand to keep himself upright, it was
often impossible to work out where all that romance and
beauty had come from. Ironically, as the group became more
adept, his voice, never the most reliable of instruments,
declined almost to the point of being unusable. If you went
to see them, you had to have the words and the tunes in your
head already as you certainly weren't going to get them from
Shane's singing. Reluctantly, after their front man became
increasingly unreliable, they realized that a parting of the
ways was inevitable. They soldiered on, but it was never
going to be the same.

I've met Shane on a number of occasions and he's a

fascinating character. He is famous for his ability to have stayed alive through a binge that seems to have lasted for his whole adult life and for having only a few rotting stumps where his teeth used to be. In some ways he is painted as a bit of a caricature by a tabloid press alerted to him by the success of 'Fairytale of New York', and I'm sure there have been times when he's played up to and cultivated that. In truth there's a lot more to him. He is first and foremost a music fan, and though sometimes difficult to understand, his voice rou tinely little more than a mumble without many discernible consonants, he always asks about new things you've heard, and rattles on about great old tracks he's recently rediscovered. He's also generally well dressed, which surprises people. I recall him coming to play a session on our late-night Radio 1 programme wearing the finest overcoat I'd ever seen. From the back, with his full washed coxcomb of hair and calf-length mohair coat with black velveteen collar, he looked like a visiting dignitary and it was only when he turned round and revealed the deathly pallor of his ruined face that you realized who it was. He can be slightly difficult to get through to at first, but as he warms to you, he opens up and it becomes apparent that his memory is much more intact than it has any right to be, as he punctuates his ramblings with that unmistakably infectious wheezing snigger so reminiscent of Dick Dastardly's dog Muttley from the cartoon series *Wacky Races*.

In 2003 I had the chance to talk to Shane, one on one, for a good few hours as part of putting together a celebration of The Pogues for Radio 2. I flew to Dublin where I met the producer Nicky Birch and we sat in the bar and waited for his manager Joey Cashman to arrive from London. Joey missed the plane, and you began to understand what the rest of The Pogues must have gone through, waiting backstage at sold-out gigs wondering whether their singer was going to show up. I suppose rock-and-roll stars are allowed to be disorganized in their private lives, it's almost expected and reinforces the view that these are extraordinary people who don't play by the same rules as the rest of us. If Shane MacGowan had had to clock on at nine on the dot every morning he'd never have lived a life that would have resulted in the songs he's written. Hunter S. Thompson couldn't have come up with *Fear and Loathing in Las Vegas* if he'd been working as a chartered accountant in Stevenage. Not least because Stevenage is a long way from Las Vegas. The commuting alone would have been hellish.

It's all about method really. For the work to ring true, you have to have lived it. Of course, I know that not every songwriter or novelist has experienced first-hand the situations they write about. One of my favourite books of recent times is *Jonathan Strange and Mr Norrell* by Susanna Clarke, which concerns the rivalry between two English magicians in the 1800s. Now quite clearly Ms Clarke couldn't experience any of the events in the novel herself because they occurred long ago, and even if you could get back there through time travel or something, they didn't really happen anyway. It's a work of fiction and a tribute to her powers of imagination. Then again, Jeffrey Archer performed his first useful public service when he got sent to prison for perjury, thereby uniting the whole nation in joy and *Schadenfreude*, and used his experiences as the basis for subsequent books, but it didn't make them any better.

I do think that for a body of work like Shane's to stand up though, you have to have seen life through a glass darkly, and that's never going to be easily combined with good time-keeping. However, you do expect the manager to kind of sort those things out on their charge's behalf. And dear Joey didn't even have the excuse of waiting for Shane. He was travelling alone to meet us and take us to Shane. But the relationship between the pair of them is a complex one that goes way beyond the normal manager and artist arrangement. To give you some idea of how it works, Joey told me that when Shane was going through a particularly extreme chemically fuelled period, they checked in to a hotel together for the weekend. They left three months later.

Eventually the skinny, twinkly and leather trench-coated Joey arrived and we were driven to the place where we were going to rendezvous with Shane. Imagining this location I'd anticipated a smoky, wood-panelled hostelry down a shadowy back alley where the Guinness was like nectar, or else a remote village inn with a flagged floor and a raggle-taggle gaggle of diddly-diddly merchants knocking out some feverish tunes in the corner. Where we ended up was an anonymous, conference-style hotel on a golf course somewhere on the outskirts of Dublin, though I couldn't tell you exactly where.

Joey checked up on Shane and reported that he was somewhere on the road from Tipperary, though his precise whereabouts were hard to pinpoint. It was clear he wasn't going to be there for the appointed eight o'clock rendezvous and so, realizing we might have a wait on our hands, we checked into our rooms, mine resplendently appointed with melamine and a sad single bed sagging beneath a silky bedspread. We then joined the jowly, Pringle knitwear enthusiasts partaking of expensive school dinners in the floral-print-festooned dining room.

Joey was delightful company as he described the adventures of The Pogues on endless tours as they 'fell around the world', and he kept our glasses well charged until Shane stumbled into the room at around a quarter to eleven, carrying a glass of what looked like Martini Rosso and asking for a light. He was wearing a good black suit, black shiny shirt and a spiky mane of black hair emphasizing the deathly whiteness of his skin. He'd gained some weight.

He joined us at the table and when asked if he wanted to order a meal he declined, saying he'd just eat 'a few spuds' that were sitting in a serving dish. This he duly did. With two forks.

For the first quarter of an hour or so he talked only to Joey. Joey kept reassuring me that this was normal and that he would start to talk to me after a couple more drinks, which was just as well as we were supposed to be conducting an interview. Gradually though, as the red wine, Baileys and Stolichnaya vodka slipped down, Shane began to chide and chat while expressing a surprising appreciation of the vocal talents of Michael Bublé.

As midnight slipped by we began to record our conversations to form the basis of the radio programme. He talked vividly of his roots as a lad growing up in London with Irish parentage and the sense of alienation that brought. In the early seventies the fear of the IRA was at its height and Shane talked of how anyone with Irish connections was treated with deep suspicion by the indigenous population. He explained how this inevitably led him to the burgeoning punk scene, where the factors that united the various clans were a sense of alienation and a strongly anti-establishment ethic most neatly summarized by The Sex Pistols' twin anthems 'Anarchy in the UK' and 'God Save the Queen'. MacGowan had been a regular face on the new-wave scene and had formed his own band The Nips, who scored a minor punk 'hit' with the rather charming ragged rockabilly of 'Venus in Bovver Boots' in 1978.

The genesis of The Pogues Shane traced to the squat scene of Burton Street, not far from Euston Station. Here the various members who would make up the band existed in run-down tenements while rehearsing and jamming in a variety of dank basements and draughty attics with leaky ceilings. They hit on this idea of playing songs in the Irish rebel tradition but with the untutored ferocity of the punk band and not the studied musicianship of the hardcore folk world. Perhaps their later collaborators The Dubliners were an influence here, as despite being Ireland's most famous folk export, they had remained determinedly rough around the edges. Sometimes to play this stuff brilliantly well was beside the point. Perhaps it was even the absolute opposite of the point.

Shane recalled how ethnic music was going through a bit of a revival in London at that time with a good deal of interest in Ukrainian sounds and particularly African hi-life. He then realized that the whole Irish subculture was sitting there intact and untapped, which led them to start playing the traditional songs Shane had learned as a child. However, the key moment came when he decided to decant the first-hand experience of being London Irish into his own original songs. He told me that the first one he wrote was the joyous romp of 'Streams of Whiskey', and after that they just began to flow from him. They were tales of things that he'd sat and seen or thought in the bars and streets of his adopted home town. The actress and director Kathy Burke, herself a Londoner with Irish parents, has spoken of hearing The Pogues and immediately recognizing that here was the voice of people growing up in their situation in that particular climate in England. Certainly songs like 'The Old Main Drag' and their first single 'Dark Streets of London' bring that whole world to life and, in the words of the man who was for many years the lead voice of The Dubliners, Ronnie Drew, 'tell it like it is'.

We talked for a long time that night. We drank quite a lot too, but Shane didn't think the drinking was all that important to The Pogues' story, as he eloquently reasoned it had been the legal lubricant for the vast majority of popular music. In fact tin-whistle player Spider Stacy thinks that though they imbibed heavily their drinking may have been overstated due to the fact that most of the songs were about booze in some way. Hmmm. Maybe.

Shane also admitted he was vain, as all lead singers are, and so I asked him how a vain man could walk around with teeth like that. He mused on this and said he might consider getting some work done in the future but didn't really want to be bothered with a new set just now as it had been 'hell getting rid of the first lot'.

I wondered if he'd enjoyed the fame his lethal live band and timeless classic songs had brought him. He said he had because it allowed him to see 'how much fun I could have being an arsehole'.

As a result of that night Shane and Joey later gave the nod for my band to support him the following St Patrick's night at the Shepherd's Bush Empire. On the same tour we played with him at the Manchester Academy when Shane and Joey didn't arrive until after ten, by which time we'd finished our already extended set, his backing band The Popes, trying valiantly to stall for time, had been subjected to a barrage of cans and bottles, and the glass frontage of the box office had been pushed in by disgruntled fans demanding a refund. And yet, when he finally wandered out onto the stage, everyone forgave him and got on with having a good night. If you enter Shane-world you have to accept his rules. I remember on one occasion hosting an edition of the Channel Four music show *The White Room* and seeing Sinead O'Connor sitting alone, elfin-like, on the stage.

'Waiting for Shane?' I asked.

She rolled her large, expressive eyes and smiled.

'Ah, we're always waiting for Shane, but you don't mind because he's a genius. Though he doesn't know it.'

When I arrived at the *Stars* recording I learned the identities of my fellow contestants for the first time. To be honest,

I hadn't really heard of them because they were from TV soaps, which I don't watch. A devilishly handsome and friendly chap called Tom Lister, who was in *Emmerdale* apparently, was going to be doing Jamie Cullum, despite being tall enough to make two Jamie Cullums. However, this hardly set a precedent for the show, as they'd previously had Boy George doing David Bowie despite being as wide as two David Bowies. Then there was a chummy, blonde woman called Jayne Tunnicliffe, someone or other in *Coronation Street*, who was transforming herself into Marianne Faithfull. There was also the beautiful though slightly more standoffish Phina Oruche, from *Footballers' Wives*, who was taking on Lauryn Hill. This seemed a pretty good idea as she looked a lot like her to begin with.

The last remaining contestant was Princess Diana's former butler Paul Burrell. He soon struck me as a man who took himself very seriously indeed and, I thought, was looking at this as a possible way into a career in musical theatre. I could be wrong, and there's nothing wrong with that even if I'm right, but he just seemed to be taking it a lot more seriously than anyone else. He also seemed strangely humourless, but perhaps he'd been a right barrel of laughs before getting sucked into all that melodrama down at St James's Palace. I asked him which vocalist he was going to be portraying, and his answer confused me slightly.

'I'm going to be Richard Gere.'

Richard Gere? Is he a singer, I thought, though it must have been out loud as 'my rock' came back at me.

'He sang "Razzle Dazzle It" in *Chicago*.'

Well yes, but Dick Van Dyke sang 'Chim-chiminee-chim-chiminee-chim-chim-cheroo' in *Mary Poppins* but that doesn't mean he's a singer in the technical sense. And how many people had a clear idea of what Richard Gere's singing voice sounded like? If the point of the show was to get as close to the original as possible, how could that be measured against something that none of us could really remember? Mind you, the singing seemed the least of Burrell's worries as he was doing the proverbial big production number with dancing girls, a bit of juggling, umbrellas and all that malarkey. It all seemed like a lot of bother to me, but then I wasn't envisaging a future in a West End theatre. I had chosen to stumble about with a drink in my hand as if envisaging a future in a West End gutter, which required far less rehearsal and therefore more time in the bar.

Rehearsals of my song 'The Irish Rover' went perfectly well as they filled the stage with enthusiastic miming fiddle and accordion players. At one point I was sent to see the vocal coach, who listened to my sandpaper rasp once through the number and then rolled about on the floor in fits of laughter.

'Well,' she said, 'there's nothing I can do with that.'

Was that a good or a bad thing? Was my performance polished to such a level of perfection that it couldn't be improved or was it so poor that it was beyond help? I didn't know and, in truth, I didn't really care. I'd only gone along for a laugh, though I was beginning to think I'd quite like Paul Burrell not to win.

After we'd all routined our numbers they talked us through the technicalities of the procedure involved in announcing the winner. This meant sitting on a plywood banquette while the audience pressed their key pads, and then once the result had been announced taking a lengthy and tortuous route through some balsa corridors to fall into the arms of the beaming Cat Deeley on some chipboard podium. If I'm honest I'd had a few jars by this stage, in the interests of method acting you understand, and wasn't paying much attention. I wasn't going to win anyway, so I didn't feel this was really stuff I needed to know.

My wife and her mate Debs, plus my chums Jamie, Andy, Gareth and James, took their seats along with the rest of the audience and the show began. I retired to the Green Room where the resourceful Marianne Faithfull had succeeded in prising open the cabinet holding the wine that was being saved for after the show. What a girl. You couldn't help but feel that the real Marianne would have been immensely proud.

The newly enlarged Jamie Cullum went on first and did a pretty good job. I didn't think he sounded enormously like the real one, which was a relief, but Tom knocked his song out with some gusto.

Then came the butler. During his interview he couldn't help but look at the screen and personally greet any of his old royal cronies who were watching down at the palace. Well, I have no idea if they were or not, but it seemed unlikely, and if 'her maj' was out there it wasn't hard to imagine her spluttering on the old Lady Grey before hurling a HobNob at the screen. Transformed into that well-known giant of popular song Richard Gere, with more than a hint of Blake Carrington, his song went off pretty well. At least there were no dropped juggling balls as there had been in rehearsal.

Phina Oruche looked, I have to say, absolutely stunning as Lauryn Hill. She wasn't the best singer on the show but she certainly had the best legs and that had to be worth a few votes, didn't it?

Jayne Tunnicliffe did a very sweet 'As Tears Go By' with some authentic sixties dancers. And then it was my turn.

They showed a little film of me doing the radio show, and then I walked out to have a chat with Cat. She was very adept at putting you at your ease, and seemed genuinely tickled at the prospect of seeing Shane. She asked me to talk about who I was going to be, and I made sure I stressed

how much I admired his songwriting, because I didn't want
to be accused of making him a figure of fun. I was determined to have fun doing the song, but really wanted people
to understand that my performance was fuelled by respect
and admiration. And Pinot Grigio. The interview at an
end, Cat delivered the cue for me to deliver that famous
line.

'Well, Mark, tell us who you're going to be.'

'Tonight, Cat, I'm going to be Shane MacGowan.'

Turns, walks towards doors with star on, gives cheery
wave, disappears into showbiz mist.

Then, of course, you have to sort out the transformation.
I'd been told to report for duty with a couple of day's stub-
ble. Jill, the playful make-up lady, then had the bright idea of
putting mascara on this when I was being interviewed as
myself, before washing it off to reveal the greying growth as
I emerged as Shane. I had a black suit, string vest, a few
Celtic necklaces, aviator shades and a spot-on wig. She then
spent an uncomfortable fifteen minutes, for both of us I'm
sure, applying black and green paint to my teeth to achieve
the trademark MacGowan 'forest of stumps' effect. My wife
didn't immediately recognize me when she turned up backstage. She didn't want to kiss me either.

Waiting behind the famous doors, dressed as Shane, tipsy
as Shane, I didn't feel remotely nervous. It was only singing
a song after all, and I'd done that hundreds of times. In fact
I was more interested in how primitive the apparatus back
there was. On telly you see the doors swish open and the
turn emerge from an atmospheric cloud of smoke. It all
looks as if it's done by computer or something. In fact
there's a bloke in a maroon sweatshirt with a hand-held
dry-ice machine the size of fan heater, and two more blokes
in two more maroon sweatshirts sliding the doors back with
bits of washing line. So preoccupied was I with goings-on

behind the scenes that when the doors did open it took me by surprise and I emerged from the mist with a bit of a stumble. Naturally, people thought this was just a bit of skilled role-play and I did nothing to disarm them of this notion.

The song, which we did twice, went really well. At least the fake musicians on the stage were really lively and I didn't forget any of the words, though they may have been in the wrong order. I thought my Shane accent was pretty good, though someone did later suggest it sounded suspiciously Cornish. I watched it back on YouTube and I'm inclined to agree. No matter. On the night the audience loved it, not least because it signalled the end of a long, hot night in a studio watching Paul Burrell turn on the smarm.

I then retired to the couch safe in the knowledge that it was all over, while the members of the audience cast their votes. I know a lot of fuss has gone on about vote rigging since then, but as far as I can ascertain this was a genuine tally. The cameras swept across our faces as Cat teased and delayed the announcement and then she said it: 'And the winner is . . . Shane MacGowan.'

People who saw it said I did a great job of looking genuinely surprised. I didn't, you know. I was quite literally gobsmacked. I then sat there for a while while my fellow contestants shook my hand and patted me on the shoulder, before realizing that I was expected back on stage and hadn't been concentrating when they were explaining how to get there.

'You took your time,' chided Cat amiably, when I eventually stumbled back on stage. She gave me some flowers that I later discovered were blooms she'd been sent herself, which was nice of her, though it seemed only fair. She hadn't won, had she?

I then did the song one more time over the closing credits,

forgetting one verse entirely, while wondering how many people watching at home were wondering what was going on. How had their favourite mainstream Saturday night show climaxed with a bloke they'd never heard of taking off another bloke they'd never heard of?

Cheers, Shane. Here's to you.

19. THE DAY I WENT TO KATE BUSH'S HOUSE FOR CHEESE FLAN

Growing up with a passion for music was problematic in the early seventies if you wanted to see bands on the television. Nowadays you've got numerous channels pumping out back-to-back videos twenty-four hours a day. Back then, there were two weekly shows and that was your lot. Unless you counted *The Black and White Minstrel Show*. Which I didn't.

Firstly there was *The Old Grey Whistle Test*. This was a 'serious' rock programme on BBC Two hosted by a large beard, through which the viewer would occasionally catch glimpses of Bob Harris. Bob is a thoroughly decent bloke and absolutely passionate about music, although it was sometimes difficult to work this out as his delivery was so laid-back it was hard to hear what he was saying. You could try lip-reading, but such was the thickness of his beard that trying to watch his mouth was like looking for a darting squirrel in dense undergrowth. Of course, Bob's mumbled delivery, rather like that of John Peel, was a signal that he was intent on pushing the music and not his personality. These DJs were a breed apart from the hyperactive, grinning berks who were just passing through music programming en route to – what they saw as – 'greater things'. Like game shows and kids' programmes. Each to their own, I suppose, though I've never really understood why those whose ambition is to present *Know Your Onions* on daytime television should be given control of radio shows where decent records ought to be played. Incidentally, *Know Your Onions* doesn't actually exist as far as I know, but as I rarely watch the idiot lantern, I can't be absolutely sure.

So Bob was the reliably downbeat custodian of *Whistle Test*, where we got to see proper, live bands doing proper, live songs in the studio. Unless they were miming, which did happen occasionally. Here it was that I caught my first glimpses of such greats as Roxy Music, The New York Dolls, Dr. Feelgood, Bob Marley and The Sensational Alex Harvey Band. It was a weekly glimpse into a distant, debauched world of sex and drugs and rock and roll, and a lifeline for the adolescent fledgling rocker.

The other programme we had access to was *Top of the Pops*, the perennial light-entertainment behemoth of popular culture, myth and legend. At least, it was perennial until it was wiped out a couple of years ago. Misguidedly in my view. If they'd stuck to the original template of popular chart acts doing their hits with someone in a jumper telling you who they were in between, no one would have had a problem with it. It was always a bit crap and it should have stayed that way. Why do these focus-group-driven consultant-mad do-gooders have to come along and spoil things by trying to make them good? Look at *Countdown*. It was the first programme on Channel 4 and it was quite patently rotten. A feeble word game hosted by a likable, though let's be honest, useless presenter in a gaudy sports jacket with his hair parted in an adjoining county and a glamorous, though chummy and unthreatening, sidekick who could also do sums. Rubbish. Addictive rubbish, maybe. But rubbish then. And still rubbish now. But what's wrong with that? There'll always be rubbish. Even if it is only collected once a fortnight these days.

Top of the Pops was rubbish, but it was good rubbish when

it knew it was rubbish. Once it got delusions of adequacy and started to think of itself as potentially quite good, it got really rubbish. They started to insist on bands playing live. Why? We just wanted to hear the hits and see someone mucking about a bit. The Faces played football to 'Maggie May' while John Peel mimed playing the mandolin. No one had a problem with that. We knew Rod Stewart was a great singer, we didn't need that to be confirmed by seeing him struggle against inadequate BBC monitoring. Look, it was an entertainment show. Mud did 'Lonely This Christmas' with a portion of the lead vocals being undertaken by a ventriloquist's dummy perched on front-man Les Gray's knee. The record went to number one. New Order performed 'Blue Monday' live, and the following week it went down. What does that tell you? That 'Lonely This Christmas' is a better song than 'Blue Monday'? That Mud were a better band than New Order? No. It tells you that the audience didn't need *Top of the Pops* to try and educate them, it just needed daft pop stars being daft pop stars. Even 'proper' pop stars understood this. Alice Cooper stumbled about with a sword, David Bowie camped it up with Mick Ronson, Marc Bolan came on to do 'Ride a White Swan' on a white swan, Morrissey had a deaf aid hanging out of his ear and a distressed bridal bouquet dangling out of his bottom. That was the stuff. But when the zealots tried to make it a real music show all that went out of the window. They even started putting bands on who weren't in the charts yet. Hello! It's called *Top of the Pops*. There was a clue in the title, you idiots. And of course their insistence that everyone played live came wholly unstuck once acid house, Balearic beat and rave became the sonic soup of the day. For these acts playing live constituted messing about with a couple of gramophones and a small panel of knobs bought at Argos, while wearing an anorak. What an arresting visual spectacle that made. Give me Noddy Holder's mirrored top hat any day.

Even worse though, presenters, of which I was one on two occasions, started to believe that people were remotely interested in what they had to say. Mistake. Other than letting you know who'd just been on, a job that can be done better and more cheaply by a caption, presenter on *Top of the Pops* was a 'non-job'. It wasn't even a much-maligned 'McJob'. A caption can't serve you a cheeseburger, can it? Of course, the host of *Top of the Pops* can disguise their basic uselessness by being desirable, glamorous and fashionable, to blend in with the desirable, glamorous and fashionable pop stars. Clearly this was not an option for me. I was one of the Radio 1 DJs who appeared in an article in the *Sun* headed: 'Too ugly for *Top of the Pops*'. With photographic evidence to back up their claim. And it wasn't just me either. My similarly besmirched easy targets were Simon Mayo, Kevin Greening, who tragically died in his sleep at the age of forty-four towards the end of 2007, and the esteemed 6Music broadcaster Marc Riley (the artist formerly known as Lard). Lard and I thought this hilarious, and certainly the photographs they'd chosen seemed to lend the newspaper's theory credibility. I mean, we were gorgeous in real life, obviously, but we did look a bit rough in those pictures.

I never spoke to Kevin about it, but I think Simon was quite rightly a little miffed to be slung into this rogue's gallery. A charming man, Simon was well groomed and had a chiselled appeal in a certain light, and had even had his own telly show and everything. And were we really less attractive than the DJs of yesteryear? Was there a time when the sight of Dave Lee Travis in a Fair Isle jumper reduced the womenfolk of the UK to gibbering wrecks? Were thousands of moistened girls riveted to the screen admiring 'Diddy' David Hamilton's meticulous comb-over? It seems unlikely, though when I did catch a glimpse of Marc and I in our matching white shirts with our arms folded introducing The Spice

Girls, it did rather look as though a pair of disgruntled waiters from a neighbouring down-at-heel trattoria had stumbled into shot. Fearne Cottons we weren't. Billy Cottons was more like it.

The point was that *Top of the Pops* had to have glamour. Its peak was in the seventies when Britain was regularly gripped by strikes and power cuts. The concept of 'urban renewal' was restricted to multi-storey car parks. They were dark times in many ways. *Top of the Pops* became a flash of fun and colour that raised the spirits every Thursday, and gave us some enthusiasm for the weekend ahead. Status Quo with their manes of hair gurning through 'Paper Plane', Slade dressed entirely in items stolen from the Christmas tree in the foyer, Ron Mael of Sparks with a Hitler moustache staring out the whole of England while his hyperactive, effeminate brother pranced around to 'This Town Ain't Big Enough For Both Of Us'. All this and the goddesses of Pan's People dancing in their knickers. These were the moments you would never forget that made *Top of the Pops* great.

And then, of course, there was Kate Bush.

When Kate Bush appeared on *Top of the Pops* in 1978 she was like nothing we'd seen before. She was beautiful of course, but in a more tantalizing and enigmatic way than anyone else. She seemed to have an untamed, gypsy side to her character, a barely concealed hint of something wild, something deliciously unbridled just beneath the skin. She was the kind of girl who looked like she'd come from 'a good family' and had been very well educated, but was also a bit of a free spirit. Not rebellious exactly, but someone well versed in flights of fancy. And her voice was simply extraordinary. The song was 'Wuthering Heights' and it must be one of the most onomatopoeic vocal performances ever committed to vinyl. She 'is' Cathy. Her voice is at the same time a romantic heroine and a shrill banshee wandering the windswept moors. If you'd never read the book you'd have got the idea from Kate's singing. And though she was wearing a bandanna and voluminous skirts as I recall, the whole package was unforgettably sexy. The blessed Pan's People may have worn blissfully little, for which I was never less than grateful and often rueful that the video recorder had yet to be invented, but Kate had that additional air of mystery. And it wasn't just a male thing. She was one of those rare pop stars who all the boys fancied, but the girls felt it as well. I guess Debbie Harry fell into that category, Chrissie Hynde maybe, but none of them had the allure of Kate. I think it was because female pop stars were supposed to be sexy in an obvious kind of way, whereas Kate's sexiness just seemed to be a by-product of what she was and the work she was doing. That was what other women liked. She was quite patently playing by her own rules and the effect was all the more powerful for that. Certainly she was an icon to my girlfriend of the time Zoe, and we added Kate to the short list of artists whose records we would listen to together in her bedroom before . . . well . . . y'know. David Bowie, Marc Bolan, Elton John, Steve Harley, Joni Mitchell, Kate Bush. Sometimes I slipped in a bit of Focus or Alex Harvey or Peter Gabriel-period Genesis, but Zoe wasn't as keen on those, which meant she was less likely to . . . well . . . y'know.

Kate Bush went on to make great albums, all of which spawned singles that sounded like nothing else around at the time – 'Army Dreamers', 'Sat in Your Lap', 'Running Up That Hill', 'Cloudbusting', 'The Sensual World' – but which became big hits anyway. It was as if a Kate record was a soundtrack to a parallel universe that lined up with ours only occasionally. Like all the greats, she did it her way. She was beyond fashion. She didn't even seem to want to be famous. In fact fame seemed to be the aspect of the job she liked least. Despite having trained in dance and being what you might think of as an ideal stage performer, she did only one short tour before retiring to the studio and sealing the enigma.

In 2004 I started presenting a late-evening show on Radio 2. One night I played a Kate track, 'This Woman's Work', and bemoaned the lack of any new material since *The Red Shoes* in 1993. I think I may have said words to the effect of 'Kate, if you're out there, phone and let us know you're OK.' It was just an off-the-cuff remark, something that hadn't been planned, but we began to count the days we hadn't heard from her. I don't know why, really. It was a link I suppose, something to talk about on those days you go live on air only to find your head empty. I guess I was also hopeful that somewhere out there, someone who knew her would tip her off and, intrigued, she might just phone. It was a long shot admittedly, but you never know.

It also seemed appropriate to have a physical manifestation of the campaign, and so 'The Bushometer' was born. As each programme dawned, and still no word from Kate, I glued a photograph of her, along with a picture of whoever was on the show that day, onto a collage spreading like a mutating damp patch up the studio wall. It was named 'The Bushometer' after the celebrated 'clapometer' used to measure audience reaction on the late and almost entirely unlamented TV talent show *Opportunity Knocks*. Presented by a smirking, brilliantined goblin called Hughie Green, this weekly parade of dismal cabaret detritus reached a climax at the end of the show when the applause for each act was recorded on this 'clapometer' contraption. What this consisted of was a cardboard-ruler affair across the bottom of the screen, across which a balsa-wood marker would make unsteady progress until, as if operated by some wheezing dwarf who'd stopped for a fag break, it settled on a particular point. Admittedly there was also a postal vote, and the whole system was probably no more arbitrary than recent polling aberrations on *Ant and Dec's Saturday Night Please Take it Away*, but careers were decided on this flimsy apparatus. Not that many of them would have had careers anyway. The acts who became famous thanks to *Opportunity Knocks* included such greats as Bonnie Langford, Little and Large, Bobby Crush, Tony Monopoly, Lena Zavaroni, Pam Ayres and, if memory serves, The Grateful Dead. It's hard to think that our lives would have been all that much poorer if opportunity had knocked but then quickly run away. To be fair, they did discover the truly great Les Dawson, but as the programme ran from 1956 to 1978, that hardly goes down as a great strike rate.

Of course, we weren't measuring Kate Bush's ability with our 'Bushometer'. It was just a handy name for what was actually more closely based on the roof appeal displays you see outside churches to show how much money they've raised. It grew as the days we hadn't heard from Kate increased, and I fully expected it to grow beyond the confines of the studio, and out into the corridor. Because Kate Bush was never going to phone. And then, in 2005, the unthinkable happened. Word began to circulate that the silence was about to be broken. Kate Bush was set to release not just a new album, but a new double album. All that anyone knew was that it was called *Aerial*. No one had seen it, no one had heard it, but it was definitely on its way. Great. Perhaps. I say perhaps because, with no activity in sight, no one really expected me to talk to Kate Bush. It was all just a feeble gag drawn out beyond its natural life. Having based a career on material that fell into that category I wasn't unduly worried about that. But now, she was back. And if she was back, I would look pretty foolish, even by DJ standards, if this extended courtship remained resolutely snubbed.

I started to phone people I knew at the record company to stake my claim. The response was not encouraging. She wasn't going to do much, if anything, and what she did do was likely to be in print. Brilliant.

'If only we knew someone high up at EMI,' said Lizzie in our office.

'Hmmm. Actually, I was at school with the head of EMI,' said me, in our office.

'Well bloody well ring him, then,' said Lizzie.

I bloody well did. His name was Tony Wadsworth. He was in the year above me at school and was the lead singer in Black Cat Bone, rivals to my band Berlin Airlift. He was one of the few people in the business who'd actually met Kate. Rumour had it that he was there at the almost mythical meeting when a small coterie of record-company big cheeses paid a visit to Bush Acres to see what she'd created of late only to be presented with a plate of cakes. That was it. No songs. No demos. Just some cakes. This may of course be an apocryphal story, but I so wanted it to be true that I never asked Tony about it just in case it wasn't. He said he'd put me near the top of the long list of people who wanted to talk to her, and would put in a word for me personally. There was a glimmer of hope. I waited. The 'Bushometer' continued to grow.

I was in Aberdeen when I got the news. We were on a tour of duty in those parts, and it was a tough assignment. Rather like our hardy troops being sent to scenes of conflict in the Middle East, so elite platoons of crack disc jockeys are occasionally airlifted to notorious radio trouble spots, which is to say places that show up as strangely immune to our collective Radio 2 charms. The plucky Aberdonians fell into this category, which, though they weren't particularly low in my estimation, made them go up in it by quite a long way.

Anyway, it was one afternoon on a routine reconnaissance record-buying patrol up there when Tina from EMI left a message on my field telephone. Word from the front had it that Kate was interested in doing an interview, had been given my number, and was going to ring to talk it over. This was fantastic news but made me as jumpy as hell. As a seasoned veteran of guerrilla campaigns dating back to the Radio 1 Roadshow I had developed the nerves of steel you need if you want to be selected for 'special services' by Wing Commander Terence Wogan. But every time my phone rang, I just turned to jelly in case it was her. Rather like expecting a call from a new girlfriend, I ran through in my head how to sound simultaneously interested, but not over-keen. I wanted her to know I was keen, not suspect I might turn into a stalker.

The day dragged on, she didn't call. The next day came and went, and the one after that. Nothing. I boarded the BBC Chinook, flew home and went with the family to visit my friends Julian and Julia in York for the weekend. It was eerily quiet. Well, York wasn't. York was quite noisy, but you know what I mean. And then, at teatime on Saturday, a message came through. Why it hadn't come through as a call I've no idea, but in a way it was better. There she was. Kate Bush on my phone with a message I could play over and over again. Just to make sure it was her.

'Hi, Mark. It's Kate Bush here. I've been told we might be meeting up for a chat. Sounds like fun. Anyway, give me a ring when you've got a minute.'

And then she left her number. Obviously, because she's ex-directory, which you can check if you don't believe me. So you won't get the number that way. You could steal my mobile I suppose, but I'm not daft enough to put her full name on there, and Kate B could be anybody.

But hearing her message was a magical moment. I know that might sound a bit over the top, but when you've grown up admiring someone from afar, and you hear their normal speaking voice on your phone, well, it's slightly surreal to say the least. I played the message a couple of times, and even let Julian hear it, and then I slipped away to phone back. Bloody hell, answerphone. I left a message and heard nothing for the remainder of that day.

The next day was Sunday, which meant breakfast, papers, roast lunch, a bit of a stroll down the Shambles and packing up the car. If she'd phoned at any point during that time I'd have been able to chat easily, but no, she had to ring while I was simultaneously driving and explaining to the kids why we couldn't have McDonald's forty-five minutes after having eaten pretty much a whole pig. I pulled over into a lay-by and finally we spoke. When she found out that I was parked up on the side of the road with impatient children hitting each other over the head with umbrellas in a VW Sharan, she thought it might be better if I called again when I got home. It was a sensible plan, though part of me didn't want to let her go. She was there, right there in person, talking just to me, and I was worried it wouldn't happen again.

Sure enough, when I called later that evening, it went to answerphone. Of course it did. Had I imagined it all? Had she really phoned, or was I just lost in a daydream to escape the kids' bickering?

But then she rang back. And we talked for ages. Which was great, because it was her phone bill. She was really chatty, and funny, and inquisitive. She was also worried about her privacy, and wanted to make sure I wasn't trying to do a tabloid-style piece that would reveal too much about her private life. Of course I had no intention of doing that. I just wanted to talk to her about the new record, and to try and understand where it had come from. Where it had all come from. There was one problem though. I hadn't heard it yet, and so not unreasonably, but with a humility not common in major recording stars, she told me to ring back when I'd heard it because there was no point in doing an interview if I didn't like it.

I did like it. I loved it. I was entranced and fascinated by it. The first album was titled *A Sea of Honey* and contained seven songs including the stately single 'King of the Mountain', a track about the mathematical value of pi, a paean to her son Bertie and a long song extolling the virtues of a washing machine. Perfect.

The second record was called *A Sky of Honey* and was, if anything, even better. Based on recordings of birdsong, its rhythms and melodies seemed to grow organically from the calls of the birds, and appeared to follow a day from dawn chorus to the trills of twilight. I didn't pretend to know what it all meant, but I did know it was special. It was bewitching, and couldn't have been made by anyone else in the whole world.

And so we arranged to meet. At no point did she ask me to phone a manager or a publicist or a press officer. She sorted it all out personally, which I know might not sound like a big deal but believe me, in this business it's pretty rare. Everyone has people. But not Kate Bush it seemed.

The thing that really surprised me though was the location she suggested for the interview. I knew she was really concerned about protecting her privacy and so the last thing I expected was for her to invite me to her house. That's pretty much unheard of. If you're lucky enough to be granted an interview with a major artist you either get them for an allotted time slot in a swish hotel suite under the watchful eye of officious press officers or, if you're lucky, they might pay you a visit to the studio. But no one ever invites you to their house. And they certainly don't ask you what you'd like for lunch. But Kate did, even apologizing in advance that because she was busy with final arrangements for the record's release, she wouldn't have time to make anything, so she'd probably just get some stuff in from the supermarket and was cheese flan OK? OK? I love cheese flan, but even if she'd suggested tripe and chitterlings marinated in battery acid, I'd have said OK.

And so the day dawned. I set off from home in the company of my regular engineer Chris Lee, who was coming along because he is a mate and fellow Kate fan and we needed to make sure it was recorded properly, and my regular producer 'Juke Box' John Leonard, who was coming along because he is a mate and really likes cheese flan.

Obviously I'm not going to tell you where Kate Bush lives, or even how long it took us to get there. Suffice to say that I eventually appeared in front of some large electronic gates with my hand on the buzzer. Once again there was no sign of 'staff' or lackeys as a disembodied but unmistakable voice crackled through the speakers.

'Hello.'

'Hi, Kate. It's Mark. Radcliffe. From the BBC.'

At this point the thought crossed my mind that it had all been an elaborate ruse and that she would say 'Who?' before calling the police. But she didn't. Instead she said, 'Righto, come through.'

We were in. Expecting a long drive through Narnia-like grounds filled with gambolling deer and perhaps the odd centaur, it was a surprise to find the house immediately on our left. A nice, big, rambling old place, Georgian maybe, but in no way what you'd think of as a mansion. Unostentatious would be one way of putting it.

And then, there she was on the doorstep. Barefoot, in jeans and what you might call a 'floaty' top, long hair unfussily clipped up, with strands trailing down to her shoulders. She was a bit smaller than I was expecting I think, and was smiling from ear to ear. If she would rather have not had her personal space invaded, then there was certainly no outward sign of that.

We made the necessary introductions and she took us into
a kitchen that was in the state of general disarray familiar to
all families. There was an Aga, lots of papers and magazines,
piles of washing – you know the kind of thing. Everything
just seemed so normal, which, in a way, seemed weird
because she'd assumed such mythical status down the years
and in the recent pursuit, that it seemed unlikely she would
just be a pleasant, funny, busy working mum.

She apologized again for not having made us anything
herself, before opening up the cheese flans and popping them
into the oven. There was salad and bread and stuff too. While
it was cooking she gave us a tour of the grounds, which
included a studio, a little guest cottage and, rather wonderfully, a weir and the remains of an old mill. It all seemed to fit
perfectly somehow.

After lunch, we set up our recording gear in the sitting
room and began to chat, for about an hour maybe.

We talked about why there'd been such a long gap
between albums and she said she wasn't quite sure herself
really but that she'd decided to take a year out after *The Red
Shoes* and, somehow, one year became twelve. She explained
that that didn't mean she'd been doing no work at all on the
record during that time, just that the desire to be a mum to
Bertie had put paid to her marathon fourteen-hour studio
sessions. This she had come to see as a good thing, as she
explained how, rather like working on a painting, it gave her
the opportunity to stand back and see how it was going,
rather than being totally immersed and losing all sense of
perspective. She revealed that she rarely does demo recordings as she has been frustrated in the past at never being able
to recapture the energy and the atmosphere of that first
attempt at the song, and so she likes to write and record the
piano and voice quite quickly before starting the long process
of enhancement and embellishment.

She was very keen to be seen to be championing the art form of the album, where the listener is taken on a journey as the tracks unfold rather than just downloading solitary tracks from iTunes. This new way of accessing music she saw as very much symptomatic of the way we live now, in search of a quick hit rather than giving something our undivided attention to fully appreciate its nuances. She was perfectly conscious that this was asking for quite a commitment from the consumer and said that she had wanted to do a double album to make sure people felt they were getting value for money in return for investing their time in the record. She was also really keen that individuals should take whatever meaning they gleaned from the often difficult to decipher lyrics. What were we to make of 'King of the Mountain' with its references to Elvis, *Citizen Kane* and washing? As far as she was concerned, you took from it what you liked and that was more important than knowing the original intention and inspiration.

Her attitude to the notion of celebrity was bewilderment. She expressed astonishment that we have come to invest so much attention on something so shallow. To her, it was the work that was important, not the notoriety that resulted from it. She explained that she wasn't withdrawn from the world in some big 'vampire castle', but just needed a quiet place where the creative process could truly function. Though she said she'd had fun being a pop star in the early days, it was never what she wanted to be. She just wanted to make the record she'd always dreamed of making since sitting at the piano and writing songs from the age of twelve.

I asked her if she'd ever play live again. She said she wouldn't rule it out but then 'hadn't ruled it out for twenty-odd years'. It was great to think there might be a possibility of seeing her perform again one day, but I won't be holding my breath. As to whether there'd be another twelve-year gap between records, she said she hoped not, but as there were no new songs just hanging around, it was difficult to say for sure. She likened the process of making records to writing a book, and that makes the gestation period more understandable I think. She did say she'd had concerns about how long it had taken to complete *Aerial* because she was 'worried that people would forget about me'. As if.

It was all very relaxed and good-natured and my lasting memory is of me rambling on with some typically addled question, at the end of which she burst out laughing. I know it might not have been the most concise and incisive enquiry she'd ever heard, but I did think that openly laughing was a bit much.

'I'm sorry,' she said, 'I was thinking about what to say and the dog just farted.'

All those years ago watching *Top of the Pops*, I never dreamed I'd be in the same room as Kate Bush, and if I was, I never expected her to be talking to me. And if she was, I never expected to hear her say the words, 'I'm sorry, the dog just farted.'

We wrapped up our chat and while Chris was coiling up the leads John and I led Kate out to the car to show her something. We'd brought 'The Bushometer'. We laid it out on her gravel forecourt and explained what it all meant. She smiled again, but to be honest, I started to wonder if she was beginning to wonder whether inviting these people to her house had been such a great idea. You could almost imagine her calling a close friend after we'd gone and saying: 'And then, you'll never guess what, they went back to their car and got out a huge, badly done collage of me glued on brown cardboard.'

On getting back to Manchester we took 'The Bushometer' out and burned it. It had done its job. The quest was at an end.

20. THE DAY I WENT TO CROPREDY

I've been in a band since I was fourteen years old and formed Berlin Airlift with my school mates Ross Warburton, Andy Wright and, sadly, the late Jimmy Leslie. I'd never been good enough at sport to warrant being included in a proper team, and always rather envied those who experienced the special camaraderie you get when you're all pushing towards a common goal. Once I was in a band, though, I realized that here was the gang I'd been looking for.

Bands are small private clubs in which peculiar roles apply, unspoken hierarchies prevail, despite lip service being paid to the vague notion of democracy, and shared adventures are guaranteed. Since I discovered all that, a band is just something I've had to have to make life seem complete.

My first book was devoted to the succession of no-hope rock bands I've been in throughout my life, and on the last page a new outfit called The Family Mahone was formed. This group, though not what you'd call massively successful, is now ten years old and has taken us to Glastonbury, and the Cambridge and Cropredy folk festivals, and seen the release of three albums, some of which have sold over a thousand copies. I know that might not sound like a lot to you, but there are groups on major labels who dream of sales figures like that, though admittedly they don't tend to hang around too long. Not for ten years anyway.

The Family Mahone began when I left Manchester behind in 1996 and moved to a picturesque village in Cheshire called Great Budworth. On the corner of the High Street, opposite the church, is a pub called the George and Dragon. Being new to the locale I often went in there on my own for a pint, knowing full well that it would only be a matter of time before I would start to get to know all the people in the area worth knowing, because obviously, people who didn't drop in for a pint at the village pub probably didn't fall into that category.

The George, and its relaxed rural approach to the licensing laws, became a fairly central part of my social life for a few years and it was here that I met Don. He was a sizable, ruddy-faced chap with a constant smile on his face that may have been the result of the constant pint that was in his hand. He knew vaguely who I was and, sharing the same keen interest in music, we regularly found ourselves in the back bar discussing the latest albums we'd heard. Occasionally we would talk about other stuff like kids and football and work, but it was mostly music. Well, I say that, but Don talked quite a lot about his fledgling computer-design business in monologues that could last up to twenty minutes, as he seemed to be able to breathe through his ears while talking continuously. As I couldn't find a gap in what he was saying to interrupt him, and being something of a Luddite, I tended to switch off during these speeches and so even though we've been good friends for well over ten years, I'm still not exactly sure what he does.

At the back of my new house was a large wooden shed with insulation and mains electricity that the previous resident had used as a workshop. Showing me round the property he was justly proud of this facility and said that it would obviously be a great place for me to keep all my tools. As all the tools I possessed at that point fitted in a carrier bag that I kept under the kitchen sink this seemed to be a waste of a lot of space. It looked like a great drum room though.

Being a drummer there's only so much playing you can do on your own. You can spend hours perfecting paradiddles, whatever they might be, and you can thump along to your favourite records. I've worked out a lot of frustrations that way. Eventually, though, you are going to need a band, and so Don came round with his guitar. Initially we were going to form a simple guitar, drums and bass trio with my great friend Andy on bass, once we'd borrowed one for him to play. I didn't want to sing, and neither did Andy, which left Don as the Kurt Cobain of the operation, although it soon became apparent that the only thing Don and Kurt had in common was that they both owned a plaid shirt. One small, the other extra large. As a lead vocalist Don was, shall we say, reticent. He had a huge box of effects and devices through which he fed his guitar yet, rather than instantaneously creating waves of glorious processed noise, these gadgets just seemed to give him something to fiddle with, shaking his head and tutting, without actually doing any proper playing. He also had his own microphone and whoever bought it off him second-hand, rather like someone buying a car from an ageing vicar, must have got a real bargain, as it was very low mileage. After rehearsing for about a month on Monday nights Andy turned to me, strawberry-blond goatee and curls shimmering in the Cheshire moonlight as we walked up the hill to the accompaniment of the echoes from the heels of his cowboy boots, heading for the George, and said, 'D'you think he's going to actually sing next week?'

I think it was at that moment I realized we were going to have to change direction. The last thing the world needed was a band of three dads doing classic rock covers. Especially with a lead vocalist who didn't show much inclination to sing.

At that time I'd rediscovered the early albums of The Pogues, and thought they might provide some material. After all, who doesn't like to hear a few diddly-diddly drinking songs when they've had a couple? Don seemed enthused at this prospect, as he too was a real fan of Shane MacGowan's songwriting. Andy was, I think, less sold on the idea but as he was the bass player, we didn't really worry too much about that. So we began to talk about a mixture of Shane originals and traditional Irish songs we thought we might be able to stumble through, and were overheard by the landlord Malcolm who said, 'Well, if you're playing all that stuff, I'll put you on in here on St Patrick's Day.'

So that was that. We had a gig to work towards in about three months' time. Simple. Except that the three of us had no chance of doing justice to that material as 'The Irish Rover' is generally little enhanced by a Telecaster treated with flange, fuzz and phasing. New recruits were going to have to be drafted in, and I knew exactly where to start.

Christy is a studio engineer at the BBC who has worked with me for longer than anyone. He could have had the misfortune of hearing more of what I've had to say than any other living soul, were it not for the fact that though he's sat on the other side of the glass for all those years, for most of it he's been watching the telly mounted high up on the studio wall. And who can blame him?

When not engrossed in repeats of *The Rockford Files*, Christy can usually be found accessing websites of particular interest on the internet. These sites cater for a very particular kind of perversion and might be loosely gathered together under the banner of 'mandolin porn'. That he is an accomplished player of this instrument is not in question, but his hours spent in front of the screen slavering at the contours of a 1922 Gibson F5 bear witness to an obsession. If we fall out before this book comes out I will revisit this paragraph and publish his address and then international mandolin thieves will descend on his house at 17 Cross Keys Street and have a field day with his pretty much unrivalled collection. He has more stringed musical instruments of all descriptions than most music shops, and spends nearly as much time playing and caring for them as he does using his teenage daughter's straighteners to tame the grey bush of hair that sits lopsidedly on his head.

I put the idea of the gig at the George to Christy and, being an absolute glutton for punishment and more addicted perhaps even than me to being in bands, he agreed immediately. He also said that he knew an accordion player, and that he'd bring him along too. This was really good news, as we now had a fighting chance of re-creating the sound of The Pogues.

The following Monday night we assembled in the hut where Cheshire's finest array of ratchet spanners had once adorned the walls. I had taken delivery from the good folk of Yahama of what is known as a cocktail kit, which basically means you can play standing up. This I was keen to do as The Pogues' drummer Andrew 'The Clobberer' Ranken had done. With just a floor tom-tom and snare, he had beaten out the ferocious, marching-band beat that had propelled their early classics and I saw no reason to veer away from that. This also enabled me to become the lead singer. I remember this coming about because I was the only member of the band who didn't absolutely refuse to do it, though the rest of them might have different memories of how that decision was arrived at and put it down to the ego having landed. To be fair to myself, there was a definite shortage of candidates. Christy and Andy didn't want to do it, Don had already tried the role on for size and found it ill fitting, which left the only other contender as the new boy on the piano accordion.

Rusty was a rover with a busking pedigree. He was a toby jug of a man – small, pot-bellied and frequently full of liquid. He was the only one of us to make a living out of music in that his gigs and street appearances afforded him the price of his rent with a modest state handout covering a few essentials like beer, fags and more beer. And more fags. Gnarled, with shoulder-length wavy hair, it was easy to picture him in a tricorn hat and waistcoat smoking a clay pipe, and he brought some much needed degeneracy to the ranks. He didn't fancy being the lead singer however, as he wanted to leave the gaps between songs for drinking and didn't want to have to talk to the audience. He would later find gaps within the songs in which to drink as well. He did agree to sing 'All For Me Grog', but otherwise it looked like the lead-vocal chores were down to me. What a good job I was so fond of the sound of my own voice. Even if no one else was.

First rehearsals with a new band are always cagey affairs. Members might not know each other and so there's always a bit of sniffing around like dogs in the park, though no bottoms were involved and no one got bitten. The first song the five of us thought we might be able to get through was Shane MacGowan's 'Streams of Whiskey', so I counted four and we leaped into the unknown. It went all right, thankfully, so we ran through perhaps seven others that sounded more or less the same and then went to the pub. Oh the joy. We had a new band, a gig, and about half an hour's material, which we considered more than enough. Then, as the first pints of Gravedigger's were plonked on the Formica-topped table, Andy informed us that he was leaving the north of England to go back to his beloved Bristol. This meant we would have to make our first line-up change before we'd even played our first gig, though he did say he would return to fulfil that one-night commitment. The ever-resourceful Christy, being a seasoned musician with lots of contacts on the folk scene, said that we didn't need to worry because he knew someone who'd be perfectly happy to step in. And that was where Doc came in.

The following week Doc turned up at rehearsal to listen to the racket we were making so he would know it when the time came for him to step into the bass player's snakeskin, Cuban-heeled Chelsea boots. Not that Doc was really a fancy-footwear kind of guy. An internationally renowned expert on train brakes and a management consultant, he had a wise and steady head on his shoulders, and some ginger hair on top of that. At later gigs he would be accused of looking like Paul Scholes's dad, which for a Liverpool fan was quite a cutting jibe. Doc and Christy were actually already band-mates in the folk group Full House, and could play a variety of instruments. It was therefore decided that rather than just sit and witness Andy grappling with the bass in search of the right notes, Doc would busk along on fiddle and banjo. Well, as soon as he started playing it was apparent that he brought so much to the sound that he would be wasted on bass. It was like hiring Michelangelo and getting him to finish off your painting-by-numbers. Well, perhaps that's overstating it slightly, but it was certainly akin to bringing in Rolf Harris to emulsion the back bedroom. We therefore needed another bass player and decided on a lad in our office called Sickly Rob, who had much to recommend him for the role as, rather like Andy, he didn't know the songs and didn't own a bass.

So now we were six, or rather seven. Because Christy, Rusty and Doc had to commute from Chester to rehearse, and because they all liked a pint or two, there could con-ceivably have been logistical problems had it not been for the key member of the clan. I've always considered the van driver to be the vital cog in the mechanism when it comes to beat groups, because you might be the finest set of musicians in the world but no one will ever know unless you can get out of the shed and onto the road. Yes, you could drive yourself but that would mean you couldn't have a drink, so what would be the point in that exactly? No matter how good you think you are, it always sounds a lot better after a few jars, or at least that's what you're hoping the audience will think. If it hadn't been for Jock we'd still be rehearsing in the shed, which would come as a bit of a shock to the present owner as I moved out several years ago.

Jock was that rarest of beasts, a teetotal Scotsman whose hobby was driving a minibus, and for a band to find someone like that is like winning the lottery. The phrase 'bear of a man' could have been invented for him, as he had a physique that tested the seam strength of the extra-large burgundy sweatshirts available to members of Chester Accordion Society, and he was also regularly baited by Christy. The final piece of the jigsaw had slotted into place and so we loaded up the van and in high spirits travelled to our first gig.

Travel time to the gig is always underestimated. I don't know why, it's just one of the rules of the road. No matter what time you set off, you will always arrive late for the sound check. On this occasion we had failed to allow for the journey being predominantly uphill, so the trip lasted about three minutes instead of the anticipated ninety seconds.

That night at the George the back bar was packed beyond capacity and a room that would comfortably hold thirty people played host to perhaps fifty or sixty. Condensation ran down the walls as we rushed through our seven or eight songs then had a four-pint beer break before playing them all again. They sounded great the second time.

And that was really going to be that. We had formed to play at the George and Dragon on St Patrick's Day 1998 and, having done that, it was unclear what the future held, if anything. Yet somehow, ten years on, we are still going. And with a proper bass player.

Charlie was another BBC studio manager who'd had the double misfortune to look after countless hours of my programmes, and also to play in a band with me called The Hunks of Burning Love. He had also engineered the first Family Mahone album, recorded in stolen BBC studio time in the dead of night. A jovial, flaxen-haired, middle-aged cherub of a chap, he proved something of a shock to the system when he joined, as he not only had several basses, but also knew the songs better than some of us who were in the band already. It was at this point we became aware that if we weren't careful we were in danger of becoming quite good.

As you might reasonably expect, there have been many, many gigs, travels and adventures over a decade. Doc estimates we've played live about 150 times and I tend to trust him on these things as he's probably got a spreadsheet to back up his figures. We've worked a lot around the Northwest, making regular visits to favourite haunts such as Telford's Warehouse in Chester, the Crewe Limelight club and Kendal's Brewery Arts Centre, where it has become a band tradition to share a dorm in the youth hostel next door. You don't get a lot of sleep but the experience makes us feel as giddy as when we were on school camp thirty-five years ago. In fact, last time we went there we had sold out in advance and the promoter offered us rooms in a nearby country house hotel. To his surprise we declined. It just wouldn't have been the same.

We've also covered huge swathes of the Midlands, North Wales and Anglesey, and occasionally visited the distant lowlands of the south to perform in London village. In fact, having not been to the capital since playing with Shane MacGowan at the Shepherd's Bush Empire in 2004, we recently celebrated our tenth anniversary by playing on St Patrick's Day 2008 at Dingwall's on Camden Lock.

We've also enjoyed our trips to the far north, having become more or less the house band at the gloriously located and fabulously friendly Loopallu festival in Ullapool, and watched pods of killer whales dance down the harbour from our hotel bedroom windows in Lerwick.

In Leeds we were part of perhaps the strangest bill we've ever played on. At a freshers' ball at the Metropolitan University we were booked to appear with a pre-Take That revival Mark Owen, Walthamstow hoody pop gnomes East 17, but without either of the two lead singers, and the Cheeky Girls, unfortunately with both lead singers. On arrival I asked the social secretary what time we'd be performing.

'I've got you down for one-thirty,' he replied chirpily.

'What, in the morning?' I expostulated. 'Are you mad?'

'Is that a problem?'

'By half-one tomorrow morning the members of this band will either be leathered or fast asleep, and quite possibly both. Can't you put us on a bit earlier? The Cheeky Girls aren't here yet and they're younger than us and so can stay up later. And another thing, we've got to get back to Chester and go to work in the morning. The Cheeky Girls won't be getting in a van to go back to Transylvania, will they? They've probably got a Travelodge or something.'

'Oh, go on then, you can go on at half-eight.'

Result. We therefore played five hours earlier than planned, to pretty much an empty hall, and left with our money at ten o'clock. Later that night, as I rose from my slumbers to take another nocturnal trip to the bathroom, I glanced at the clock and saw that it was a quarter to two. As I stumbled back to bed and dragged the duvet around me I was so grateful not to be on stage over the Pennines in front of a gaggle of inebriated undergraduates who were miffed to discover that the only two they recognized out of East 17 were the backing dancers.

Mind you, I'm not criticizing anyone for drinking. Though I drink a fraction of what I did in the early days of the band, boozing has been a central tenet of our existence. There is a generally accepted rule that you need three pints, at least, before you feel in the right zone to go on and play. Often, like the three slices of pizza rule (as if you eat four you feel too stuffed to give it your all), these regulations are flouted. At St Helen's Citadel one Christmas a bottle of absinthe was introduced into the mix. This had a noted effect on several of our number, most particularly myself. The concert ended when I tried, in my haze, to sit on a stool behind the drum kit. This proved a miscalculation, as it wasn't so much that the stool wasn't there any more, but rather that it had never been there in the first place. Losing my balance in front of three hundred paying customers I keeled over backwards, pulling the drums, microphones and strings of fairy lights with me. I'm not proud of this. It is hardly dignified behaviour for a fifty-year-old father of three and I think that explains why I tried to hide my embarrassment by making camp under the overcoats in the bottom of a large cloaks cupboard in the dressing room. For over an hour.

Perhaps the pinnacle, or nadir, of our drinking prowess came at another freshers' event at an agricultural university somewhere in deepest, darkest Shropshire. We had in fact played there once before and enjoyed a lovely day out for part of which we had exclusive use of the dodgems while the students were having their dinner. On this occasion proceedings didn't appear so well organized. The committee had set up a stage and PA system, but had forgotten to sort out any lighting. This was resolved by a burly bloke in a rugby shirt and kilt driving a mud-splattered old Land Rover into the marquee and turning its headlights on in the direction of the stage. That's the kind of place it was.

We did our sound check and then retired to a nearby pub to enjoy a handsome four-course meal accompanied by fine wines and liqueurs. The 'three pint and three slices of pizza' rules having been abandoned, we returned to the venue at around ten only to be told that things had been running a bit late, which came as no surprise, and that we wouldn't be required to play until half past midnight. In contrast to the Leeds situation, this filled us with utter glee as it enabled us to start on the generous drinks rider that had been laid on back-stage. The whole site was awash with booze. Students were queuing at what was billed as a cocktail bar. In reality this consisted of dustbins filled with all manner of spirits and sold in plastic glasses for eight pounds a pint. It had been calculated that each glass contained twelve pub measures. There were people there who could barely see, let alone walk. For their own benefit I can only hope they couldn't hear too well either.

Back in the dressing room we had fallen on the combination of Guinness and Baileys. Initially decorum had prevailed and we had imbibed these unlikely bedfellows of the alcoholic world in separate glasses. As time wore on though, and half past midnight came and went, it was suggested that it was easier if you just put both drinks into a single pint pot. The curdling effect that was all too visible did give you some indication of what was going on inside your stomach. Still, there wasn't time to worry about details like that as there was a gig to do. Or at least there would be once the crucial game of ice-cube cricket had been completed. This involved ice cubes being 'bowled' towards a 'batsman' brandishing a tray, who would then score four if he could knock the frozen block out of the skylight. Engrossed, we finally made the stage at around one forty-five, having made the dubious last-minute decision to alter the set-list to include lots of songs we hadn't played for months. Well, it probably didn't matter, as we couldn't remember the ones we'd played the previous week either. At least the cocktail bar didn't run dry.

The evening finished with Jock, the only sober one, losing his footing and crashing down into the backstage mud. Accordingly he drove us back to the hotel bare-chested, though I didn't initially realize this as he had so much wiry hair on his upper body that I just assumed he was wearing an Angora sweater. Once back at our accommodation I downed a quick Armagnac before bidding everyone good morning and going off to enjoy a couple of hours of much needed sleep. On the stairs.

The gig that I hold perhaps most dear came in 2004 when we first played at the Cropredy festival. Held in the lustrous Oxfordshire countryside near Banbury, it is curated by the seminal folk-rock band Fairport Convention. For Doc and Christy, who had grown up listening to Fairport, this was one of the highlights of their lives and their excitement was infectious.

Having arrived late the previous night after doing a radio show in Manchester and sharing Christy's camper van, I emerged on the Friday morning to take in the scene. To be honest, I was unprepared for how big it was. It was no Glastonbury or anything, but there were 15,000 people in attendance and, as there is only the one stage, they would all be forced to watch us. As I wandered the site it became apparent just what a responsibility this was. Even the bar was completely open-air. If it rained, or you didn't like the music, it was tough. We were all stuck with each other. There was simply nowhere else to go.

Playing at festivals is always a bit unnerving as not only are the crowds much bigger than you're used to seeing, but you also tend not to get a chance to balance your sound before you play, as bands just roll on and off all day. This is doubly stressful, as you not only feel unsettled by the sight of people stretching far into the distance, but the sound coming through the monitor speakers can sound like a different band completely until they get it sorted out by the third or fourth song.

We took to the stage in fine weather, shouted a cheery hello, rolled up our sleeves and cracked into the first song. It's at moments like this that being in a band makes your nerve ends tingle like nothing else I've ever experienced. It also makes you feel very close to the guys on stage with you. You're in it together and you're utterly dependent on each other to make it work. I imagine Doc the management consultant might call it 'team building'.

We were onstage for a mammoth hour and a quarter, which is a very long time to be on the only stage at a festival where most of the people haven't heard you before. Because our music is a rousing, raggle-taggle racket we anticipated a few hundred party animals jigging around in the pit, but it took us a while to win over the more sedate section of the crowd sitting in their foldable chairs away up the vale. Gradually, however, you could see sandals and socks begin to tap, straw hats begin to nod and polypins of ale starting to be quaffed. We were winning them over and it felt fantastic.

For me, it was especially pleasurable as we were playing lots of songs that I'd written myself. It's an amazing feeling to come up with something and play it to the boys and for them to then take it up and run with it, making it sound much, much better. For me, this is the collaborative part of the process. I've never been able to sit down and write with anyone else, as it's such a personal and protracted experience. Having said that, Christy and I wrote ten songs in a week for an album we made as a fictitious beat group of the sixties called The Four Counts. I actually like those songs a lot and it proves that you can produce quality very quickly under the right circumstances, or how else do you explain that album achieving worldwide sales approaching seventy copies?

And that's really why life without a band, without this band, is unimaginable to me. To stand on stage at Cropredy that day and to hear our crew in full flight performing tunes I'd knocked together in my back kitchen while 15,000 people drank it all in, well, it was a long way from the back bar of the George. Even Jock had a cider.

21. THE DAY MY MOTHER HIT ME WITH A GOLF CLUB

I have only twice in my life suffered visible head trauma.

The first occasion was when I stuck the suction pad of a baby's rattle to my forehead in an attempt to entertain the infant Jessica Michaelides with a Dalek-like appendage. Once the gurgling and giggling had subsided, mission accomplished, I reached for the toy and attempted to prise it off. This proved considerably more difficult than it should have been. It was the early eighties and I can't be sure that superglue was widely available, but it was as if some had been smeared onto the sucker, as in the base of the novelty and not the foolhardy wearer, such was the degree of grip it had taken on the front of my head. As Jessica's parents Tony and Marie took turns at trying to end my ordeal, using all the strength they could muster while laughing hysterically, I could feel a distinct tingling on the skin.

Finally, by pooling their joint strength, the limpet rattle eventually relinquished its hold with a loud pop, and Tony and Marie fell backwards into the Welsh dresser. However, one look at their faces, with tears of mirth streaming down their reddened cheeks, told me that all was not well.

'I think you'd better look in the mirror, Mark.'

There in the centre of my forehead was a perfect circle of deep crimson. Burst blood vessels, I suppose. In a way it was quite beautiful, as if the sun had set just above my eyebrows. I toyed with the idea of painting Japanese lettering across it and trying to pass it off as some mysterious martial arts symbol, thinking that people would be loath to make fun of me in case I proved to be a grandmaster of the ancient oriental art of tearing your arm off and shoving it down your throat.

Thankfully the facial Jupiter red spot went down of its own accord after only two or three weeks, but those weeks were spent in full-time employment at Manchester's Piccadilly Radio, where I had to explain what had happened to naturally inquisitive interviewees on a daily basis. I thought about telling people it was a birthmark, but that was difficult with colleagues who'd known me beforehand, as birthmarks rarely spring up on people who are in their early twenties.

The other time my forehead was subjected to an unprovoked attack was on a pitch-and-putt course in Southport, and it is this incident that probably lies at the root of my deep distrust of golf.

The Radcliffe family holidays of my childhood were perfectly normal affairs. We didn't go abroad until I was fourteen, but then, no one did really. Well, only rich people, and we certainly didn't fall into that category. We weren't poor or anything. I'm not attempting to paint myself as a working-class hero because I am neither heroic, nor working class, but then, neither was John Lennon really. Imagine no possessions? Yes, John, but what were you going to fill all those apartments in the Dakota Building with? All the bread you'd baked?

My family lived a comfortable semi-detached existence and we had our own car and everything, but we weren't well off. I knew this because we had some family friends, or possibly distant relations, who lived near Harrogate and were somehow connected to Tetley's brewery. I had no idea what 'rich' meant until I visited their house. I'd been to smaller places on school trips.

Actually though, I'm pretty sure the Radcliffes were a rich dynasty once upon a time because should you undertake a comprehensive tour of the many and varied tourist attractions Bolton has to offer, as I'm sure you will, you'll be paying a visit to the Tudor manor Smithill's Hall. Here, over the main fireplace, hang coats of arms of notable families of the time, and the noble heraldic shield of the Radcliffes hangs there proudly. By rights, I'm pretty sure we should be able to claim that house as a holiday home or something, at least in a time-share arrangement with the other, probably lesser, families hanging there. Alas, no such law appears to exist and so we are left to relative penury, denied our birthright, the family fortune lost. Well, unless it's under my dad's mattress.

In the absence of the misplaced private income and army of dutiful footmen, our holidays were taken at guesthouses and bed and breakfasts at a variety of English resorts. Often these would be on the south coast, in order to maximize the journey time, possibly to cut the number of days spent at the resort, thereby minimizing expenditure.

There didn't seem to be all that many motorways in operation in the late sixties either, so a trip from Bolton to, say, Bournemouth would take approximately a day and a half. Or so it seemed. These days, car journeys are comparatively painless for kids. They are normally lounging on seats you'd have to pay first-class fares for in a 747, watching DVDs out of one eye while texting or playing hand-held video games with the other.

Due to flooding, it once took me and my wife about eight hours to do the normal two-hour hop from Cheshire to Anglesey. My two youngest daughters, Mia and Rose, spent the trip happily reclining on their banquettes watching a DVD playing from a machine that sat on a small coffee table,

enjoying a range of M&S finger foods. It was as if they had
their own loft-style apartment back there. I know that sounds
like we had a really posh, expensive car, but we didn't. We
had a scraped Sharan, the DVD player was eighty quid from
Argos, and, not being in the habit of furnishing our vehicles
from Ikea, the coffee table was on its way to a more permanent home. What I'm saying is that road travel for nippers is
a doddle compared to how it was when we were small,
although perhaps the balance is being redressed now that
journey times are again increasing due to the number of cars
on the road and the fact that the Highways Agency insist on
closing the motorway every time someone loses a wheel nut.

In-car entertainment in my young days consisted of, if
you were lucky, a crackly AM radio, punching my sister in
the thigh and a *Big Chief I-Spy* book. These publications
were a series of pamphlets intended to give kids something to
look out for on endless road trips. They were available in a
range of fascinating subjects including road signs, trees and
makes of lorry. All you had to do was sit quietly staring out
of the window, pencil in hand, waiting for the sight of an
adverse camber sign, silver birch or Bedford TJ6, and you'd
be in Bournemouth in no time. The hours just flew by. Now,
I'm prepared to accept that somewhere there were swotty
kids, probably eager contestants on *Ask the Family*, for whom
this plan was perfectly executed every single time. Perhaps
there were eager beavers who stayed silent and vigilant just
hoping for a glimpse of a Foden S36 flatbed somewhere
between Carlisle and Polperro. I tried valiantly, really I did,
but it just didn't have the same appeal as flicking elastic bands
at my sister Jaine's ears.

The weirdest thing about these *Big Chief I-Spy* books was
that we were encouraged to believe there was an actual Red
Indian chief overseeing all this spotting stuff. If you spotted
everything in whichever book you happened to be on, you

sent it off to Big Chief I-Spy, who would send you something back. I forget what it was now, but it was probably a
badge or certificate or something. I know it can't have been
anything exciting because if it had been a genuine bit of
Red Indian paraphernalia, I might have tried a bit harder. My
sister would have had to share her Maltesers if threatened
with a genuine tomahawk. So I never bothered sending anything off to this great Sitting Bull of the English trunk-road
network. And to be honest, even at the age of nine I was
sceptical about his existence. The idea that a fearsome
Mohawk warlord would give up scalping and squawing for a
desk job in the Home Counties seemed unlikely to say the
least.

Another difference between my young travelling days and
the present is the markedly different attitude towards child
safety. Nowadays, no right-minded person sets out without
making sure any small child is strapped into a seat that would
probably survive atmospheric re-entry. Back then, you just
chucked all the kids in the back and let them fight it out. If
it all got too much for my younger brother Joe, he would
complete the journey on my mum's knee in the front passenger seat, where he could gleefully reach for the handbrake
or gear stick being wholly unencumbered by a seatbelt. I'm
not trying to suggest that my parents weren't bothered about
our well-being, it was just that nobody seemed to give it
much thought. To be fair, there wasn't much more consideration given to the seating arrangements for the adults. Most
cars had simple, vinyl, low-backed, non-adjustable chairs
without any refinements whatsoever. A headrest was seen as
the height of luxury. Even if you could never quite get your
head to rest on it. So my mum and dad didn't travel in appre-
ciably greater comfort than we did. Well, not until we got the
Cortina anyway.

The Cortina was a bit of a break with tradition in our

family, as we'd always had Volkswagens up to that point. This Cortina, a silver Mark II model, had an irresistible selling point though. It had, and if you could pause briefly here to give this moment the drama it deserves I'd appreciate it, reclining front seats. Unbelievable. Just one lift of a little lever and you could lean right back as if you were in the dentist's chair, all in the comfort of your own car. How about that?

My dad was quite ridiculously pleased with this innovation and it led to one of the strangest memories I have of Radcliffe family trips. We were going to London to see something or other. The Trooping of the Colour, perhaps. Something you could watch for free anyway. The night before we were due to go, we were playing out in the street when my mum appeared with a thrilling announcement.

'We're going to go now and travel overnight.'

These days lots of people do that to get a clear run, but back then it was a fantastically romantic notion. And if it was dark there was no way you could do a *Big Chief I-Spy* airborne gnats book, so mindless violence against my sister was the only obvious alternative. Brilliant!

The thing that made the trip memorable for me though wasn't the night riding, or the sights and sounds of the capital, but the sleeping arrangements. We couldn't go straight from Bolton to London without a stop-off. It was nearly two hundred miles, for goodness' sake. You didn't tackle distances like that in one go. Accordingly we pulled into a motorway service station and prepared to bed down . . . in the car. My dad had decided this was possible because, and I know you're ahead of me here, we had reclining seats. This meant that my mother and father could recline to what looked like a peculiarly back-breaking posture, while Jaine and I dossed down head to toe, top to tail, on the back seat, millimetres from the tops of our parents' heads. My young brother Joe was installed in splendid isolation on the parcel

shelf. That is to say the three- to four-inch ledge you find
behind the rear seats in a standard family saloon. We knew
how to live. Roll on breakfast.

The next morning we rose refreshed after two and a half
hours restless dozing, interrupted only by yelps as one of us
kicked some part of someone else, and congratulated ourselves on being up in time to watch dawn break. We
subsequently reached journey's end exhausted and fractious,
though to be honest, that pretty much describes the relationship I enjoyed with my sister at the best of times.

I can't remember what we had for breakfast, but most of
our meals were prepared by my mum on a Primus stove in a
Quality Street tin to keep the wind off. Of course, the fare
on offer to families in those days bore little resemblance to
what you can get now. Not for us the Captain Barnacle
young pirate platter with free eye patch and colouring book.
No way did we get the Luke Skywalker Junior Galactic
Warrior Cheesy Feast Star Pizza with complimentary light-
sabre cutlery.

In the sixties and early seventies the dining-out options for
families were, to say the least, limited. There were self-serv-
ice cafeterias serving fish and chips, sausage and chips or egg
and chips; tea shops serving fish and chips or sandwiches;
cafes with waitresses serving fish and chips or pie and chips;
Berni Inns, for special occasions, serving fish and chips, steak
and chips, or gammon, egg and chips, and fish and chip
shops serving . . . well, you get the picture. Oh, and pubs.
Which served beer. And lemonade and crisps to children
provided they didn't actually enter the bar area.

None of this was actually my parents' fault, you understand. In truth, I think we fared better than most. At least we
had regular holidays, and looking back, some of them can't
have been a barrel of laughs for my mum and dad. I recall
one holiday in a bed and breakfast near Swanage where they

slept on a camp bed in front of the property's only television set. They had to wait for all the other guests to retire before they could start letting the bed settee down and making preparations for the night. Oh, for a reclining seat.

I'm also haunted by the thoughts of a fortnight in a guest-house in Morecambe that was a perfectly nice establishment that had few rules apart from 'No dogs'. You can guess what we did, can't you? That's right. We took the dog, a cute but irascible West Highland terrier called Rags. He had to be smuggled in and out of the place in a shopping bag. No, really. If the proprietor of the digs caught sight of us playing with him on the beach, we just had to pretend he belonged to someone else. No, really.

But all those sunny weeks, smothered in calamine lotion to tackle the prickly heat, are treasured times. Babbacombe, Ilfracombe, Widdecombe, Castle Combe – you name it, if it ended in Combe we went and had good, simple, fun family holidays there. Even if it did take us half a week to get there. They were wonderful times. Well, except for Southport.

I've actually got a great deal of affection for Southport, with its colonnaded shopping arcades and promenade nowhere near the actual sea. It's a place where you can still feel the dignity and grandeur of the Victorian seaside resort. However, it is also a place of particular horror, for it is here that my mother hit me with a golf club.

It was on a windswept pitch-and-putt course that she half brained me to death. She didn't mean to. I was just standing too close on the sixth tee and got caught in the forehead with the full force of her backswing. It created a lump the size of a tangerine, which might not sound too dramatic, but my head was itself only about the size of a grapefruit at that time. In the ensuing days this pulsating growth turned all kinds of lurid colours, from vivid purple to phlegm yellow. I felt sure it was going to burst and cover everyone in a thirty-foot radius with noxious slime. It didn't, of course. It disappeared like the suction circle from Jessica's rattle, leaving only the mental scars.

Overall, you'd have to say that if that's the worst memory from fourteen or fifteen years of family holidays, then that's pretty good going. More than that though, there's a really positive side to this story. Just after my mum's club had connected with my frontal lobe, my dad helpfully smacked me on the rear of my head for 'getting in the way'. Inspired. Quite what effect he thought this would have on me I don't know. Having felt the impact of an Exocet missile on the front of my bonce, it was obviously going to make little difference getting a clout from his hand on the back. The effect on him though was quite profound. So racked by guilt was he, and remains to this day, that he never took up playing golf. Equally scarred for life, neither did I. If that's not something to be happy about then I don't know what is.

22. THE DAY I SAVED NEIL HANNON'S BACON

My television career need not detain us long. In a cheap and nasty bright-green shirt I hosted a series about football with Marc Riley, wearing a cheap and nasty bright-yellow shirt, called *Match of the Nineties*. For the first few episodes of this we appeared to be avoiding eye contact either with the camera or each other, leading people to speculate that we'd fallen out in a big way. We hadn't. We'd simply been told that in television you do something called 'cheating the angle'. This involves turning half towards each other and half towards the camera so that on screen it looks like you're having a cosy chat, but you can still see plenty of face. Well, either they got it wrong or we did as the end result looked like two delegates at a village idiot convention staring into the middle distance and talking to no one in particular.

Another triumph co-hosted with Marc was *Pop Upstairs Downstairs*, a title that makes very little sense to this day. This project was basically a pop quiz based on *University Challenge*, except in our version one team really did sit on top of the other thanks to a job lot of scaffolding we had delivered to the studio. I also sat above Marc in a sort of double-decker garden shed. That was where the 'upstairs/downstairs' bit came in, though I have no idea why it was set in a garden.

This programme was actually moderately successful by the standards of the fledgling digital channel UK Play, now BBC3, and ran for about three years. Not that this involved much of a commitment from us as they were all filmed across one weekend and then just got shown over and over again. You might reasonably consider this to be quite a lucrative project thanks to the accumulation of repeat fees. You'd be wrong. Checking back through contractual documents in the name of exhaustive research I can reveal that the figure we got every time one of those shows was repeated was £0. Mind you, that was each.

I also hosted four series of *The White Room* for Channel 4. This was actually a pretty good music show with terrific staging, brilliant lights and mercifully short links. They also got me some new suits specially made to measure by a bloke in leather trousers and shark's-tooth necklaces called, rather wonderfully, Kaveh Savage. Suitably attired in emerald-green velveteen or shiny silver-grey, I got the chance to introduce the likes of Prince, Bowie, Stevie Wonder, Pulp, Oasis and Iggy Pop in alarming transparent trousers. I'm a big fan of Iggy but I remember thinking that the primal beat of 'Lust for Life' was little enhanced by the sight of a gyrating pensioner's shrink-wrapped genitals. I also got to introduce Little Richard, who took issue with me calling him 'one of the godfathers of rock and roll', and made me do it again losing the words 'one of' and the 's' off 'godfathers'. Fair enough. Chuck and Jerry Lee weren't there to argue the toss and I certainly wasn't going to argue with him. I know he's only small, but he had a wild look in his eye and I didn't want to run the risk of being nutted by a quiff with that much lacquer on it. Even if it would have only hit me in the sternum.

I thought, and hoped, that *The White Room* might last a very long time, as *Later with Jools Holland* has, but it wasn't to

be. I don't know why really, though I did warn them against
booking East 17 for what became the last series.

That I never secured a regular job on telly I now look
upon as a bit of a blessing, to be honest. So many DJs I used
to know seemed far more intent on getting a game show
than actually concentrating on playing good records. Radio
they saw as the poor relation to the great god television, and
was just something you had to do to get noticed by the TV
bosses. I could never understand that. All I've ever wanted was
to play the best music I could possibly find and to have a bit
of a laugh in between, and not being on the telly has enabled
me to keep doing that. Well, perhaps I'm not being entirely
candid there. Somewhere lie the tapes of countless rejected
pilot shows for television including 'Mark and Lard's Chat
Show' and the big-budget team game 'Conspiracy Theory',
in which Marc had a small island built on his head so that he
could emerge from a large tank of water representing the
Bermuda Triangle. Inspired. But uncommissioned.

The only television presenting I've ever really enjoyed has
been from festivals. I've had two stints hosting Glastonbury,
firstly for Channel 4 in the early nineties, and then again
when I was given a surprise recall by BBC 2. It meant access
all areas at the festival, a bit of cash, free food and drink, and
very little work. What's not to like? As it turned out I finished up being on screen quite a lot and, unlike the other
in-vision work I've done, nerves don't seem to trouble me at
all. I don't suppose it's all that surprising. All you've got to do
is sit in your wellies on a big ethnic futon that might have
come from Lenny Kravitz's bedchamber, swig a pint of Black
Sheep and chat about bands with the fragrant Jo Whiley.
Occasionally I might find myself in the company of the
equally fragrant Lauren Laverne or the only slightly less fragrant Phill Jupitus, with whom I took time out from the
festival site a couple of years ago to visit a local shoe museum.

It's usually me who ends up doing the helicopter links too, and though I tried to get out of it last time I was told I had to do it as Jo was afraid of going up there, Lauren was pregnant and they weren't sure if they could fit Phill inside it.

I've also been a regular presenter of the television coverage of the Cambridge Folk Festival on BBC4. This event happens at the end of July and is pretty much my favourite weekend of the year. It's set in the grounds of Cherry Hinton Hall in parkland on the outskirts of the city, and is a place of annual pilgrimage for around 10,000 good-natured souls. Coming off the back of Glastonbury's 120,000 punters the previous month, it always feels like a bit of a holiday. It's also a relatively small site, which restricts the numbers and makes it easy to get around. If you want to see a troupe of Hungarian gypsy fiddlers on the second stage at twenty past two, and who wouldn't, you don't need to leave the beer tent until quarter past. If you want to see a band on an outlying stage at Glastonbury at twenty past two, and the weather's as bad as it usually is, you have to set off the previous day. Last time I was there I decided to go and have a look at the newly installed Park Stage. It was muddy underfoot which meant sticking, often literally, to the already thronging paths, as cutting across the fields ran the risk of sinking into unseen pools of dubious slurry. It took me about an hour and a half to get there and on arrival I was greeted by the sight and sound of Chas and Dave. Now, I have no particular aversion to this pair of gruff Cockney gargoyles, and might even wander into a pub where they were appearing and down a couple of convivial pints of London Pride to the strains of 'Gertcha', but I didn't consider their oeuvre to be adequate reward for the routemarch I'd just undertaken. Cambridge is big enough to feel like it matters, but small enough to be easily manageable. Not unlike myself.

The crowds at Cambridge, and folk festivals in general, are

also the warmest and easiest-going you could ever meet at a
large event. You can be any age, follow any fashion, wear the
least-flattering skirt woven out of raffia or sport the most
ludicrous facial hair outside of Dickensian drama, and
nobody gives a stuff. They're all there to make friends, drink
beer and listen. And when I first went I was astonished how
intently they listened. To see someone like Ralph McTell,
armed only with an acoustic guitar, hold that many people in
the palm of his hand was like nothing I've ever seen before.
And it's not just the music they pay careful attention to. On
Sunday morning everyone spreads out their travelling rugs
and flicks through the papers while the omnibus edition of
The Archers is played through the main PA system. Personally
I've never been a fan of *The Archers*, but what a seductively
heart-warming and quintessentially English scene that is.

I also love the fact that at Cambridge you experience
bands you'd probably be unlikely to hear or see elsewhere. I
remember vividly standing at the side of the main stage with
Eliza Carthy and being hypnotized by the exhilarating speed
and dexterity of the Romanian peasant orchestra Taraf de
Haidouks. On another occasion, glass of Bombardier in
hand, I became fixed on two men stripped to the waist hitting a giant xylophone made out of railway sleepers with
what looked like broom handles. They were in a band led by
a diatonic-accordion player from the Basque country, and if
someone asked you if you'd like to go out and see that on a
rainy night in Ilford you would probably say no unless you
were a native of the Basque country or an aficionado of the
diatonic accordion, whatever that might be exactly. But for
half an hour at Cambridge, with the sun on your back and a
pint in your hand, it's a really great way to pass the time.

The mix of acts at this most homely of festivals is nothing
if not eclectic. There are traditional folk artists to be sure, but
you'll also hear country, world music, blues and anything

that really depends on the quality of the song. There are also bigger, more familiar names in the stew. I've witnessed great sets there by the likes of Joe Strummer, Emmylou Harris and The Divine Comedy, and in fact it was during the live transmission of The Divine Comedy's set from Cambridge that my proudest moment in television occurred.

I'm a big fan of Neil Hannon who is, to all intents and purposes, The Divine Comedy. His songs manage to combine musical sophistication with wit and genuinely catchy pop hooks. He may be the missing link between Noël Coward and The Pet Shop Boys. He's also a cheerful, charming, dapper and highly portable chap with a very natty line in floral-print chemises.

On the night in question I introduced the band to the live audience both at the festival and watching on TV, and then retired to the side of the stage to enjoy the show. Towards the end of the set Neil led the band into perhaps his most famous song, 'National Express'. Overcome with joy and lost in the moment as the crowd spiritedly joined in with the song, the impish Neil clambered down into the pit in front of the stage, and went along the front row giving beaming punters the chance to sing the refrain through his microphone. It was a lovely moment, and one you couldn't see on the box without smiling and wanting to be there. This section of crowd participation over, Neil then turned, put his hands on the lip of the stage, and attempted to put his feet against the front of the platform in order to pull himself back up into position. Unfortunately, the front of the stage at Cambridge is a curtain and not a hard surface, meaning that the hapless Hannon could not get a foothold and was in danger of disappearing underneath the boards rather than being returned triumphantly to stand on them once more. The band, bemused but well drilled, simply played round the chord sequence while peering at their petite leader as he made ever more feverish, but futile, attempts to escape the orchestra pit. After a couple of minutes of this, and realizing that no one was going to help him, I decided I had to at least try and bring the situation to some sort of conclusion. And so, as I had my access all areas pass, I scurried down to join Neil and, clasping two hands together, gave him a foothold which enabled him to claw his way back to where he'd come from, and finish the show in style. This was all captured by the cameras and beamed out live, and I consider it to be the one truly useful thing I've ever done on television. The other good point in relation to this incident was that, as Neil is a slight individual, the ease with which I threw him back up made me look almost as macho as those blokes without shirts battering the big marimba thing. If it had been Boy George down there I'd have been in trouble.

23. THE DAY I SWORE ON THE RADIO

It was in spring 2004. It's only ever happened once and, though I'm not saying that excuses having done it, I think one transgression in all that time is pretty amazing. After all, it's not like I don't swear in everyday life. I don't think I use profanities any more or less than most people I know and I'm certainly not saying you can be content with a smaller vocabulary if you use them liberally. Thick people who swear in every sentence are just that, thick, not smart like you and me. We know words like oxymoron, susurration and recalcitrant, but I do think having a few well-placed swear words in your arsenal can help give things a little emphasis, and can sometimes make things much, much funnier.

I'll give you an example in the form of a joke. A bloke goes for a job on a building site and the foreman says to him, 'Can you make tea?'

To which the applicant replies, 'Yes, I can.'

Then the foreman asks, 'And can you drive a fork-lift truck?'

To which the bloke replies, 'Why, how big's the fucking teapot?'

Now, that is one of my favourite jokes, but it's considerably less funny if you don't swear in the punchline. It's not just that he's using a word you would never use in a job interview, but something to do with the rhythm of the thing. Try the gag without the f-word and it just doesn't work as well. Like Jarvis Cocker said, sometimes, contrary to what you're told as a kid, swearing is big and quite clever in the right context.

It's often stated that what we once considered shocking words have seen their effect largely diluted. I'm not sure that's entirely true. Certainly it's hard to envisage use of the f-word causing the same sense of outrage as it did when the theatre critic Kenneth Tynan became the first person to say it on the television in a discussion about censorship in 1965, or when John Lennon put it in the lyric of 'Working Class Hero'. Wow, The Beatles swear. And they seemed like such nice boys.

But there are still lots of situations where we still consider it wholly inappropriate and unnecessary. Would you use that word in a conversation with your mother? Well I wouldn't. Would your mother use it in a conversation with you? If you said yes I'd be genuinely surprised. Would you make a speech at a wedding where you called the bride and groom 'a really fucking great couple'? You wouldn't, would you? Or if you did, I bet you haven't been asked to speak in public since. There are just some circumstances in which it's just not the done thing, and one of those is on live, daytime radio.

Some might say this is a bit puritanical and that the language used on radio should reflect the everyday common vernacular. There's some truth in this. If there hadn't been a degree of acceptance of that axiom then radio would still be the exclusive domain of gentlemen in bow ties reading tightly scripted bulletins in clipped tones of received pronunciation. So I'm sure we all agree that radio has been a richer linguistic experience since regional accents have been allowed onto the airwaves, and not just when being interviewed as eyewitnesses to crime. I certainly think so, but then there may be a bit of a vested interest there. And so what? Aren't my vested interests as a broadcaster with a northern accent as important as those of someone who talks like Prince Philip? That those listening should be able to identify presenters as the kind of people you might readily strike up a conversation with in a pub, or on a train, or at a concert, or at a football match, seems to me to be a really healthy situation.

However, that still doesn't mean you can swear when you want to. If you swear in front of people then you've scanned the assembled company and assessed whether using an expletive is likely to cause offence. When you do it on the radio, you can't do that. You can't know if someone is listening in the car with their kids or sitting in the kitchen with their old mum. I wouldn't want to hear it myself and I don't think I'm narrow-minded when it comes to freedom of expression. I'll tell you how broad-minded I am. If I had narrow-minded friends, which I don't, I would treat them just as broad-mindedly as my broad-minded friends.

I must say, though, that the frequency with which the f-word, or even the dreaded 'c' word, crops up in daily newspapers without warning surprises me. I kind of feel that unless they know exactly who's going to be reading every copy, they should be subject to the same checks and balances as radio and television. After all, the stray swear words that do pepper live broadcasts are usually spur of the moment things and, though undesirable, are often unavoidable. It's live. A newspaper isn't. So I suppose my message to editors is, 'Come on guys, get a fucking grip.'

It's actually something of a mystery to me how I don't swear on the radio more often. I know fellow presenters who make it a rule never to use foul language in a studio at all, just in case the microphones are live and you hadn't realized it. I don't. I can happily rattle off a stream of colourful light-hearted invective to a member of the team immediately before going back on air and delivering a speech of sublime erudition. Well, I won't use any expressions likely to cause offence anyway. And I might say 'errm' quite a lot, but at least I won't say the f-word. I don't have to make a conscious effort not to. It's like a valve switches somewhere inside the brain that won't allow any swear words through, and it's been foolproof for thirty years of broadcasting. Except on one occasion.

Naturally there are times when a word of this type might slip out on air when you don't intend it to. You might be frustrated with an interviewee who refuses to give you anything more than one-word answers or be incensed by the views being expounded by a guest or caller. You might possibly have had a drink or two. The weird thing about the occasion on which I swore is that it wasn't in any of these situations.

It was a routine afternoon show on Radio 1. Marc Riley and I were sitting opposite each other across a hessian-topped table. We had a caller on the line, as we were coming to the end of one of our celebrated quizzes. I couldn't tell you which particular one it was as we'd had so many. Perhaps it was 'Bird or Bloke' or 'Dobbins or Bobbins' or 'The Spice is Right' or maybe 'The Craptown Factor'. They were all creations of genius anyway, and how they never got made for television is a mystery to me. No wonder ITV continues to struggle if it can't see a golden nugget of a quiz show in the sludge of popular culture.

Anyway, the exhilarating cut and thrust of the game over with, we would give the winner details of whatever we had lying round the office that we didn't want and couldn't sell, that we'd decided to give them for a prize. On that particular day the victor was to be sent a DVD, if Michelle remembered to post it, featuring episodes of seventies cop show *The Sweeney* starring John Thaw and Dennis Waterman.

Marc, nobly attempting to make the prize appear a bit more desirable than it was, said he'd recently bought this very artefact himself. This must have been why we were giving it away. Nobody wanted it except him, and he'd already got it.

He then began to extol the virtues of this 'classic' series depicting a time when villains 'looked after their own', men were men, women were women, violence was violence and truisms were truisms. For some reason I began to get bored with this exposition and decided to intervene. I'm pretty sure these are my exact words.

'Oh, honestly, you'll buy anything, you will. They stick out all this rubbish on DVD and you just fucking lap it up.'

I have no idea where it came from. I wasn't angry. I hadn't been arguing with Marc. I didn't even have a strong opinion either way about the bloody *Sweeney*. Why, after all those years with a clean record, had I sworn at that moment? I still can't explain it.

Immediately the word had left my lips it was as if everything stopped. Marc and I just sat there looking at each other. The engineering and production team through the glass raised their eyebrows, bit their lips or covered their mouths in shock. In fact the first person to react was the caller on the line, who chuckled and expressed, not unreasonably, surprise at the kind of language he was hearing.

Within about five or ten seconds, which can seem like an age at times like that, I recovered some sort of equilibrium and apologized straight away. I absolutely held my hands up and admitted that, though it was in no way premeditated, I accepted I was totally in the wrong, solely at fault and said sorry for what offence I'd caused. I was pretty distraught about it to be honest. I mean, we were doing a fairly knock-about, unscripted show but you were trusted with the airtime on the understanding that strict professional etiquette would be maintained. And I failed to keep my end of the bargain that day.

After the programme had finished I phoned the controller Andy Parfitt, told him what had happened and apologized to him personally. He was OK about it and didn't even tell me not to do it again, as that would have been pointless. I hadn't meant to do it at all and had never done it before. He did warn me that I'd probably get a rap across the knuckles from the regulatory body, Ofcom, as people were bound to have complained. And they did. That's fair enough, I suppose, but I can't really see what would compel someone to write to the BBC about something like that. It was a mistake that had been apologized for straight away. It wasn't as if I'd scripted it to deliberately push the boundaries of what was acceptable on daytime radio. I hadn't tried to laugh it off and pretend it didn't really matter. A few people wrote in to complain anyway to try and get me into as much trouble as possible. Thanks for that, you guys. Thanks a fucking bunch.

That was pretty much the end of it, though. I didn't get fired, or receive an official warning or have my pay docked. I went back on air the following day and apologized again. That's all you can do really, isn't it? To say sorry for what offence you've caused whether you meant to or not, and for that reason, I apologize for the dreadful language in this chapter. Sorry.

24. THE DAY I GOT SACKED FROM THE *RADIO 1 BREAKFAST SHOW*

I remember the day it began as well as the day it ended. On a Friday afternoon in January 1997, Marc Riley and I, safe in the knowledge that we were leaving our night-time roost for a new slot in the afternoons, were misusing BBC studio time in an effort to complete the latest Shirehorses hit over-long player. It would later enter the album charts at number twenty, where it would stay for the grand total of one week, thereby making me a bona fide chart artist, though I don't boast about it on my CV. As we were packing up and discussing plans for the weekend there was a call on my newfangled portable phone, of which I was inordinately proud, it being one of the latest lightweight models being slightly smaller and lighter than the average house brick. Amazing! Marc had one too and wore it clipped to his belt, an arrangement that threatened to pull the waistband of his jeans down to builder level and reveal a good deal of under-panted backside, which would later become the fashionable mode amongst the nation's youth. I think Marc was very much a trendsetter in this regard.

On the other end of my Vodaphone breeze block was an agitated-sounding Matthew Bannister, the relatively new, modernizing controller of Radio 1 who had promoted me up the batting order on his arrival. His regime of sweeping change was long overdue, although in retrospect, perhaps a little swiftly carried out. I was right behind him at the time, and remain so to this day, but if you take over a football team it's probably better to implement change gradually rather than all at once. I believe the appropriate cliché would be 'a blend of youth and experience'. The Radio 1 Matthew inherited had a blend of late middle age and experience, and that was always going to need drastic surgery if it was to continue to be regarded as a youth station. The fact that Matthew threw everybody out within months was later viewed as a mistake, but at least it cleared some space and, to use another well-worn cliché, you can't make an omelette without letting Simon Bates go.

Not all the changes Matthew made went desperately well, however. Programmes anchored by Danny Baker and Emma Freud went considerably less smoothly than anyone could have predicted, but there was always going to be a period of transition. Radio audiences at that time were notoriously resistant to change and so the ratings suffered an inevitable drop. This became a test of corporate nerve, as it was generally accepted that the downturn would stop at some point and a brave new core listenership would emerge and grow. This had to be the case. I daresay fewer people shopped at Marks and Spencers in Manchester city centre after it had been blown up by the IRA and was being rebuilt. That doesn't mean the new Marks and Spencers is less good than the old one, does it? Similarly, Matthew and those loyal to him, including myself, had to stand amidst the shards of shattered egos that littered the old Radio 1, confident that a bright new version would eventually stand there.

That it did is probably due to Chris Evans more than anyone else. At that time Chris seemed to be absolutely at the centre of the zeitgeist in his presentation of the breakfast show and he gave the rest of us the platform and stability we needed. I took some personal gratification from this as I had once saved him from the sack back at Piccadilly Radio in Manchester. I had somehow managed to become head of music while Chris was a lowly technical operator. One night shift he inadvertently erased an interview with Bob Geldof, that we had secured in the immediate aftermath of *Live Aid*, before it had been broadcast. The station manager was not unreasonably infuriated by this and wanted to give Chris his marching orders. I persuaded him to give the errant, ginger rockabilly-headed tape slave another chance. I have reminded Chris that he owes his whole career to me on several occasions and, while he concedes that the incident happened, he puts forward the controversial view that his own ability has been a factor since then and refuses point-blank to give me the half of his wealth that I consider to be my due.

Chris's show became a huge success and sent out just the kind of positive vibes about the new Radio 1 that Matthew desperately needed. So when Evans asked for Fridays off to attend to his television commitments, Matthew had a major problem. Breakfast shows had always been five days a week, and still are, but if Chris was determined to play a game of brinkmanship, and he was, could Matthew retain his personal credibility if he gave in to Chris's demands? Was it better to have four days a week of Evans than no Evans at all?

The upshot of their battle was that Chris departed, which left Matthew, and his deputy Andy Parfitt, needing someone to take over. And fast.

That they chose us is a decision I suspect they regret to this day.

That Friday Matthew informed me that Evans had gone. He talked about the future of the station as he saw it and it became clear, to my genuine amazement, that he wanted us to take on the breakfast slot. Admittedly, we had done the occasional week on the programme when Chris had been on holiday, and had got away with it, but that was very different to taking it on full time. For a start, we were very happy going into the afternoons, as that didn't involve getting up early. We were also very pleased with the pay rise we'd been offered and just wanted to get on with what we'd planned. It also represented a massive gamble for Matthew, as we had performed pretty successfully at night, but were largely unknown to huge swathes of the daytime audience. I have to say though that this only occurred to me in hindsight, as at that point we'd had so much good press it never crossed my mind that we wouldn't be up to the job.

I told Matthew straight away that I didn't really fancy it.

'Oh,' he said, 'I hadn't really been expecting you to say that.'

Which was understandable. This was the biggest radio show in Europe and if you were lucky enough to be offered it, then it was generally accepted that you said thank you and got on with it. But I didn't want to do it and neither, I think, did Marc, although he might have been slightly less set against the idea than I was. There then followed a few days of contractual wrangling as we tried to find ways of making them change their minds. We asked for 50 per cent more money, thinking that would do the trick. It didn't. We insisted on doing the show from Manchester, not as some great battle waged on behalf of the North, but because we thought they would never let that happen and so we'd be off the hook. They agreed to that too. And so we were stuck with it.

When it was announced that we were taking over the press went into overdrive. Because Chris's show had been so successful, and his departure so publicly acrimonious, the *Radio 1 Breakfast Show* had become a regular tabloid story, and we were wholly unprepared for the glare of publicity that came our way. Reporters came to my house wanting photographs of my wife, one paper had people in my dad's garden, another, one of the evil titles that peddles garbage while hiding behind a veneer of Middle England respectability, whatever that constitutes, offered money to my ex-wife for her story. To her eternal credit she refused, but it did force me into revealing everything that could conceivably be used against me, which wasn't a lot, to Matthew Wright at the *Mirror*. Matthew assured me he'd put it all across in a sensitive and non-sensationalist way, and even though when you see your private life examined in tabloid-speak you wince slightly, he was true to his word and I'll always be grateful to him for that.

Our misconceived and ill-fated breakfast show began on 17 February 1997. I have to confess to being crippled with nerves, which I hadn't really expected. I know that sounds a bit daft and arrogant, with it having such a huge audience, but it never crossed my mind that we wouldn't be successful and so I didn't really think I had anything to be nervous about. The first show was pretty poor and though everyone seemed confident that we'd recover from a bit of a shaky start, I'm not sure we ever truly did. I know that whenever you make a big change in your life, like leaving home, going to a new school or college, starting a new job or moving house, it feels strange initially and you have to give it some time. Occasionally, though, you just know you have made a mistake from the very beginning and I honestly think we knew at the end of that first show that it would never work.

For a start it was too bloody early. I have the utmost respect for people who can shape their thoughts and speech patterns at that time of day like Terry Wogan and Chris Moyles. I certainly couldn't do it. Marc and I had to stand by the coffee machine binge-drinking double espressos to get our mouths working, and that made us so hyped up on caffeine, as well as nerves and sleep deprivation, that when we got on air we

sounded like gibbering idiots. We would later turn this rather
spectacularly to our advantage on the afternoon show, but no
one wants to hear two Northern lumps haranguing each other
at that time of the morning.

Another reason for our downfall is that, put simply, we
weren't Chris Evans, and at least we can regard ourselves as
blameless on this count. Simon Mayo had looked after proceedings for an interim period after Chris's departure, but
everyone knew that was a temporary measure. Simon, a thoroughly safe pair of hands and all-round good egg, had
enjoyed a successful stint as breakfast presenter himself and
had no problems stepping into the breach. It might have
been better for everyone, apart from Mrs Mayo possibly, if
he'd stayed there. But we were the permanent replacements,
and Evans had set the bar high. Too high as it turned out,
which we should all have foreseen, because one glance at
Marc and I would tell you that we weren't built for the high
jump.

Another nail in the coffin was that the content of the programme was, well, a bit rubbish really. All our material at
night hinged on a common understanding with the audience
that it was laced with irony. That didn't really work at breakfast time. I remember being on tour with The Shirehorses
and sharing a people carrier with the support act, a young
comedian called Peter Kay. Every morning, as the rest of us
nursed hangovers, the non-drinking Peter would commence
the string of never-ending wisecracks and observations that
would continue until he got on the stage that night.

'Peter,' I used to say, 'it's too early for comedy.'

Evidently the Radio 1 breakfast shift was too early for
irony. We knew that quizzes like 'Dobbins or Bobbins', where
you had to identify real and false names of horses running that
day, were crap. That was the point, though it didn't stop you
participating in and enjoying the game. 'Fish or Fowl' and

'Bird or Bloke' followed the same ingenious template. Other items like 'The Busy Buzzy Bee Game' and 'Wheel of Misfortune' went on for what seemed like hours. 'Trivial Hirsute' involved an appointment book of chance, a hairdryer of doom and a live haircut carried out by resident studio barber Keith. You could get up with 'Trivial Hirsute' on your radio alarm clock, have a shower, drive to work and get to your desk, and the item would still be going on. Of course, I see now that no one has the time or inclination to concentrate on something like that in the morning, especially as it wasn't exactly riveting anyway, but at the time we just blundered on regardless with the hare-brained schemes Marc and I had hatched in the pub with producer Rhys Hughes. I put an effect on my voice to become the beached whale of love Fat Harry White, who treated the school run to innuendo-rid-dled tales of window boxes and 'planting seed in the woman next door's dirtbox'. We had an item called 'We Love Us' where bands were tested on their knowledge of themselves. And though I do smile at the memory of The Spice Girls winner Sporty being presented with her prize of a foot spa, it was clear that nothing was working.

At one point things got so bad that management, heavily influenced by focus groups, had decided that it might be better if there was less chat in the early part of the show. Poor old Marc was basically told to shut up, which made it seem like he was carrying the can and was grossly unfair. If any-thing it was his irrepressible spirit that kept it going for as long as it did. As ever, we had to twist this situation into some wacky notion and so 'Five Words for Lard' was born. The idea was that he could only say five words between six-thirty and seven, and when he said the fifth, you could ring in and win a prize. Probably a pot of jam or a teapot or something. It might have been better if we'd had five words between us and just played some good records.

Eventually audience figures were tumbling at such an alarming rate that it became clear to the heavy-hearted Matthew Bannister that something had to be done. We had for some time had to have a conference phone call after each show so they could point out to us which bits had been passable before moving on to whipping us for the far greater number of segments that had been poor. And if that sounds a bit like I think we were treated harshly, then rest assured I don't. We were screwing up not just the show but, because the breakfast show on any station needs to perform well as the audience declines from that high watermark throughout the rest of the day, potentially the whole output.

One morning in studio 5, Manchester, I wearily picked up the phone to go through another post-mortem and Andy Parfitt was on the other end.

'Hi, Andy. What did you think of it today?'

'Yes, it was all right, but Matthew and I want to come and see you tomorrow.'

'Right. Are we getting the sack?'

'We'll see you tomorrow.'

I put the phone down and repeated the short conversation to the team, and I think we all knew what was coming. Nevertheless, it was a difficult twenty-four hours, as we not only had to go home and speculate on what our future, or lack of it, might hold, but also had to come back into work and knock out another shoddy show the following morning. This we duly did, and it wasn't a noticeably poorer show than all the others as, whatever else you want to throw at us, we always had pride in our ability to turn up on time and not cause any trouble.

Following the show Andy went into the office to talk to the team, and Matthew took Marc and I to the Palace Hotel next door for some posh coffee.

'I'll come straight to the point,' said Matthew, looking

genuinely sorrowful, 'the figures just aren't good enough and we are going to have to make a change.'

Momentarily, though he was saying exactly what we'd expected him to say, there was a bit of a shock. We really were getting the chop. We'd only been doing the programme for about five months and it did seem that the axe had fallen comparatively swiftly. Then again, if we knew it wasn't working, why should they have felt any differently? The day before, Rhys had asked me what I'd say if they told me that I'd been fired. I said I'd ask if they had anything else I could do at the station and if they said yes, I'd say thanks very much and get on with it. If Matthew's regime had taught us anything it was that no one was irreplaceable, not even Chris Evans, although at that juncture it was looking rather like he might be. So I immediately asked Matthew what plans he had for us, if any, and he said that as Nicky Campbell was leaving to go to Radio Five Live, would we like to take on the early afternoons. Looking back on it, this was incredibly loyal of Matthew, as he could have just paid up the first year of our contracts and got rid of us. With the stench of failure clinging to us, we'd have been lucky to get on national radio again, and would forever have been known as those two plonkers who couldn't cut it at breakfast.

'So what do you think you might do in the afternoons, then?' he asked us.

Thinking of all the tortuous machinations of 'Trivial Hirsute' I thought about it for a moment and then said, 'We've been thinking we might play some records and talk in between.'

Matthew smiled, said that sounded fine and told us that the breakfast show was going to be taken over by Zoë Ball and Kevin Greening. We nipped out and bought them a congratulations card, which we signed and gave to Matthew to pass on to them, and that was pretty much that.

Coming out of the hotel I had the feeling of a man who'd been let out of jail. The show could not have been turned around, the audience having lost all faith in it, and I felt an enormous sense of relief to be free of it. As I'm sure the listeners did. Ironically, after the pressure lifted and we knew we were leaving, we turned in by far the best month's programmes we achieved in that slot. There are also people who regard our short tenure of the breakfast slot as some sort of Dadaist deconstruction of the art of early morning radio, but I'm not sure I'm one of them. Though I've come to regard failure on that scale as quite interesting, I still think we messed up pretty miserably.

Our final breakfast show was broadcast on 10 October 1997 from Rome, where we'd been allowed to go and see the England football team draw nil–nil with Italy, and qualify for the World Cup. We started our afternoon show the following Monday. That one lasted a bit longer.

25. THE DAY PAUL MCCARTNEY WAS SECOND CHOICE

You can't help but get a bit excited when meeting Paul McCartney because he's the most famous musician alive. I know that sounds like a pretty bold statement, but if you think about it there isn't anywhere in the world that hasn't heard of The Beatles. They were the biggest band that has ever existed and, for any number of reasons, that will never be topped. They were right there at the birth of what we think of as pop music and had a whole untapped world of hitherto uncatered-for youth to go at. That won't happen again. Also, consumers are far more sophisticated and selective these days, to the extent that their buying habits have pretty much resulted in bringing about the end of the record business as we know it. The Beatles, and a few others like Presley, Dylan and The Stones, pretty much invented it. If you wanted in on this newfangled pop music you bought a Beatles record. It was as simple as that. So they became the most famous band in the world, and Paul and John, as the main writers and singers, became more famous than George and Ringo. John is dead. Paul is not. Ergo, Paul is the most famous musician alive.

Perhaps if they'd known they were going to be the biggest group in the world they'd have thought of a better name, because The Beatles is pretty poor. I suppose it's become so ubiquitous that we don't notice it any more, but it's not good. As a pun, it's feeble, and the end result sounds like it's something to do with the film *A Bug's Life*. By rights The Beatles should be four jaunty animated scarabs and not the most celebrated pop stars who ever walked the earth. Why couldn't they have thought up a good name like The Rolling Stones or Velvet Underground or Led Zeppelin or Roxy Music or Aerosmith? Admittedly they're not right down there with The Police, Yes, Kiss, Busted, McFly and Take That, but they're hardly on a par with Talking Heads, The Ramones, Stone Roses or Throbbing Gristle, are they? Throbbing Gristle. Now there's a name to conjure with, and if I'm being honest, it's rather wasted on Genesis P-Orridge and his industrial grindcore accomplices. As rock adventurers and committed avant-gardists, their legacy is assured, but you're not going to want to listen to the records all that often. Far better for them to have been The Beatles and for the legendary creators of *Revolver* and *Sergeant Pepper* to be renamed Throbbing Gristle. How wonderful for the greatest musical gift this island has given the world to be known for eternity as Throbbing Gristle. Who would I see about getting that sorted out, d'you think? Well, Paul McCartney maybe.

The first time I met him was in 2001 when he came to visit the studio in Manchester where Marc Riley and I broadcast our Radio 1 afternoon show. There was always a discernible buzz around the building on the infrequent occasions we had a big name dropping by. If Kylie was due you would get both men and women taking twice as long to fetch a round of teas from the canteen in the hope of coming up against the pint-sized glamour popstrel. When Robbie Williams paid us a call it seemed like the entire female population of the BBC had coincidentally chosen the same day to finally get round to taking a closer look at the unremarkable paintings hanging in those unremarkable corridors, on the off chance of bumping into the remarkable Robster. I don't recall the male drones being that bothered.

When Paul came everybody came out for a gawp. Or at least it seemed that way. I suppose it's only natural to want to see one of the world's most famous people in the flesh, although I can't see what's actually to be gained by it. He's only like he is in the pictures but mobile when all's said and done. Still, at least you can tell your friends that you walked past him and he was using his own legs to get around on. And maybe that he was slightly taller than you were expecting.

In my experience, which is not limitless but it's all I've got to draw on, very famous people have an act, a persona, that they use for meeting mere mortals. They're always friendly, because having been doing the job for so long, they're good at it, and, knowing that they don't really need to do any promotion, once they've decided to do something, they do it with good grace. But there's always a little character they've created to use in such situations. Bowie adopts a slightly madcap approach as if he's a character in an Ealing comedy. Jagger is not without warmth but retains a hint of superiority. Paul McCartney's act is to make you think he's a completely regular, normal bloke. I know what you're thinking. How do I know it's an act? Perhaps he is a regular, normal bloke. Well, you may be right, though it would be the first time that someone has had that degree of success, and been propelled to that level of fame, and not been screwed up in the process. To have lived for so long with everybody telling you how great you are, laughing at all your jokes and never saying no to you must change you at least a little bit, mustn't it? Of course, it might change you for the better, and when they tell you how great you are they may well be speaking the truth, but it's got to shift your critical faculties. Shielded from everyday reality by aides-de-camp and cash, you see a different world to the rest of us. That's why show business is littered with the likes of Michael Jackson, Elvis Presley and Britney Spears. The world you inhabit becomes a reality of your own creation and once you, as the omnipotent being at the centre of this private universe, falter, either through failing health or declining income, the illusion begins to unravel. There can be no greater image of this than Jackson's rusting fairground at his crumbling Neverland ranch complex. So if McCartney has managed to live through the whole Beatles thing and emerge as a regular, normal bloke, then that's a remarkable achievement. Let me be clear on this one. I'm not saying he hasn't managed it, but I am saying that it's impossible for the rest of us to know for sure.

And yet, when I met George Harrison I was really tempted to believe that it was a trick he'd managed to pull off. I went to his private office at Handmade Films to talk to him for a programme I was making about Rickenbacker guitars. Shown into an office that felt like a headmaster's study at a British public school, I waited alone for my first meeting with a Beatle. And the role I'd chosen to adopt was that of someone who met people as famous as Beatles every day, as I didn't want to come over as a gushing imbecile. I saved that persona for my DJ-ing work.

When George arrived he was dressed in dark clothes you barely noticed, which generally means they cost a fortune, and was as friendly and open as if he'd wandered in to chat to an old mate about football or gardening or the weather. He was also absolutely beautiful. I mean, I'm not gay or anything, but I know a good-looking chap when I see one, and George Harrison was way beyond handsome. His dark hair was still lustrous, and he peered from beneath it with deep, twinkling eyes and the suggestion of a Merseybeat-era cheeky grin. He was carrying a plain, brown paper bag, which he put on the coffee table. What does George Harrison carry around in a brown paper bag, I wondered? Well, that was his business and I didn't feel it was appropriate to ask.

We conducted the interview and he recalled how difficult it was to get hold of good instruments in the early days, and the joys of finally getting his hands on a decent guitar like a Rickenbacker. After the tapes had been turned off he poured us a cup of tea, picked up the paper bag and said, 'Oh, there's some flapjacks my wife has made here. Would you like one?'

I don't know why I remember that moment so vividly, but it just seemed amazing that in his position, when he could send any one of a number of lackeys out to buy whatever pastries his heart desired, that he would choose to carry around home-baked flapjacks in a brown paper bag. It seemed indicative of a man who'd been able to maintain a degree of normality despite having lived one of the most extraordinary lives anyone had lived ever. Look, I'm not claiming to have been a mate of George Harrison's, I've no idea what he was really like or what made him tick, but offering people your wife's home baking has got to be an indication of a person who's more in touch with reality than someone who's built their own private funfair, hasn't it?

Paul was very amiable though. He was using his own legs to get around on and was slightly taller than I was expecting. He looked trim, happy and was accompanied by Heather Mills who, I'm ashamed to say, I didn't notice at first as I was a bit discombobulated at meeting Macca. At that time Paul and Heather seemed pretty much inseparable, and she had been the muse for his new album *Driving Rain* in many ways. I thought that perhaps my failing to have immediately clocked who she was might offend the besotted Paul in some way, but if it did, he didn't show it, and relatively quickly I regained my poise and shook her by the hand. She was taller than I was expecting too, and was very good looking, though not in the George Harrison league.

Paul, though surely possessed of ego, showed none of it that day as he cheerfully participated in the organized laddish chaos of the show, and even agreed to an impromptu live rendition of his latest single 'Freedom', using us as his backing band.

Marc Riley played lead guitar, or at least he was holding one. Possibly conscious that not only was this Paul McCartney, but also that the guitar part on the record had been played by a bloke arguably slightly better on guitar than Marc called Eric Clapton, he opted to play at very low volume. This was most out of character for him, as a hundred tinnitus-inducing sound checks with The Shirehorses had demonstrated. Even when Macca indicated the point at which the solo kicked in, Marc adhered to the infallible theory that you can't be accused of making a mistake, or dropping a bollock to use the right technical lingo, if nobody can hear you. No matter. He can still say without fear of contradiction that he has played guitar for Paul McCartney. Even if it was inaudible.

Bass duties were taken on by our long-standing, long-suffering, long-haired, long-faced engineer Chris Lee. Chris is not only a bit of a musician but a Beatles fanatic. Accordingly, he had the exact same model of Hofner violin bass that has become Paul's trademark. He picked up the song with irritating ease, though we are only talking bass, which has four strings and is therefore two easier than guitar, and jammed along without giving the slightest outward sign that this was the greatest moment of his musical life. How many kids who loved The Beatles have grown up to play a song live on the radio with Paul McCartney? After the song was completed Chris got Sir Paul to sign his bass down the edge of the body. An original 1960s Hofner violin bass signed by Paul

McCartney. How much is that worth? Well, I can make a reasonable estimate and if Chris persists in sending ear-splitting tone down my headphones then it'll be mysteriously turning up on eBay.

I played the drums and that would have been enough to brag about, but I subsequently got the chance to meet Paul again, and in a location that Beatles fans regard as some sort of shrine: Abbey Road studios.

The Cavern may be where the Beatles legend was born, but Abbey Road studios is where it was assured. There in St John's Wood, under the watchful eye of George Martin, they made the records that would change recording for ever as they combined peerless pop songs with pioneering sonic innovation. They also ensured that London would have one more obstacle to traffic as generations of pilgrims posed on that zebra crossing to have their photographs taken.

As part of a Radio 2 series called *Sold on Song*, Paul agreed to be interviewed at Abbey Road to talk about how he approached the art of songwriting, and the chosen inquisitor was me. McCartney at Abbey Road. It was better than chatting to Elvis at Graceland where, when all's said and done, all he really did was watch television, gorge on Zeppelin-sized sandwiches and experience some bathroom difficulties. The Beatles had actually created their masterpieces in Abbey Road.

So here I was, sitting opposite Paul once again, and it was impossible not to feel a certain sense of occasion. I listened back to the pre-edited tapes of that programme recently and in the general chitchat before we get down to the interview proper I sound terribly nervous. Once we get down to business, though, I seem completely at ease. I don't know how that works really. I guess that's just what you learn to do if you've been doing this job for a while. You still feel apprehensive but you find ways of dealing with it so that, like a duck, you appear outwardly calm and serene but no one can see your feet paddling frantically just beneath the surface.

Quizzing Paul on how he goes about writing a song, I was surprised to learn that he hardly ever starts with even a vague idea of a tune in his head. He explained that he will often sit at the piano and hit random chords and progressions until he likes the sound of something. This single phrase will then form the base to which other bits are added to build up a number. I suppose the key to that technique is knowing a good bit when you hear it amidst the randomness. For example, he knew he had something when he stumbled across the first line of the immortal melody of 'Yesterday'. He could tell it was good but had to keep singing it to the others to check it wasn't something someone else had composed already. And just so he had some random words to sing along to the tune and establish the metre, he sang 'Scrambled Eggs' at the opening of the first line before eventually coming up with 'Yesterday'.

He admitted that he sometimes feels insecure about this way of working, as if he should have a more academic and theoretical approach to what's often called the craft of song-writing. Presumably the instinctive way is great when the songs are flowing, but pretty scary when you're going through a fallow period. He said that lots of really big-name songwriters who don't have formal musical training experience this sense of panic from time to time. I thought it amazing that a man who has written some of the world's most enduring popular songs should feel any insecurity at all.

He talked engagingly about his early days in The Beatles, and particularly their collective obsession with the art of rock-and-roll guitar. Their idol was Eddie Cochran and he recalled how impressed John Lennon was at the audition when Paul played 'Twenty Flight Rock' note perfect on an upside-down guitar, as there wasn't a left-handed one avail-

able. He then told how Brian Epstein once gave them a week
to write an album and, rather than thinking that was a tough
assignment, they were grateful to have a whole seven days to
spend just writing songs. He explained how he and John
would then sit opposite each other on two single beds in a
rented room and swap chords and ideas on old acoustics. He
remembered 'She Loves You' coming together at one of
those early sessions. It was also worth noting, he said, that all
the songs had to be really catchy because they had no way of
recording demos. Reel-to-reel tapes and machines were
hideously expensive, and there were no cassette decks in
those days. Accordingly you just had to keep the tunes in
your head until you got to the studio. He reckoned that this
was no bad thing, as if you couldn't recall it the next day, it
obviously wasn't memorable enough and so was better forgotten. You couldn't help but wonder how many possible
classics had just been lost for ever back there. He told me that
the songs they did remember weren't guaranteed to make the
cut even then, because everyone in the band had a right of
veto, so if George, Ringo or even George Martin didn't like
it, it didn't go on the album.

Paul's new record at the time was called *Chaos and Creation
in the Backyard* and there's a track on there called 'Jenny
Wren', which seemed to hark back to one of his most
admired compositions, 'Blackbird' from the *White Album*.
He admitted this was deliberate and revealed that the original had arisen from a Bach-influenced duet he and George
used to play to surprise people who thought that these noisy,
long-haired beat bums couldn't really play properly. But how
extraordinary to sit in Abbey Road and have Paul McCartney
play that famous tune on his guitar right in front of you.
Fortunately things had moved on a bit since his audition and
there was a left-handed guitar he could use.

In the weeks leading up to this meeting I'd been reading

my daughter Mia the book of *Yellow Submarine*. Someone had given it to her for her sixth birthday and she'd become fascinated by the surreal tale of the Blue Meanies, the apple bonkers, the suckophant, Jeremy Hilary Boob, PhD (The Nowhere Man) and four men called John, Paul, George and Ringo. While reading the story aloud to her I'd attempted to use different voices for different characters and, naturally, attempted a Scouse accent for The Beatles themselves. In truth, my ability to mimic regional dialect is not great. On the Radio 1 shows I often left the accents to Marc Riley, who had a natural gift in this area. I could just about manage the odd Welshman, David Bowie, and Cockneys with speech impediments. My Liverpudlian was passable but only, bizarrely, if delivered in a very high-pitched register, as it had been based on a record-dealer friend of ours called Russ Taylor who shouted in relentless falsetto. This then was the voice I used for Paul, George and John. Ringo, who always had a more lugubrious delivery, I tried to give a lower tone, which resulted in the already dubious Scouse approximation giving way to an unmistakable West Midlands twang.

One night when we'd finished the book, again, Mia asked me why I was using those 'funny voices'. I explained that I was just choosing them at random to suit the characters in the book, but in the cases of the four heroes I was using the accent they used in real life. She paused and looked at me wide-eyed.

'Dad, do you mean The Beatles are actually real?'

And then it struck me. I'd never thought to mention that they were a real live group and so, naturally, presented with this dream world in a story book, she had assumed they were fictitious characters like the Moomins, who sound like they should be a band, and the other fab four: Ratty, Mole, Badger and Toad.

She asked me all about the band and wanted to know if

they were still alive. I told her that George and John had died, but that Paul and Ringo were still with us. She thought about this for a moment and then asked me something that made me feel like the world's best dad at that moment.

'Dad?'

'Yes?'

'Do you think you could get this book signed by a Beatle?'

Not many dads, faced with that question, are able to reply, 'Funnily enough, love, yes I could.'

However, the sweetness of the moment was tarnished by a stupid mistake on my part. Instead of just saying I could sort it out, I added a further question.

'And which Beatle would you like?'

As soon as I'd said it I knew what I'd done. But it was too late. Inevitably, she replied, 'Well, ideally Ringo.'

Of course. The small one with the different voice from the other three. Little, cutesy, Brummie Ringo.

As Paul was signing the inside front cover I felt obliged to tell him that he was second choice. He smiled, inscribed the dedication and drew a cartoon face over half of the page, leaving plenty of room for Ringo to do the same should I ever bump into him. Whenever you're ready, Ringo.

26. THE DAY I TURNED FIFTY

Turning fifty didn't cause me any great angst, which is more than you can say for my mum, who found it rather hard to accept that she had a son whose birthday was announced in *Saga* magazine. My nine-year-old daughter Mia was equally indignant.

'I don't want you to be fifty, Dad.'

'Why not, love?'

'Because it's too old.'

I don't really like parties much but I thought I'd better have one. It seemed to be an occasion that needed marking in some way. I took the back room of my local pub, the Spinner and Bergamot, and we had beer and music. Oh, and some food. My wife and I sorted the menu out. She was keen to have rocket and Parmesan salad. I wanted pork pies. I reminded her whose party this was. We had rocket and Parmesan. And pies.

I didn't want it to be too big a 'do' so I kept it to family and the usual gang of close friends. Bono, Archbishop Desmond Tutu, Beyoncé, Ronaldinho. My three daughters Mia, Rose and Holly were there, Holly blooming in pregnancy to make it a landmark year in more ways than one. Fifty and a granddad. Blimey.

We held the party a week early as I spent my actual birthday at the 2008 Glastonbury Festival, where I was presenting the television coverage for BBC 2 with the ever chummy, eternally cool and also heavily pregnant Jo Whiley. We went on air at midnight on Saturday the 28th of June and so it was mildly disconcerting to hear the director Helen in my earpiece saying, 'Fifteen seconds to transmission, and fifteen seconds of your forties left, Mark.'

That Sunday I celebrated my half-century. The Family Mahone appeared on the Avalon Stage in front of a crowd of around 4,000 who, having been whipped into shape by a hip-beat-poetry-riffing Zane Lowe, sang 'Happy Birthday' to me as I walked on stage. After our set I was then whisked away to go up in a helicopter to describe the sprawling wonder of the Glastonbury site to the millions watching on TV. That done, I took advantage of my stage pass to watch the stately and majestic Leonard Cohen lead 100,000 people through a communal 'Hallelujah' as the sun went down. Not a bad way to spend your fiftieth birthday, eh?

And as you leave me, lost in a reverie on the side of the Pyramid Stage, I can only be deeply thankful for how lucky I've been to do the things I've done. That's why I wrote this book. And if that sounds a bit self-important, then I'll leave the last words with my youngest daughter Rose, six, when she saw the manuscript lying on my desk.

'Is that your book, Dad?'

'Yes.'

'Wow! That is a waste of a lot of ink.'

ABOUT THE AUTHOR

Mark Radcliffe was born in Bolton and attended Manchester University. He has been employed by the BBC to talk in between records for over twenty years, many of these with Lard (aka Marc Riley) and currently with Stuart Maconie on Radio 2. He has won 6 Gold Sony Awards and has recorded five albums with two bands. He is married with three daughters and lives in Cheshire.